CIVIL WAR

Photography
UPI/Bettmann Archives
National Archives, Washington, D.C.
Archive Publishing

Design
Marnie Searchwell

Commissioning Editor
Andrew Preston

Commissioning Assistant
Edward Doling

Picture Research
Leora Kahn

Editorial
Peter Rea
Jane Adams

Production
Ruth Arthur
David Proffit
Sally Connolly

Director of Production
Gerald Hughes

MALLARD PRESS

*An imprint of BDD Promotional Book Company,
Inc, 666 Fifth Avenue, New York, NY 10103.*

*Mallard Press and its accompanying design
and logo are trademarks of BDD Promotional
Book Company, Inc.*

CLB 2432
© 1991 Colour Library Books Ltd, Godalming,
Surrey, England.
First published in the United States of America
in 1991 by The Mallard Press.
Printed and bound in Singapore.
All rights reserved.
ISBN 0 792 45376 X

CIVIL WAR

Clark G. Reynolds

MALLARD PRESS

CONTENTS

CONTENTS

Foreword

WAR FOR THE WORLD

by Abraham Lincoln, President of the United States

Excerpted from his war message before a joint session of Congress July 4, 1861

•••*A*t Fort Sumter ... the assailants of the Government began the conflict of arms. ... In this act, discarding all else, they have forced upon the country the distinct issue "Immediate dissolution, or blood." And this issue embraces more than the fate of these United States. It presents to the whole family of man the question whether a democracy – a government of the people, by the same people – can, or cannot, maintain its territorial integrity against all its domestic foes. It presents the question, whether discontented individuals, too few in numbers to control administration according to organic law, in any case can ... break up their Government and thus practically put an end to free government upon the earth. It forces us to ask: "Is there, in all republics, this inherent and fatal weakness?" "Must a government, of necessity, be too strong for the liberties of its own people, or too weak to maintain its own existence?"*

So viewing the issue, the administration had no choice left but to call out the war-power of the Government and so to resist force employed for its destruction by force for its preservation. ... A right result ... will be worth more to the world than ten times the men and ten times the money it will cost. ...

This is essentially a people's contest. On the side of the Union, it is a struggle for maintaining in the world that form and substance of government whose leading object is to elebate the condition of men – to lift artificial weights from all shoulders – to clear the paths of laudable pursuit for all – to afford all an unfettered start and a fair chance in the race of life ... This is the leading object of the government for whose existence we contend. ...

Eng.d by A.H. Ritchie.

Abraham Lincoln
This steel engraving – one of several in the present work – appeared in the 1864 book Portrait Gallery of the War, *edited by Frank Moore. Each engraving was taken from a photograph, inasmuch as no process then existed for reproducing photos in publications.*

17

Introduction

THE GREATEST WAR OF MODERN TIMES

Amidst the blazing July heat which engulfed the southern Pennsylvania countryside around the hamlet of Gettysburg, soldiers in blue and soldiers in gray uniforms approached a stone wall on Cemetery Ridge from opposite sides. The sounds and sights of war had been all about them for three days, passing in review – howitzers of the field artillery, heavy cannon of the coast artillery, machine guns, antiaircraft guns, mechanized tanks, and, roaring overhead, B-17 Flying Fortress strategic bombers, attack planes, and fighters. When the men reached the wall – the "high water mark of the Confederacy" – they stretched out their right arms across it and shook hands.

The date was July 4, 1938, the 75th anniversary of the epic Battle of Gettysburg and the Final Reunion of the Blue and the Gray – the last time veterans of the American Civil War would meet in a formal encampment. All of the 3,690 men present were over the age of 90, the oldest 107; two dozen of them had fought in this particular battle. At that time, July 1863, over 80,000 men of Lee's Army of Northern Virginia had battled a like number of Meade's Army of the Potomac in the one clash which, more than any other, would decide the future course of America – and the world.

For although President Franklin D. Roosevelt dedicated the Eternal Peace Light Memorial at this final reunion, across the ocean Adolf Hitler was threatening to engulf Europe in war over the Munich crisis. A year later he attacked Poland to begin World War II, and by the end of 1940 neutral America had become the "arsenal of democracy" to provide weapons to beleaguered Britain and China. The Japanese attack on Pearl Harbor a year later brought the United States into the fight to lead the Allies to ultimate victory in Europe and the Pacific. And then the mighty republic assumed the heavy task of policing the world against militant communism during the Cold War. Finally, by the 1990s, the example of American democracy and free enterprise was being embraced across the globe – not simply the high water mark of a free people but reaching flood tide on a planetary scale.

By no stretch of the imagination could this ultimate triumph have been achieved if America had been divided into two nations. A unified American people accomplished the feat – "one nation, under God, indivisible, with liberty and justice for all," in the words of the flag salute. The Civil War cemented this nation – a war of national unification which forevermore put an end to American sectionalism and slavery and which forged the American colossus.

Although the combatants and civilians of North and South appreciated the scale of the conflict for their own future, no one of that day – least of all the European powers concerned only with each other – could begin to imagine the full magnitude and global consequences of the American Civil War. But in setting the stage for the new America-led and America-inspired world, the Civil War must rank as the greatest war of modern times.

To understand it and to know it is to realize that this struggle was nothing less than a war for the future of the world.

1

THE TWO AMERICAS

North and South, Fort Sumter,
1st Bull Run to mid-1861

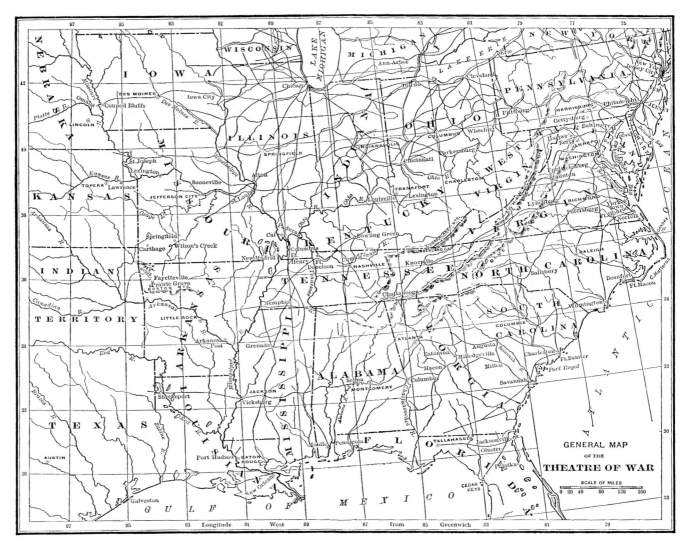

GENERAL MAP
OF THE
THEATRE OF WAR

SCALE OF MILES
0 20 40   80   120   160

Thomas Jefferson, revered as the apostle of democracy in America, died on July 4, 1826 – fifty years to the day that the young republic had adopted the great document he had authored, the Declaration of Independence. Four years later, on April 13, 1830, on the anniversary of Jefferson's birthday, the nation's leaders gathered at a formal dinner to honor his memory. At the conclusion of the meal, toasts were called for, whereupon the President of the United States, tall, stern Andrew Jackson, rose, held up his glass, and proclaimed, "The Federal Union: It must be preserved!"

At that, the Vice President, John Calhoun, stood up and made his

Facing page: the black slave in the cotton field became a symbol and focus of the war for the world, unifying a divided American republic into a true, uncompromising democracy for all its people and serving as a beacon for the oppressed masses around the globe.

toast, "The Union: next to our liberty the most dear. May we all remember that it can only be preserved by respecting the rights of the states and distributing equally the benefit and burden of the Union."

Thus did ardent Unionists and states-righters proclaim the battle lines with strong words, but their guns did not open fire until thirty-one years after that memorable evening, on April 12-13, 1861, with the bombardment of the government's Fort Sumter by Southern rebels in Calhoun's home state of South Carolina. This artillery duel dramatically announced the intention of the Southern states to exert their individual rights over the central authority of the Federal Union by severing their ties and forming an independent nation of their own – the Confederate States of America.

In the intervening years between the Jefferson banquet of 1830 and the shelling of Fort Sumter in 1861 the Union of North American states had grown apart into two virtually separate entities. Before 1830, the Union had been held together by its very architects, the last Founding Fathers who had fashioned it as an unprecedented experiment in democracy – political liberalism exercised by a willingness to compromise over political differences. This spirit was epitomized by Jefferson, the Virginia plantation aristocrat, and by John Adams, the Massachusetts merchant patrician who had helped Jefferson write the Declaration of Independence and who, remarkably, died on the very same day as Jefferson.

With both men and their entire generation gone, the two sections began to drift apart as the nation expanded

THE TWO AMERICAS

westward, bringing frontiersmen like the Tennessean Jackson to the fore. The men of Northern mercantile, business-oriented New England, New York, and Pennsylvania vied with the Southern agrarian planters of Virginia and the Deep South to attract the new Western states to their sides. The specific point of issue became the Negro slavery so vital to sustaining Southern economic and social institutions and thus political strength.

In fact, the birth of the American Republic had occurred at a significant period in world history. Its Constitution, adopted in 1787, happened to create the world's last major nation state of the pre-industrial era – for the Industrial Revolution had begun in Great Britain just a few years earlier. Neither France and the other continental states of Europe, absorbed in the wars of the French Revolution and Napoleon, nor the young United States, struggling through its national adolescence, even began to develop factories on the British model until after the global wars ended in 1815. But in America only the mercantile, British-inspired North progressed along nineteenth-century commercial, industrial lines. The South remained rooted in the eighteenth century – a French- modeled agricultural society of plantations and small farms.

The new states to the west of the Appalachian Mountains and then west of the Mississippi River were all agrarian in character, each linked to the mercantile and shipping centers of the commercial Northeast – New York City, Boston, and Philadelphia – by the new steam technology which had spawned the Industrial Revolution. Beginning in the 1830s, steam locomotives crisscrossed the North and steamboats used canals, the Great Lakes, and the Mississippi-Ohio-Tennessee-Cumberland river network to create new business centers at Pittsburgh, Chicago, and St. Louis. By the 1850s, Western wheat and Southern cotton were being moved by rail and river steamer to the great ports of the Northeast and New

Although the Northern and Midwestern states were as agricultural as those of the South, producing grain as opposed to cotton, by the 1850s they had begun to industrialize on a vast scale – as suggested by this lithograph of several factory mills at Lawrence, Massachusetts.

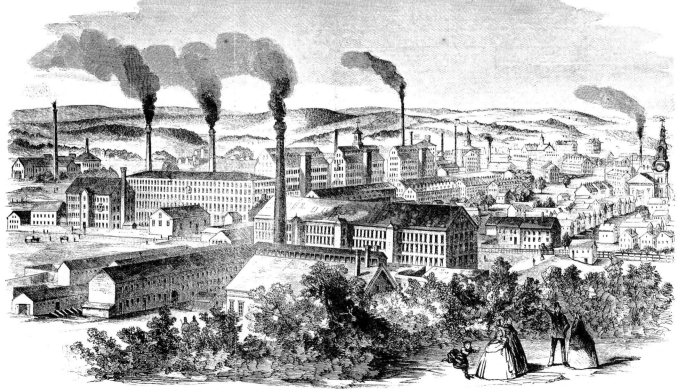

24

"King Cotton" is seen on one of Charleston's wharves ready for shipment North and abroad before the war. Although the great South Carolina seaport had a thriving, independent merchant class, the cotton economy and the slave labor which sustained it kept the businessmen allied to the predominant Southern planter aristocracy.

By mid-century, the United States shared the distinction of practicing slavery with only a handful of lesser nations – Ottoman Turkey, Brazil, and the Spanish in Cuba. Even Brazil was adopting gradual emancipation.

Overleaf: a Southern slave market.

THE TWO AMERICAS

Orleans for transhipping overseas on sleek Clipper sailing ships and sail-steamships. The nation's economic hub for this vast activity remained Wall Street and the port of New York; the major trade route was the transatlantic New York-to-Liverpool run which connected America with industrial England. Except for the cities of New Orleans on the Gulf of Mexico and Nashville on the Cumberland River, the rural South steadily fell behind the burgeoning North.

The dynamic economic life of the North – like that of Britain – created a cosmopolitan urban culture based on a capitalistic, liberal-minded middle class of businessmen, bankers, and professional men. Not only did they thrive on cultural diversity from exposure to European ideas and immigrants, but they – and many active women – adopted and espoused liberal causes embodied in the Constitution and already transforming Britain. Not least of these was a mounting revulsion to Negro slavery. The British Empire outlawed slavery in 1833, and virtually every other European country followed suit – save Spain and Ottoman Turkey. The eradication of such an antiquated social institution within the young American democracy became the crusade of vocal Northern abolitionists. In contrast to the North, the South persisted in feudalistic ways, dominated by its planter aristocracy of landowners who depended for their prosperity upon white small farmers and black slaves. The South had no real middle class of merchants – or where it did, as in coastal Charleston, they were kept subordinated by

inland planters. Suspicious of foreign and Yankee ideas and reformers, Southern leaders resisted the future.

The growing sectional split affected American military institutions as well. The United States had inherited the English militia system, depending on armed townsmen to defend each community from foreign intruders, Indians, and outlaws. A small professional army provided the nucleus for a wartime force swelled by volunteers as in the War of 1812 and the Mexican War of 1846-48. Since defense of the coast, rivers, and frontier settlements required fixed fortifications, the U.S. Military Academy had been founded at West Point in 1802 to train engineers to build, defend, and attack forts. In the South, however, fear of slave revolts inspired state military schools to train sons of planters to prevent or crush uprisings. Like Britain, America's first line of defense – of the coasts and of its vital merchant shipping – became the navy, which by the 1840s had small squadrons stationed throughout the world. These warships also suppressed the slave trade from Africa under general British leadership, although Southern captains were less enthusiastic about this mission for obvious reasons. The introduction of steam propulsion resulted in the creation of the U.S. Naval Academy at Annapolis in 1845 to train officers in marine engineering. By European standards, however, the U.S. Navy remained small and never fashioned a traditional battle fleet.

As long as the South had an equal number of states as the North represented in Congress, it could insure

Ride for Liberty: The Fugitive Slaves, a painting by Eastman Johnson, portrays a Negro family escaping north. Although the Fugitive Slave Act of 1850 guaranteed their return to the owners when captured, abolition-minded Northern states assured their freedom by enacting personal liberty laws.

Left: an escapee from slavery in Baltimore in 1838, Frederick Douglass settled in Massachusetts, where he became the leading black anti-slavery lecturer and reformer of the antebellum era. He edited the North Star *abolitionist paper, which also championed equality for women. During the war, Douglass helped raise Negro regiments.*

This 1845 song cover (below) honors the best-known alumnus of what the South called its "peculiar institution" – slavery.

The Underground Railroad, as portrayed by C.T. Weber, depicts fugitive slaves being given refuge at a "station" along this escape route – an abolitionist's farm in Indiana. Some of the escaped slaves were spirited away as far north as Canada.

THE ARISTOCRATIC, AGRICULTURAL SOUTH

A Southern View

by **Louis T. Wigfall**, Texas Representative, Provisional Confederate Congress. Wigfall, a "fireater" – or rabid secessionist – made these remarks in May 1861 to the correspondent of the London *Times*, William Howard Russell, who recorded them. Wigfall soon became a Senator in the permanent Congress, having held the same office in the U.S. Senate.

We are a peculiar people, sir! ... We are an agricultural people; we are a primitive but a civilised people. We have no cities – we don't want them. We have no literature – we don't need any yet.... We do not require a press because we go out and discuss all public questions from the stump with our people. We have no commercial marine – no navy – we don't want them. We are better without them. Your ships carry our produce, and you can protect your own vessels. We want no manufactures: we desire no trading, no mechanical or manufacturing classes. As long as we have our rice, our sugar, our tobacco, and our cotton, we can command wealth to purchase all we want from those nations with which we are in amity, and to lay up money besides. But with the Yankees we will never trade – never.

A Northern View

by **Ulysses S. Grant**, Colonel, United States Volunteers. Native of Ohio and a West Point graduate in 1843, Grant had left the Army as a captain after eleven years in order to engage in farming and then business in Missouri, but returned to lead the 21st Illinois Infantry in June 1861. This is an extract from his memoirs.

There was no time during the rebellion when I did not think, and often say, that the South was more to be benefited by defeat than the North. The latter had the people, the institutions, and the territory to make a great and prosperous nation. The former was burdened with an institution abhorrent to all civilized peoples not brought up under it, and one which degraded labor, kept it in ignorance, and enervated the governing class. With the outside world at war with this institution, they could not have extended their territory.

The labor of the country was not skilled, nor allowed to become so. The whites could not toil without becoming degraded, and those who did were denominated "poor white trash." The system of labor would have soon exhausted the soil and left the people poor. The non-slaveholders would have left the country, and the small slaveholder must have sold out to his more fortunate neighbors.…

The war was expensive to the South as well as to the North, both in blood and treasure; but it was worth all it cost.

political compromises which protected its unique identity. The victory over Mexico in 1848, however, added so much new territory to the Union – mostly west and north of the cotton-growing climate – that it became only a matter of time before many more new states would be created as "free" and thus give overwhelming superiority to the North in the national legislature. A series of hotly-disputed laws and Supreme Court decisions addressing slavery and new states during the 1850s threatened to tear the Union apart. These focused on the "border" areas of the upper South where Northerners and Southerners coexisted – the counties of western Virginia and eastern

William Lloyd Garrison was a moralist who was calling for emancipation from 1831 and who later supported the war as a vehicle for freedom.

THE TWO
AMERICAS

Democrat James Buchanan held the nation together as President from 1857 to 1861, but only just. By supporting, albeit reluctantly, a pro-slavery constitution for the territory of Kansas in 1857, he drove an irreconcilable wedge between the Northern and Southern wings of his party.

Tennessee; the states of Maryland, Kentucky, and Missouri; and the territories of Nebraska and Kansas. The sharpest dispute occurred in "bleeding Kansas" from 1854, where John Brown and other militant abolitionists fought a bloody struggle with pro-slavery groups over whether or not Kansas would be admitted as a free or slave state. When Brown had to be captured and hanged for seizing the government arsenal at Harper's Ferry, Virginia in 1859 to promote a slave insurrection, tensions between North and South were stretched nearly to the breaking point.

The final thread of Union depended upon the national political parties producing superior leaders to save the republic from disintegration. But the political turbulence of the 1850s would not permit this. The Whig Party collapsed and was replaced by the new Republican Party at mid-decade. The Democratic Party became a shaky coalition dependent on solid Southern participation. Highlighted by the slavery issue, however, the Democrats divided as the Southern wing bolted the party in 1860 to nominate Vice President John C. Breckinridge as its candidate for President. The northern wing nominated Stephen A. Douglas of Illinois, while a compromise party

A famed explorer of the Rocky Mountains, John C. Frémont garnered the Presidential nomination of the young Republican Party in 1856. Something of a misfit, he had been expelled from the College of Charleston (S.C.) and court-martialed during the Mexican War, and then proved only meddlesome as a Union general.

BLACK REPUBLICAN.

FREMONT AND DAYTON.

This anti-Republican handbill castigates Frémont and his running mate William L. Dayton as pro-black reformers in the election of 1856. Four years later, the South regarded a Republican victory as truly lethal to Southern rights and thus cause for secession.

THE TWO AMERICAS

Dred Scott lost his long-fought case for freedom before the Supreme Court in 1857. His claim had been based on his eventual residence in Northern states. The pro-slavery decision threw open the territories to slavery, making the Civil War virtually inevitable. Scott was freed by his new owner anyway, but died in 1858 at about 63 years of age.

This Currier & Ives anti-secession political cartoon of early 1861 blames South Carolina for the disastrous course of the Deep South. Free of the late President, "Old Hickory" Andrew Jackson, who had put down that state's attempt to nullify the Union in 1832, the South, led by South Carolina, pursued the goal of secession. Note South Carolina's riding on "the whole bog," the others on jackasses.

picked yet another candidate. The Republicans nominated Abraham Lincoln, also from Illinois. Lincoln, like Breckinridge, had been born in the border state of Kentucky but had migrated west and north. Also born there a year before Lincoln, in 1808, was Jefferson Davis, who however had moved south to Mississippi, from which he would be chosen as President of the new Confederacy. As the U.S. election neared, even the Army threatened to break up over the suspected disloyalty of Southern officers.

With the vote split between four candidates, Lincoln won the election in November 1860 on a plurality – the candidate with the most votes but not a majority of the total votes cast. Lincoln's simple avowed policy of maintaining the integrity of the Union came as no comfort to the South, which feared his opposition to slavery. Before he could assume office on March 4, 1861, the states of the Deep South intended to sever their ties with

SOUTHERN OFFICERS IN THE ARMY

By **Captain George W. Hazzard**, U.S. Army (Letter to Presidential nominee Abraham Lincoln from Cincinnati, Ohio on October 21, 1860)

So long has southern influence and southern patronage controlled our army that I know only one officer of any rank in it [Col. Edwin V. Sumner] who is not an avowed admirer of the peculiar institution [slavery].... The command of the army [Winfield Scott] and of the military geographical departments of Texas, Utah, and New Mexico is conferred on Virginians. Every Military Bureau is presided over by a Virginian or the husband of a Virginia wife. The Colonels of four of our five mounted regiments are southernors; the Adjutant General is brother in law of Senator [James M.] Mason of Virginia; the Acting Commissary General, the Surgeon General, the Judge Advocate General and his assistant, and the Quartermaster General all Virginians. The grossest favoritism has been practiced to secure this result....

Gen. [Albert Sidney] Johnston, the pet & protege of Jeff. Davis, is ... on leave – so is Lt. Col. [William J.] Hardee of the 1st Cavalry, the gallant Col. [John B.] Magruder of Va., ... and Maj. [P. G. T.] Beauregard of Louisiana who will be the Vauban [seventeenth-century French fortifications expert] of the southern army. All these officers are in intimate relations with secession senators and ... will go to all lengths, so I believe would our Quartermaster General J. E. Johnston....

(By talent more than conspiracy, all the above named Southern officers became senior Confederate generals. Captain Hazzard, while commanding the guns of a division and two batteries of the 4th U.S. Artillery, fell mortally wounded at White Oak Bridge in the Seven Days Battles in Virginia, July 1, 1862.)

THE TWO
AMERICAS

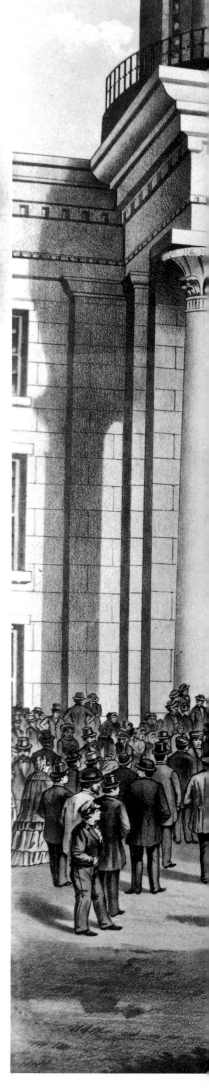

the United States in order to preserve their special way of life. They had no other recourse, for the political union of all the American states had by 1860 become a fiction. If the South was to survive as its own master, it would have to fight a war against Lincoln's resolve to preserve the Northern-dominated Union.

South Carolina led the way. In December 1860 it passed an ordinance of secession, proclaiming its independence from the United States. The battery of U.S. artillery stationed at vulnerable Fort Moultrie, abutting the entrance to Charleston harbor, quietly moved to the uncompleted Fort Sumter, situated atop a land spit astride the channel, and refused to leave. Early in the new year, the other states of the Deep South seceded almost simultaneously – Mississippi, Florida, Alabama, Georgia, Louisiana, and Texas. In February 1861 they created the Confederate States government at Montgomery, Alabama, and elected as President Jefferson Davis, a West Point graduate, veteran Mexican War regimental commander, former Secretary of War, and U.S. Senator. In March he issued a call for 100,000 12-month volunteers to man the new Confederate army and sent its Brigadier General P. G. T. Beauregard to Charleston to force the surrender of Fort Sumter.

Abraham Lincoln assumed the Presidency of the United States on schedule, March 4, dedicated to preserving the Union at all costs but uncertain over how to defuse the mounting crisis over Fort Sumter. In the event, the Confederacy settled the issue by bombarding the fort over two days in April until the defenders under Major

The inauguration of President Davis on the steps of the Alabama state capitol at Montgomery, February 18, 1861. After Virginia joined the Confederacy two months later, the Confederate States' capital was moved from Montgomery to Richmond. Note the weeping slave girl with the basket (foreground).

THE TWO AMERICAS

Robert Anderson capitulated. Though the battle was bloodless – incredibly, there were no casualties – it triggered the Civil War. Lincoln immediately exercised his authority under the Constitution as commander in chief by issuing a call for 75,000 three-month volunteers and declaring an economic blockade of Southern seaports. Whereupon Virginia seceded, followed shortly by Arkansas, North Carolina, and Tennessee, which joined the Confederacy. Davis moved the seat of government to Richmond to cement Virginia's prominent role in the new nation. Lincoln, to secure the sharply divided border states, boldly moved troops into Maryland, Kentucky, and Missouri and welcomed the secession of the western counties of Virginia to form the new territory of West Virginia. And Kansas achieved Union statehood. For the South, the addition of these two new free states to the

President Abraham Lincoln delivers his inaugural address on the steps of the uncompleted national capitol building in Washington, D.C., March 4, 1861.

Union (West Virginia officially in 1863) meant there was no turning back; free states would forevermore dominate the Congress.

On paper, no one could doubt the numerical superiority of the Union over the fledgling Confederacy. The population of the North stood at 21 million in contrast to the South's 12 million (one-third of them slaves). A general rule of thumb is that about 10 percent of any population, but only males, can be spared to don uniforms and fight. And, in fact, before the war ended, the U.S.A. would field some 2,500,000 troops, the C.S.A. somewhere between 850,000 and 1,000,000. The key to success lay, however, in how effectively the remaining 90 percent of civilians were mobilized to operate the separate wartime economies and how well the troops themselves were divided and properly employed on the

Negro slaves are depicted mounting a Confederate cannon on Morris Island preparatory to the bombardment of Fort Sumter in Charleston harbor early in 1861. The artist is A. R. Waud, whose sketches throughout the war formed the basis for woodcuts in Harper's Weekly.

Above: this watercolor by Waud depicts Southern troops at Charleston signaling by torches and reading signals at night. Their semaphore flag (right) could only be seen during daytime.

several war fronts. Such requirements were neither understood nor appreciated by either government. The call to arms was little more than a blind rush into the unknown, devoid of coherent planning or strategic design.

In truth, the Union and the Confederacy went to war virtually equal in every respect. Northern industry was not geared up for war, while early Southern seizures of government arsenals and forts like Sumter and the Norfolk navy yard gave the Confederate army sufficient arms and ammunition to equal those of the Union army. The existing U.S. Army was spread out in garrisons across

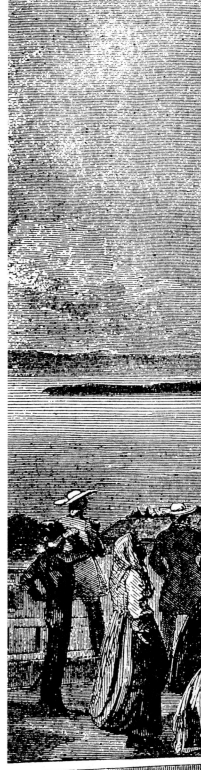

the Great Plains, the few effective vessels of the U.S. Navy around the world protecting merchant shipping. So the North and South each raised armies of volunteers that would have to be trained by the few professional officers on both sides – and neither government knew how to do it on a large scale. The only examples to guide planners of both countries were European, but history could – and would – be misused because analogies between Europe and America often proved false.

The war aims of the two belligerents shaped the course of the conflict, for national policy determines how strategy is devised and executed. Without a clear, coherent goal, any nation can be reduced to half-solutions or even chaos in prosecuting a war. The great Prussian philosopher of war, Karl von Clausewitz, whose writings were untranslated and unknown in America, had written that the aim of any embattled nation should be to wage "absolute war." That is, it should have the entire population, the nation's collective will, aligned in common cause, "absolutely" committed to break the enemy's will to resist. This could be done, he said, by a "total war" designed to destroy the very fabric of the enemy state, or it might be achieved by a "limited war," fighting for lesser, but well-defined, objectives.

Both the Union and Confederate governments in April 1861 fell into two of the same categories defined by Clausewitz. Both rallied their people with patriotic fervor to defeat the other side – absolute war. But both also had limited war aims. Lincoln remained determined to restore the Union at any cost, even if it meant a negotiated settlement by which the Southern states would agree to return to the fold and even keep their slaves. So he hoped that one or two victories in battle would convince the rebellious states to stop fighting. Similarly, the Confederacy had no desire to destroy the Union government. Jefferson Davis planned to fight a

Above: Artillery Lieutenant Adam J. Slemmer refused rebel demands that he surrender Ft. Pickens on the tip of Santa Rosa Island, guarding the approaches to Pensacola Bay, Florida. The fort is seen being reinforced by 500 Union troops on April 12, 1861. To prevent a similar relief of Fort Sumter, General Beauregard began his bombardment of that place the same day.

Right: residents of Charleston, those in the foreground mourning the outbreak of war, watch the bombardment of Fort Sumter from rooftops in the city, April 12, 1861. Guns fired on the fort from virtually every direction, yet, incredibly, inflicted no casualties.

41

defensive war only, not even to invade the North, while seeking formal recognition of the legitimacy of the Confederacy from Britain and France. He believed that a few victories in battle would result in this recognition, whereupon the European powers would openly challenge the Union blockade and supply the Confederacy. The people of the North, wearied of the struggle, would then sue for peace and grant Southern independence.

Yet, both governments misjudged the other from the very outset. Northern leaders underestimated the fierce determination of the Confederates to fight on absolutely for independence and would spend more than a year believing that the rebellion would collapse under the weight of Union arms. Southern leaders, looking at the great expanse of their territory – equal in size to western Europe, could not see how the Union could possibly raise and equip enough troops to conquer the Confederacy. They believed further (like Clausewitz, unknown to them) that by fighting on the defensive in familiar territory for home and hearth they held an immense advantage. Such a belief was rooted in the examples of Spain and Russia destroying the superb invading armies of Napoleon Bonaparte during 1812-13.

Geography, said Clausewitz, is the "bones of strategy." And the geography and topography – the lay of the land and water – of America dictated three different strategic

scenarios. First, a war fought in the North and West, above the Potomac and Ohio rivers, would be one of rapid mobility made possible by the well-developed railroad network connecting Northern cities. Had the fighting concentrated there, the war probably would have been short, like the mid-nineteenth-century wars in Europe. The fighting would in fact rarely reach north of Kentucky, but the rails gave the Union great mobility to concentrate troops at threatened points. Second, a war fought in Virginia would be restricted and plodding due to the Wilderness – tangled thickets and woods lacing the countryside between Washington and Richmond, sparse in the open ground essential for maneuver but conducive to guerrilla operations and cavalry raids. The Appalachian Mountains cut off Virginia from the third geo-strategic region, the sprawling Mississippi Valley with its open ground suitable for maneuvering armies and pierced by navigable rivers conducive to defensive fortifications and naval operations. Warfare here would be of the old, Napoleonic type exploited by the British Army and Navy which defeated both Napoleon in the Peninsular War of 1809-13 and Russia in the Crimean War of 1854-56.

None of this was realized by any leaders, North or South. Had it been, the Union could have prepared for a long war and developed a systematic strategy of driving through the valley of the Mississippi and its tributaries,

A Kentuckian by birth and married to a Georgia woman, Robert Anderson nevertheless defended Fort Sumter against the South. He was allowed to return North with his defeated garrison where he was regarded as a hero. Though promoted to brigadier general, ill health forced his early retirement.

The Norfolk Navy Yard and the receiving ship Pennsylvania (on the right), formerly a ship-of-the-line, are put to the torch by the U.S. Navy as it evacuates, April 20, 1861. The Confederate forces captured immense numbers of cannon and the hull of the frigate Merrimac, burned to the waterline.

Their Country's Call, 1861, *a painting by J. L. G. Ferris, captures the emotional anguish of a loved one's departure. The letter in the young Union officer's belt no doubt contains his orders. The portrait of George Washington over the mantel symbolizes the call to duty.*

and the South would not have felt so immune to invasion. But the West Point graduates of the preceding forty years had no training and little experience in strategic thinking. And they had been schooled in the tactical examples of Napoleon described by Henri Jomini and translated into U.S. Army manuals by Professor Dennis Hart Mahan and Captain William J. Hardee. This school of tactical thought advocated boldness and mobility, to concentrate most of

one's troops on the enemy's flank, turn it, cut off his supply lines (lines of communication) with the rear, and then capture the exposed enemy city. It was a simple formula developed by the French emperor and learned by his enemies to use against him. In America, however, real mobility was only possible in the open ground west of the Appalachians. But generals on both sides would try it repeatedly in Virginia and in otherwise unfavorable

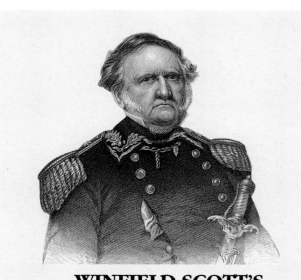

WINFIELD SCOTT'S "ANACONDA"

May 2, 1861

Lieutenant General Winfield Scott, as General-in-Chief of the U.S. Army the only officer to hold that exalted three-star rank (though by brevet, honorary), was the most experienced and well-read military officer on the North American continent when the Civil War began. Like Lincoln and most Northern leaders, he viewed the conflict as a limited struggle in which the Union army and navy had only to coerce the South to end its rebellion and return to the flag.

Unlike popular opinion and the younger Ohio militia leader George B. McClellan, who wanted a direct invasion of Virginia and Tennessee, the 74-year-old Scott on May 2, 1861 recommended a grand strategy of encircling the rebellious states, strangling them economically to enable pro-Unionist sentiment in the South to demand reconciliation.

While the Navy's blockade sealed off the Atlantic and Gulf ports, an army of 60,000 troops could move down the Mississippi from its junction with the Ohio River to the Gulf, turning the great river into a third coastline and held by "a cordon of posts." A student of the great commanders of the seventeenth and eighteenth centuries (Maurice of Nassau, Gustavus Adolphus, Frederick the Great and the theorist Jomini), Scott knew the efficacy of using rivers and sea power, and from his own experiences as a leading general in the War of 1812 and Mexican War he was a master of coastal operations and topography, and he knew the danger of debilitating tropical diseases in the South. The Confederacy, as big as western Europe, would take time to subdue. But Scott's view did not prevail, and he was replaced by McClellan six months after his plan was derided as an anaconda or giant snake. Yet in retirement Scott lived to see his basic strategy eventually implemented and succeed.

On April 19, 1861 – five days after the surrender of Fort Sumter – Southern sympathizers fire on the 6th Massachusetts Infantry Regiment passing through on its way to Washington. Nevertheless, when the Stars and Stripes was raised over the custom house, Baltimore and Maryland declared for the Union.

situations in the Western theater, resulting in heavy casualties, stalemate, or victories that could not be exploited by the exhausted winner of the battle.

While they overestimated the applicability of the Napoleonic experience to the Civil War, Northern and Southern leaders underestimated the role of sea power, which would have no Clausewitzian philosopher until Professor Mahan's son, Alfred Thayer Mahan of the U.S.

Navy, first defined naval strategy three decades after the war. Alone among American leaders, Union General Winfield Scott understood the subtle advantages of applied naval power and advocated such a strategy in his "Anaconda Plan" to blockade the Southern coasts and advance down the Mississippi. But the U.S. Navy had traditionally followed a policy of waging war on an enemy's commerce along the

THE TWO AMERICAS

French model (*guerre de course*), using cruisers to sink or capture enemy merchant vessels and gunboats to augment coastal fortifications. The Confederacy immediately adopted this traditional American naval strategy, but the Union navy had only the experience of the Mexican War to develop techniques of blockading Southern ports and attacking coastal forts. And if naval power required anything, it was time; the effects of blockade and amphibious operations took years to wear down an enemy. The quick Napoleonic attack by land held out a more attractive prospect for the North.

Both governments therefore hastily organized their forces to fight and win what they expected to be a short war. General Scott superintended the buildup of the Union army and could not convince Lincoln's able Secretary of the Navy, Gideon Welles, to follow a maritime strategy of strangling the South into submission. Scott said further that the volunteers in the new army needed six months of training before they could fight effectively. To wait until November 1861, Welles argued, would buy time for the Confederacy to forge a militant nation. The new troops, signed up for only three months, should be committed to battle as soon as possible by attacking the rebels in Virginia and capturing their capital at Richmond. This view was shared by the people of the North, enraged over the insolence of the South and anxious to crush the rebels. The battle cry "On to

Above, above right, and right: Philadelphia's spontaneous welcome of volunteer Union regiments en route to Baltimore and Washington underscored the determination of the North to crush the rebellion.

46

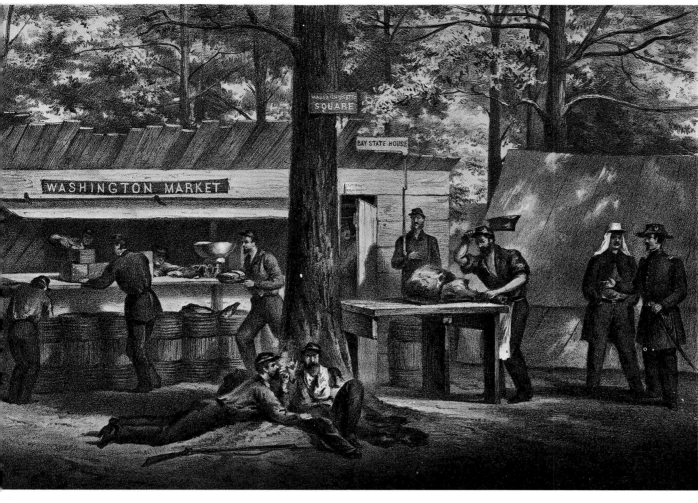

When Major General Benjamin F. Butler and his Massachusetts militia occupied Baltimore in May 1861, they encamped just outside the city. Seen here is the commissary of the Massachusetts 6th. Alfred Ordway was the artist.

*"A Confederate Bull Battery"
is the label for a bull-drawn
battery of three guns (below),
seen entering a rebel camp in
Virginia on July 8, 1861.
Since "horse artillery" meant
the gunners rode the horses,
this is bull artillery (though
the bugler rides a donkey).
Note the Stars and Bars, the
first rebel national flag.*

Federal troops attack from the right at the First Battle of Bull Run, July 21, 1861, while wounded men are tended in the foreground. This initial major action of the war degenerated into a virtual melee before Southern arms prevailed.

THE TWO AMERICAS

Richmond!" echoed in Washington and across the North.

During the three months following the opening of hostilities at Fort Sumter, both sides mustered state regiments, elevated career officers to high rank, and permitted their state-raised troops to elect their own officers. Virtually all of them were therefore inexperienced amateurs. The Union army needed a leader of genius to muster its offensive effectively, and at Scott's suggestion Lincoln had offered command of it to Colonel Robert E.

Lee. Being a Virginian, however, Lee declined and accepted a generalcy in the Confederate army. Therefore, Scott (also a Virginian, but loyal to the colors) kept the reins and saw to it that regular officers were elevated to general of volunteer ranks, while retaining their lower regular commissions until the war ended. Consequently, Major Irwin McDowell of the artillery was appointed brigadier general of volunteers in May and given command of the army assembling just south of

the Potomac River for the advance on Richmond. President Davis of the Confederacy ordered Brigadier General Beauregard – a former brevet major of U.S. engineers – to command Southern forces gathering at Manassas Junction in northern Virginia to prevent McDowell's advance. Brigadier General Joseph E. Johnston – who had held the same rank when he resigned from the U.S. Army – occupied Harper's Ferry, assembling a second force to hold

At the critical moment in the First Battle of Bull Run, Jackson's Virginians hold Henry House Hill, enabling the 1st Virginia Cavalry Regiment to drive the 1st New York Fire Zouaves and two Union artillery batteries right flank back across the creek.

JACKSON AT BULL RUN

July 21, 1861

by **Major William M. Robbins**, 4th Alabama Infantry

...Jackson, with his brigade, was struggling desperately to arrest the Federal columns; but immovable as Jackson and his men stood, the surging tides of the enemy were beating upon him with such a mighty force that it seemed as if he must give way.... Our brigadier, General Barnard E. Bee ... came galloping to the 4th Alabama and said, "My brigade is scattered over the field and you are all of it I can find. Men, can you make a charge of bayonets?" "Yes, General," was the prompt response, "we will go wherever you lead and do whatever you say." Pointing toward where Jackson and his brigade were desperately battling, Bee said, "Over yonder stands Jackson, like a stone wall! Let us go to his assistance." Saying that, Bee dismounted and led the 4th Alabama to Jackson's position. Other reinforcements coming up, a vigorous charge was made, pressing the Federals back. In this charge Bee fell mortally wounded.... Before the Federals recovered ... they saw Kirby Smith's men advancing down the Warrenton pike upon their right rear, and this unexpected appearance in that quarter struck them with an overpowering panic and caused their precipitate retreat from the field.

that vital arsenal on the upper Potomac.

Beyond northern Virginia, the new Union and Confederate regiments collected along the border areas separating their two countries, forming almost what in military terms is known as a "frontier." But not quite. That is, a frontier usually constitutes a barrier of fixed fortifications on both sides in the seventeenth- and eighteenth-century manner. Brigadier General J.F.K.

Mansfield of the regular army, an 1822 West Pointer placed in command of the defenses of Washington, proposed that the Union create just such a frontier, while state and Confederate leaders in Tennessee laid plans to erect forts for commanding the rivers along the Kentucky border. But the distances were too great, the topography too varied, and military operations too fluid to follow a frontier concept, and skirmishes, raids, and minor battles

occurred across northern Virginia, the Tennessee-Kentucky border region, and southern Missouri. The first real campaign developed in the seceding counties comprising West Virginia, where Major General George B. McClellan with a force of 20,000 men drove back a Confederate army one-fourth his strength in a campaign of maneuver and several pitched battles during June and July 1861.

Besides, fixed fortifications and frontiers, like a naval blockade, implied the long war that neither side anticipated or desired. In mid-July, the U.S. War Department ordered General McDowell to use his army of 30,000 volunteers to attack Beauregard's 20,000 at Manassas, while Robert Patterson, a major general of Pennsylvania militia, advanced into the Shenandoah Valley to the west with 18,000 to prevent Johnston's 12,000 from reinforcing

THE TWO AMERICAS

After his victories at Fort Sumter and Bull Run, P.G.T. Beauregard was promoted to full general, the last of five, following – in order of seniority – Samuel Cooper, the Adjutant and Inspector General; A.S. Johnston; Robert E. Lee; and J.E. Johnston. He never attained similar success thereafter, however, and was shifted between theaters the rest of the war.

Beauregard. Presumably, McDowell could overwhelm Beauregard, leaving the way open to Richmond. But when the 69-year-old Patterson failed to press forward against Johnston, the latter whisked most of his forces by rail to the environs of Manassas on July 20. The two armies clashed next day along the creek known as Bull Run.

What history would eventually label the First Battle of Bull Run started out as a Napoleonic set piece but degenerated into a wild melee due to the inexperience of officers and troops alike, unable to control or even execute precise tactical maneuvers. While McDowell feinted against the rebel right flank he sent his main force in a sluggish attempt to turn the Confederate left. Beauregard conducted the general battle, while Johnston rushed his own brigades from the right to the threatened left flank. Brigadier General T.J. Jackson's brigade stood so firmly that Jackson earned the nickname "Stonewall."

An actual sketch, made on the spot by one of the Special Artists of Frank Leslie's Illustrated Newspaper.
Mr. Leslie holds the copyright and reserves the exclusive right of publication.

Scapegoats were sought to account for the disaster at Bull Run, even officers not fully engaged in the battle. One was the young Colonel James E. Kerrigan (seated at the fireplace), 25th New York Infantry, seen at his court-martial for drunkenness, being friendly with the enemy, and seven other charges.

54

The Southern troops counterattacked, and as the Union forces began to fall back they suddenly panicked. In the wild rout that ensued, they fled for twenty miles back to Washington, and many sightseeing civilians were captured along with soldiers. But the exhausted Confederates could not be organized to pursue McDowell, and the action ended with about 3,000 Union soldiers killed, wounded, and captured and 2,000 casualties for the South.

The Confederate victory excited the people of the South and stunned those of the North. It would be a longer war after all, and four days after the battle, General McClellan was given command of the defeated Union forces around Washington and charged with creating, training, and leading a powerful army with which to crush the rebellion. Old General Scott soon retired, and fresh calls for troops went out from both governments. The war for the world now began in earnest.

Brevet Lieutenant General Winfield Scott had to retire as General-in-Chief after Bull Run, due to age. His regular rank and pay was that of major general, the "brevet" being an honorary title bestowed by the U.S. Army to honor a meritorious deed, in lieu of medals.

Overleaf: under a flag of truce, Southern citizens are transferred from a Union vessel to Confederate boats near Norfolk for passage to Southern lines in the late summer of 1861. The rebels evacuated Norfolk the following May. Drawing by A.R. Waud.

2
OFFENSIVE BY SEA

Coastal Operations, the High Seas, and the Peninsular Campaign 1861–62

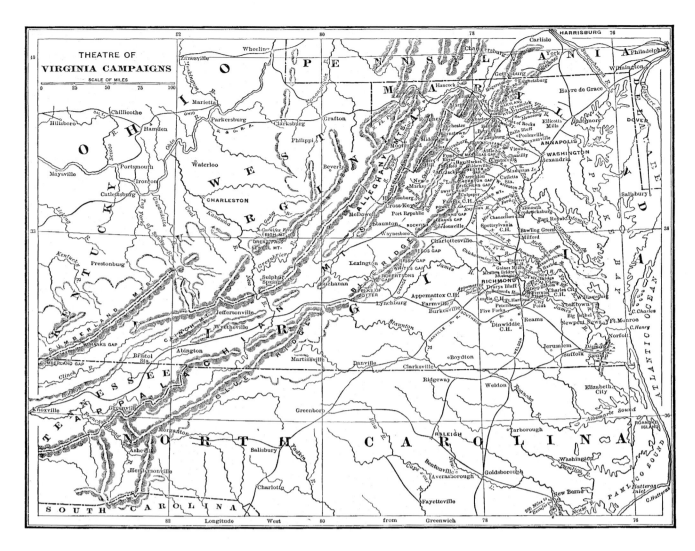

THEATRE OF
VIRGINIA CAMPAIGNS
SCALE OF MILES

Beat! beat! drums! – blow! bugles! blow
Through the windows – through doors – burst
like a ruthless force,
Into the solemn church, and scatter the congregation,
Into the school where the scholar is studying;
Leave not the bridegroom quiet – no happiness must
he have now with his bride,
Nor the peaceful farmer any peace, ploughing his field
or gathering his grain,
So fierce you whirr and pound you drums –
so shrill you bugles blow.

Thus did poet Walt Whitman capture the heartbeat of the
land in 1861 as tens of thousands of young men rushed
to the colors – the Stars and Stripes of the blue, the new
Stars and Bars of the gray. Most of them – perhaps 80
percent on both sides – came from farms, and as soon as
the late summer harvest was gathered 500,000 signed up
for three-year hitches in the Union army,
400,000 for one to three years in the
Confederate. Like all soldiers, they
learned to march, pitch tents, dig
in to the good earth for
protection, and run
for cover if
need be.

*Union warships bombard
forts Hatteras and Clark at
Hatteras Inlet, North
Carolina, August 28 and 29,
1861. Flag Officer Silas H.
Stringham's guns forced the
forts to submit, although a
small landing force under
Major General Benjamin F.
Butler received much of the
credit.*

Naval shells from Flag Officer DuPont's fleet lying in Port Royal Sound burst inside Fort Walker at Hilton Head, South Carolina, November 7, 1861. Note the idled guns facing landward. After forts Clark and Beauregard surrendered, the U.S. Navy established a major blockading base here.

OFFENSIVE BY SEA

Paradoxically, however, the fate of these landsmen would to a large extent be governed by the sea. This was especially true for the Confederacy, whose states before the war had relied completely for manufactured goods on the North and on foreign goods transshipped south in coastal vessels via New York. Now military goods would have to come directly to Southern ports.

While the opposing armies of volunteers swelled and were trained under the handful of career officers throughout the autumn and winter of 1861-62, the maritime dimensions of the war were taken in hand by professionals, for warships are machines whose officers require years of training in seamanship, navigation, and water-borne logistics (supply). Fortunately, unlike their counterparts in the army, American naval officers could take leaves of absence during peacetime to command merchant ships and thus keep their skills well honed until wartime required their return to duty. On the other hand, Americans had harbored suspicions of naval elitism ever since repressions by the British navy in the Revolution. So instead of any top uniformed officer like the U.S.

Army's general-in-chief, control over the Navy was vested in the civilian Secretary. Indeed, the high-sounding rank of admiral had even been forbidden, the most senior captains by 1861 being called "flag officers." Both the Union and Confederate navies continued these practices, although the latter allowed a few admiral ranks to be bestowed for meritorious service, and the U.S. Navy finally adopted the rank of rear admiral in mid-1862. But the opposing secretaries never surrendered their powers to the senior officers.

Fortunately the Union navy enjoyed two dynamic, experienced New Englanders at the helm. Secretary Gideon Welles of Connecticut had had invaluable experience as the bureau chief who clothed and fed the navy during the Mexican War, and Massachusetts-born Assistant Secretary Gustavus V. Fox had been a naval officer before serving as captain of several merchant ships, including oceanic steamers. Both men brought to the wartime navy wide experience in the economics, logistics, and technology of sea power. Fox quickly became the dominant figure, selecting key officers,

Above: two Confederate artillerymen lug a cannon ball during their futile defense of Port Royal Sound, S.C., November 7, 1861.

Unlike Fort Sumter, Union troops did not give up Fort Pickens (right) in Pensacola harbor. The fort was not attacked, enabling its garrison to prevent blockade runners from using the excellent port.

Ten casemate batteries inside Fort Pickens bombarded Fort McRae on the opposite side of the channel in late November 1861 and again on New Year's Day, 1862. The damage to Fort McRae was so great that it helped convince the Confederacy to abandon Pensacola in May 1862.

Overleaf: the Federal Congress is caricatured early in December 1861 furiously debating their response to the Trent affair, during which Britain loudly protested the Yankee seizure of two Confederate diplomats from the British mail packet Trent by the USS San Jacinto.

dealing with the army, and deciding on ship construction and naval strategy. The Confederacy had the services of a civilian Secretary of similar talents, Stephen R. Mallory of Florida, a customs inspector, marine lawyer, and former U.S. Congressman. He singlehandedly directed the fortunes of the Confederate sea service.

Economics lies at the heart of naval policy – the crippling of an enemy's overseas trade. Lincoln's blockade of Southern seaports aimed at choking off not only imported arms but all manufactured goods which sustained the Southern war effort. And the South intended to challenge that blockade by keeping its ports open and by attacking Yankee merchant ships. Great Britain ruled the seas, its navy enforcing the international law dictated by the British government in this century of the *Pax Britannica*. In the peace settlement ending the Crimean War in 1856, Britain prevailed upon the other powers to sign the Declaration of Paris, ruling that warring nations must allow ships of neutral countries to carry noncontraband (non-military) materials into enemy ports. Most importantly, any declared blockade had to be effective if it was to be observed as legal by neutral carriers. In the Civil War, this meant that if a British warship found no Union warships patrolling off the entrance to a Southern harbor, the blockade was null, and neutral merchant ships could enter. If warships were on station, the merchantmen could not enter. Since the 2,700-mile coastline of the Confederacy would require a

The brilliant General Robert E. Lee (above) looked young and fresh when he turned down command of the Union army at fifty-four and helped organize Virginia's troops for the Confederacy. However, his hair turned gray as he unsuccessfully defended the South Atlantic coast during 1861-62 and then assumed command of the Army of Northern Virginia.

As Lincoln's Secretary of State, William H. Seward (right) first thought that a war with Great Britain might unify the North and South but then thought better of it and soothed British pride over the Trent affair. Assisted by Ambassador Charles Francis Adams in London, he managed to maintain Britain's neutrality throughout the war.

OFFENSIVE BY SEA

huge Northern fleet to create an effective blockade, the Davis administration banked on Britain's testing and rejecting the ineffective Yankee blockade.

Although the United States had not signed the Declaration of Paris, the British had every right as the dominant maritime power to enforce the provisions of the pact in this war. Britain, which imported over 75 percent of the South's entire cotton crop in 1859, certainly needed Southern cotton for its busy textile mills — especially as the Confederacy in the summer of 1861 shortsightedly imposed an embargo on its own cotton exports in order to hasten British support. Also, Britain had been closely pressed by the U.S. as its greatest trade competitor. But Britain saw a dangerous precedent if it denied the North's blockade; the tables could be turned

in a future European war when Britain might declare a blockade and the U.S. could test it — as indeed would be the case half a century later in World War I. The neutral British, also needing Northern wheat and friendship, decided on a safe middle course. They would allow swift private British merchantmen — often commanded by Royal Navy officers on leave of absence — to run the blockade from British Bermuda and Nassau in the Bahamas and Havana in Spanish Cuba, thus keeping open the trade routes without a formal test of the blockade. And they even turned a blind eye to Confederate warships being illegally constructed in British shipyards.

Britain insisted that the Union observe the rules of international law. When these were violated, diplomatic relations between Britain and the Union became strained.

The major incident was the *Trent* affair in November 1861 when the Union steam frigate *San Jacinto* under Captain Charles Wilkes forcibly removed Confederate diplomats James M. Mason and John Slidell from the British mail packet *Trent* en route to England. The mounting war scare between the U.S. and Britain abated only after Union Secretary of State William H. Seward wisely released the two men on a legal technicality.

Application of sea power takes time in any war, and time clearly favored the Union, if that time was used wisely. At least the North had a firm shipbuilding base in eight naval shipyards, an immense merchant marine, and a nucleus of powerful steam warships to initiate the North and South Atlantic and East and West Gulf blockading squadrons. Welles and Fox agreed that the oceans were too vast for an occasional rebel cruiser to locate and sink more than a few merchant ships, so no Northern convoys were established – save for one warship escorting mail steamers carrying California gold through the Caribbean to New York. On the technological side, the industrial base of the Union enabled builders of Yankee warships to experiment with iron plating over wooden hulls, which had just been introduced in Europe, although applying such untried technology in time of war was risky should it fail to work.

Secretary Mallory had considerably less to work with in the South – two shipyards, one iron works, and only 200 career officers. But he contracted with British firms to build commerce raiding cruisers, began the construction of gunboats to help defend Southern harbors and rivers,

A New York infantry regiment, variously identified as the 67th or the 74th, is encamped near Washington during the autumn of 1861. The ten companies and their regimental band initially had an authorized strength of between 845 and 1,045 officers and men, soon to be whittled down by battle.

OFFENSIVE
BY SEA

All quiet along the Potomac for Union outposts bivouacked on the river bank while guarding the nation's capital.

and – like any second-rate navy – looked to technological shortcuts with which to neutralize enemy warships. These were ironclad steamers like the former *Merrimac* (renamed *Virginia*), underwater "torpedoes" (actually free-floating mines or powder charges attached to a spar), and even coastal "submarines" (really submersibles, since they never operated at depths below the immediate surface of the water). All these weapons would take their toll in many incidents but none proved decisive. Worse, the small Southern railroad network needed to bring wood, iron, and coal from the interior to the coastal shipyards and bases was commandeered by the army, which also eventually drafted skilled carpenters and mechanics away from navy construction projects.

In one respect, however, the Confederate Navy won a major campaign – the attack on Yankee commerce. At the outset, President Davis issued letters of marque to private merchant captains, authorizing them to serve as privateers for attacking Northern shipping. Such an ancient practice had been outlawed by the Declaration of Paris, and when 17 Union merchant ships fell victim to the first Southern privateers in 1861, an enraged Northern court sentenced a captured privateer crew to hang as pirates. But when Davis responded by randomly selecting three Union army prisoners to hang, Lincoln commuted the capital punishment. Still, the incident generally finished the practice of privateering, except for a vessel seized in 1863 by the Union sloop *Cyane* in San Francisco before the ship could be deployed by rebel sympathizers. So instead, Mallory turned to British-built cruisers, notably the *Alabama*, which under the command of Captain Raphael Semmes operated worldwide for two years, destroying over sixty merchantmen and cargos worth almost $6 million before being sunk by the Union screw sloop *Kearsarge* off Cherbourg, France in 1864.

This 15-inch cast-iron smoothbore Rodman gun was part of the extensive system of fortifications built to protect Washington, D.C. It formed part of Battery Rodgers, located near Alexandria on the Virginia side of the Potomac River, and swiveled on two rails within the timber revetment.

The powder magazine inside Battery Rodgers was covered by more than seventeen feet of dirt to absorb enemy shellfire. For its 15-inch Parrott gun, the battery contained these stacked solid 428-pound balls, each fired at ranges of up to two miles by a 40-pound powder charge.

Although only five of these large raiders operated during the course of the war – never more than two concurrently – they and a few lesser vessels sank 261 Yankee merchantmen totaling 110,000 tons. Worse, they frightened Northern shipowners sufficiently to shift 800,000 tons of merchant shipping from U.S. to neutral British registry and its attendant lower marine insurance rates and naval protection. Although Yankee shippers still met the wartime trading needs of the North, the American merchant marine was fatally weakened over the long term – for an unsympathetic postwar Congress would not permit these vessels to return to American registry.

While this commerce warfare gradually developed, the U.S. Navy took immediate steps to make the blockade work. In June 1861 Assistant Secretary Fox appointed Captain Samuel F. DuPont as senior member of a strategy board which recommended that joint army-navy expeditions seize positions along the Southern coast for blockading stations. Once secured, these places could be manned and fortified as enclaves from which Union blockading steamers could be resupplied with coal and provisions, giving them sufficient staying power to remain on station and chase down blockade runners. Since, strategically, the Confederacy was a hollow shell on the interior, with its main armies concentrated in Virginia and Tennessee, the only opposition expected by the Union along the coasts would be from seaport forts and makeshift gunboats. Thus began the fleet-vs.-fort character of coastal operations. In August 1861 the first expedition easily captured the forts at Hatteras Inlet, North Carolina, and three months later Flag Officer DuPont, newly appointed commander of the South Atlantic Blockading Squadron, seized Port Royal Roads and Beaufort, South Carolina.

Such reverses led Jefferson Davis in November to transfer General Robert E. Lee, unsuccessful in trying to regain West Virginia for the Confederacy, to command of the coast defenses of South Carolina, Georgia, and East Florida. Lacking sufficient manpower to defend the long

The romantic view of the gathering armies is typified in this oil painting of Maine and Rhode Island volunteers by James Walker. So uniform are the soldiers that they are all of the same height! Only their beards and mustaches differ.

General McClellan is
caricatured by a Northern
newspaper as a policeman
enforcing the Constitution
during the Peninsular
Campaign. Jefferson Davis'
hand organ plays a tune of
retreat, "Skedaddle!" – the
soldier's word for running
away in the face of the
enemy.

coastline, Lee elected a strategy of defense-in-depth. He pulled his meager ground forces away from the coast, keeping them beyond the range of Union naval guns and logistical support, with a view toward luring the Union troops inland where he could defeat them. The strategem failed completely, however, since the mission of these Union forces was to remain on the coast. Therefore, joint Union expeditionary forces had little opposition in capturing several more positions along the coast early in 1862, notably St. Augustine and Jacksonville, Florida, and Fort Pulaski, commanding the approaches to Savannah, Georgia – the latter operation again led by DuPont. Secretary Mallory hurriedly authorized gunboat construction to defend the Chesapeake Bay; Wilmington, North Carolina; Charleston; Savannah; Mobile, Alabama; and New Orleans, but the early losses of territory to Union blockading squadrons and amphibious expeditions seriously weakened the Confederacy's defenses.

The South therefore adopted a continental strategy, assuming a defensive character, with armies positioned along its border with the Union and with forts, supported by the gunboats, defending its seaports and river courses. Under various and often changing geographic names, its armies and departments generally reflected the states in which they operated. In the Eastern theater of war, what came to be known in mid-1862 as the Army of Northern Virginia protected Richmond and most of Virginia. In the Western theater, several smaller armies held the line across southern Kentucky and southern Missouri. Strategically, the South thus had the theoretical advantage of operating from interior lines, able to shift troops to whatever positions were threatened by Union advances. But any real mobility was compromised by the fact that only one railroad connected East and West, the Memphis and Charleston across the Appalachians, meaning that the shifting of major forces could only be accomplished by long, overland marches.

The Union, by contrast, adopted an offensive strategy with a distinctive maritime character. That is, to invade the South, it could move ground forces by rail and river

*Using hand-held lanterns,
Confederate soldiers of Major
General John B. Magruder's
command reconnoiter
outside their defensive works
at Yorktown, Virginia, during
McClellan's siege of the place
in April 1862.*

steamer to advanced bases around Washington and St. Louis, then advance along the lines of the rivers dissecting the South: the Potomac and James in Virginia, the Mississippi, Ohio, Tennessee, and Cumberland in the West. The Union armies were therefore named for these rivers. As these armies followed the watercourses, gunboats could provide fire support and help reduce Confederate fortifications. And where rivers proved less suitable or absent, Union army railroads could be constructed to maintain supply links with the North. If the Union advanced simultaneously on all fronts, the Confederacy could never hope to meet each penetration. But in 1861 no such grand strategy existed, and coordination between theater commanders immediately proved difficult.

In August 1861 Lincoln appointed Major General McClellan to command of the new Army of the Potomac and three months later also to succeed Scott as general-

in-chief of the Union armies. At the same time the brilliant tactician Henry Wager Halleck was recalled to active duty as major general in the regular army to direct Union fortunes in the West. McClellan, however, kept his initial focus on the Eastern theater and planned to exploit Union maritime advantage by moving the Army of the Potomac – once trained, equipped, and ready – by water from the environs of Washington, down the Potomac and the Chesapeake Bay to Fortress Monroe on the tip of the Virginia "peninsula" formed by the York and James rivers. The fortress, after resisting Confederate attempts at capture, would act as McClellan's base of operations as he moved up the peninsula and along the James River to take Richmond. Unfortunately, because McClellan delayed his advance so long, Lincoln relieved him as general-in-chief in March 1862, an act which helped convince McClellan to commence the campaign still as the head of the Army of the Potomac. In addition, that January, Lincoln replaced the ineffective Secretary of War Simon Cameron with the dynamic Edwin McMasters Stanton.

Despite his delays, McClellan adeptly organized the Army of the Potomac into a force of over 100,000 men, organized into five corps commanded by major generals. Each corps comprised two divisions, each division three brigades plus artillery, and each brigade five 1,000-man regiments. The cavalry was separate. The opposing Confederate army under General Joseph E. Johnston, about 85,000 strong, was organized along similar lines, except that corps designations were not yet applied. The

Union guards, one (left foreground) armed with a carbine, others with stacked musket rifles, watch over Confederate prisoners taken during Jackson's Shenandoah Valley campaign in May 1862. The pointed Sibley tent (center background) allowed campfire smoke to escape through the top.

Mud-splattered 20-pounder Parrott rifled guns belonging to the 1st New York Battery of McClellan's army on the Peninsula. This standard rifled artillery piece, used by both sides, doubled the range of the smoothbores to over two miles. Inventor Robert P. Parrott headed the West Point Iron and Gun Foundry throughout the war.

Previous pages: following the rebel evacuation of Yorktown, Union troops attack the Confederate rear at Williamsburg, Virginia. Brigadier General Winfield S. Hancock's brigade is seen driving in the enemy left wing, May 5, 1862.

This civilian-operated sutler's store at Yorktown provides sundry army-approved articles that McClellan's soldiers could purchase to augment the bare necessities issued them by the Quartermaster Department.

Inside a Union telegrapher's tent at Camp Winfield Scott near Yorktown on the Virginia Peninsula.

ALL QUIET ALONG THE POTOMAC

McClellan's inaction with his growing army on the north bank of the Potomac River caused great frustration among the people of the Union during the autumn of 1861. One simple and oft-repeated descriptive War Department news bulletin increased the bitterness: "All quiet along the Potomac." The only military actions occurred between Union and Confederate soldiers standing picket duty on the opposite shores taking occasional pot-shots at each other. And because these private soldiers, rather than officers, were the victims, such casualties were not newsworthy; everything, officially, remained quiet.

Harper's Weekly published a poem entitled "The Picket Guard" in its November 30, 1861 issue which captured the irony of this injustice. Although it carried no by-line, the moving verse was authored by a New York woman, Mrs. Ethel Lynn Eliot Beers. Five different composers, North and South, set the poem to music, but the version by the Confederate John Hill Hewitt in 1863 won the widest acceptance on both sides. The first verse of the slow, sad refrain of "All Quiet Along the Potomac Tonight" told the story:

All quiet along the Potomac tonight,
Except here and there a stray picket
Is shot, as he walks on his beat to and fro,
By a rifleman hid in the thicket:
'Tis nothing, a private or two now and then
Will not count in the news of the battle;
Not an officer lost, only one of the men,
Moaning out all alone the death rattle.
All quiet along the Potomac tonight!

OFFENSIVE BY SEA

South had a more logical ranking system for its general officers: generals led armies, lieutenant generals corps, major generals divisions, and brigadier generals brigades, unlike the Union, which settled for the lower two ranks.

A Confederate secret weapon suddenly frustrated McClellan's plan of campaign. The ironclad C.S.S. *Virginia*, swiftly converted from the frigate hull of the captured U.S.S. *Merrimac*, steamed out of Norfolk at the mouth of the James River to easily sink two wooden Union frigates in Hampton Roads on March 8, 1862. As near panic spread across the North in fear of this monster possibly ravaging New York harbor, next day a revolutionary Union warship arrived off Fortress Monroe in the form of the *Monitor*, a turreted platform looking like a "cheesebox on a raft." The two vessels slugged it out to a standstill, after which the *Virginia* withdrew to Norfolk. Remaining there instead of challenging the *Monitor* again, she discouraged McClellan and the navy from advancing up the peninsula via the James. So he elected to advance along the less navigable York River, with minimal support from his navy, which remained more concerned with keeping watch over the *Virginia* at Norfolk.

After most of the Army of the Potomac arrived on the peninsula aboard transport vessels from Washington during late March, McClellan moved against Yorktown on April 4, only to stop short next day when he encountered 17,000 rebel troops well dug in. In typical engineering fashion, he elected to lay siege to Yorktown, meaning an artillery bombardment that consumed an entire month. McClellan's caution and textbook approach to capturing Richmond cost him the elements of initiative and surprise, but he counted on the arrival of yet another corps under McDowell from Washington and a force from the upper Shenandoah Valley to give him overwhelming strength for investing the Confederate capital city.

The Confederates quickly exploited McClellan's sluggishness. General Lee, recalled to Richmond from his

Norfolk Navy Yard, reoccupied by Union forces in May 1862, was so thoroughly devastated as a result of its burning – first by Union forces and then by the retreating rebels – that immense repairs were necessary. The yard continued to aid the blockade, but in a much reduced capacity.

Currier & Ives prints often romanticized the war, as in the image (right) of the Battle of Fair Oakes, or Seven Pines, where, on May 31, 1862, Union assaults seem to move in rigid waves. One of "Professor" Thaddeus S. C. Lowe's seven hydrogen-filled balloons was used to telegraph Confederate movements to McClellan. The cumbersome tethered gas bags were rarely used again.

After the rebel evacuation of Williamsburg, McClellan's army presses through the woods and across the streams of the Virginia Peninsula toward Richmond. Large tree trunks have been felled by the enemy to slow their advance.

Overleaf: the Army of the Potomac collects its dead and burns the carcasses of horses at Fair Oaks Station after the battle.

83

OFFENSIVE
BY SEA

86

Enemies shake hands (left) as they collect their wounded under a flag of truce. Sketch by A. R. Waud for Harper's Weekly.

A two-wheel Finley ambulance (above) disgorges wounded Union soldiers onto a railroad flatcar for passage to a hospital on June 3, 1862, after the Battle of Fair Oaks. The flimsy carriage badly jolted its human cargoes, thereby exacerbating their wounds and pain. Drawing probably by Arthur Lumley.

THE NAVAL BATTLE WITH THE *MERRIMAC (VIRGINIA)*

March 9, 1862

By **Samuel Lewis**, Gun-loader, U.S.S. *Monitor* (and veteran sailor of the U.S., British, and Russian navies who enlisted under the alias Peter Truskitt in the event he "might have to decamp [desert] at the first port" to escape a bad captain or a bad ship)

You can see surprise in a ship just the same as you can see it in a human being, and there was surprise all over the Merrimac. *She fired a shot across us, but Captain [John L.] Worden, our commander, said, "Wait till you get close, boys, and then let her have it." In a moment the ball had opened. Our guns were so low down that it was practically point-blank firing, and we made every shot as far as possible tell. At first the* Merrimac *directed her fire at the turret, and was evidently trying hard to put a shell in. … The din inside the turret was something terrific. The noise of every solid ball that hit fell upon our ears with a crash that deafened us. … Screw-heads [which held the turret plates] began to fly off from the concussion of the shots. Several of the men were badly bruised by them. …*

The immense volume of smoke and narrow apertures to see through made maneuvering very difficult, and at times we had hard work telling where the enemy was. Twice she tried to ram us, but we got out of the way. We looked for an attack by a boarding party, and had a supply of hand grenades to throw out of the turret if one succeeded in gaining the deck. Our men were confident and hopeful all through. Once Lieutenant [Samuel Dana] Greene [the executive officer] called out, "They are going to board us!" but instead of scaring anybody it seemed to please the crew. "Let 'em come!" sings out one, "we will amuse them some!" After the fight had been in progress for a couple of hours, I was knocked senseless by [the shock of] a shot. …

The Merrimac *turned tail after a little over four hours of fighting. The enthusiasm of our men was at fever heat.*

OFFENSIVE
BY SEA

Union guns atop Malvern Hill pummel Lee's army on July 1, 1862, bringing an end to the Seven Days' Battles: Oak Grove, June 25; Mechanicsville (or Beaver Dam Creek), June 26; Gaines' Mill, June 27-28; Garnett's and Golding's Farms, June 27-28; Savage's Station, June 29; and White Oak Swamp (or Glendale), June 30.

coast defense command to advise Davis, had Johnston shift the main army overland from northern Virginia to the peninsula and Stonewall Jackson with 10,000 men to attack several Union brigades in the Shenandoah Valley as a potential threat to Washington. Lincoln and Secretary Stanton, suitably alarmed, refused permission for McDowell and the other reinforcements to join McClellan and even forced the latter to send a corps from the peninsula to help defend Washington against Jackson. For the entire month of May Jackson thrusted and parried against three uncoordinated and larger Union forces in the Valley campaign, achieving great mobility with his "foot cavalry" – infantry marching at the double-quick for an hour then resting flat on their backs for ten minutes. The net effect was to deprive McClellan of the forces preoccupied with Jackson, who then rejoined the main army on the peninsula in early June. Major culprits in the wasted effort against Jackson were Lincoln and Secretary Stanton for ignoring their military advisers who understood

Jackson's diversionary strategy.

Meanwhile, the Peninsular Campaign continued as Johnston abandoned Yorktown and Norfolk early in May in favor of stronger defenses closer to Richmond. McClellan moved slowly up the York, hoping to link up with McDowell but mired in the broken ground and marshlands about the smaller Chickahominy River. Meanwhile, the Confederates had to destroy their deep-draft *Virginia* – unable to escape from Norfolk up the shallow James River – whereupon shallow-draft Union gunboats pressed up the James as far as Drewry's Bluff, only seven miles from Richmond. There, however, on May 15, Confederate cannon drove them back, revealing the danger of warships attacking fixed fortifications without assaulting infantry in support. Johnston then planned to attack the part of McClellan's army south of the Chickahominy before the rest could cross over. On May 31 the rebels struck and nearly succeeded, but poor staff coordination and a determined Union counterattack frustrated the

This military bridge was thrown across the Chickahominy River by the 15th New York Infantry, enabling McClellan to move his troops between both banks in the drive on Richmond. Though hardly level, the timbered roadway did its job.

HOW IT SEEMS TO KILL A MAN

by **Charles F. Manderson**, Major, 19th Ohio Infantry

The first man I killed was before Richmond, when McClellan was in command. I was doing picket duty late one night near the bank of a creek and had been cautioned to be specially watchful, as an attack was expected. I carried my musket half-cocked, and was startled by every rustle the wind made among the trees and dead leaves. It was sometime after midnight that I saw a Confederate cavalryman dashing down the opposite side of the creek in my direction. As he was opposite I fired upon the horse and it fell. The cavalryman regained his feet in a moment and had drawn his pistols. I called him to surrender, but his only reply was a discharge from each revolver, one bullet inflicting a flesh wound in my arm. Then I let him have it full in the breast.

He leaped three feet in the air, and fell with his face down. I knew I had finished him. I ran and jumped across the creek, picked him up and laid him on his back. The blood was running out of his nose and mouth, and poured in a torrent from the ragged hole in his breast. In less time than it takes to tell it, he was dead, without having said a word. Then my head began to swim, and I was sick at my stomach. I was overcome by an indescribable horror of the deed I had done. I trembled all over, and felt faint and weak. It was with the greatest difficulty that I managed to get into camp. There they laughed at me, but it was weeks before my nervous system had recovered from the shock.

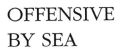

OFFENSIVE BY SEA

move, and Johnston himself was severely wounded in this two-day Battle of Fair Oaks (or Seven Pines). Robert E. Lee replaced Johnston, welcomed Stonewall Jackson's return from the Valley, and prepared to crush the one remaining Union corps now left north of the Chickahominy. In mid-June, he sent his flamboyant cavalry leader Brigadier General J.E.B. "Jeb" Stuart on a reconnaissance in force, but Stuart overplayed his mission by riding north and east completely around McClellan's army. In capturing Union supplies on this foray, he alerted McClellan to the vulnerability of the Union base of operations on the north side of the peninsula.

McClellan, determined to preserve his strategic maritime advantage, thereupon decided to shift his base from the York to the James, where the Navy could not only support him but deliver McDowell's reinforcements now finally en route by sea from Fredericksburg on Virginia's Rappahannock River. Since Lee's Army of Northern Virginia stood in the way of the movement from the north to the south side of the peninsula, McClellan had to fight his way across. The result was the Seven Days' Battles, beginning on June 25, 1862 – seven different engagements in which the two armies slugged it out before McClellan reached the James on July 1, on which day 250 Union cannon emplanted on Malvern Hill slaughtered frontal

assaults by Lee's infantry. McClellan had succeeded in reaching the succor of Union gunboats at Harrison's Landing, but the Army of the Potomac had not gotten one foot closer to Richmond. With casualties of 16,000 men (against 20,000 for the South), McClellan was not permitted by his superiors to proceed up the James against Petersburg, the southern flank of Richmond's defenses. The Union invasion of Virginia by sea had failed, due in large part to the brief, unanticipated presence of the ironclad *Virginia.*

McClellan's failure on the peninsula thus discredited the idea of a seaward invasion for the foreseeable future, thus sacrificing the unique Union strategic advantage. Army–Navy rivalry was part of the reason, especially the determination of Assistant Navy Secretary Fox to dominate Union strategy along the Southern coast. Dazzled by the

A Confederate Rodman gun, probably captured at the Norfolk Navy Yard in April 1861, commands the approaches to Richmond at Drewry's Bluff on the James River. These defenses prevented Union warships from pressing beyond toward the Confederate capital.

performance of the *Monitor* at Hampton Roads, Fox ignored his own experts and contracted with John Ericsson, the vessel's inventor, to build ten more. The problem was that the 1,000-ton two-gun monitors were best suited to harbor defense – just like the new Confederate ironclads – and not for offensive assaults on coastal fortifications which required a large and fairly rapid volume of fire as achieved during the capture of Port Royal, South Carolina. The victor there, Rear Admiral DuPont, and his uniformed colleagues instead welcomed the ironclad steamer *New Ironsides* in August, a 3,500-ton behemoth mounting broadside batteries of fourteen 11-inch smoothbore guns and two 150-pound Parrott rifles. DuPont made the *New Ironsides* his flagship on the blockade of Charleston in January 1863. Fox, however, ordered DuPont to attack the six forts guarding Charleston with nine monitors on April 7 that year. In the action, the forts' gunners scored 20 percent hits of 2,200 rounds fired, sinking one monitor and damaging and driving off the rest, though the *New Ironsides* suffered only minimal damage. When DuPont refused to renew the suicidal attack, Fox fired him.

Fox would not give up his obsession to capture the "hell-hole of secession" – the seaport where South Carolina had initiated the rebellion – and he delayed efforts to seize the increasingly important port of Wilmington, North Carolina, by continued efforts against Charleston. Fox promoted a joint Army–Navy attack on Battery Wagner of Charleston's Morris Island during the summer of 1863. It finally succeeded in September but not before the first Union Negro troops as well as white recruits had been butchered in several assaults. Rear Admiral John A.B. Dahlgren, DuPont's replacement, kept up the pressure on Charleston and a close watch on three Confederate ironclads inside the harbor. The *New Ironsides* proved durable as ever, not only engaging other rebel forts but even absorbing a hit from a spar torpedo by the submersible *David* in October. "Miracle weapons" like monitors and mines blinded Fox and others to the larger traditional problems of fleets-versus-forts which required more conventional though armored warships. Such strategic shortsightedness consequently delayed the prompt application of Union naval superiority along the Atlantic seaboard. Fortunately for the Union, this was not the case in the Western theater.

Confederate guns on Morris Island (foreground) fire on DuPont's monitors as they approach Fort Sumter, April 7, 1863. Intersecting rebel fire was also provided from Sumter itself and from Fort Moultrie on Sullivan's Island (far right background).

A Yankee shell bursts inside Fort Sumter.

U.S. Navy gunners aboard one of Admiral DuPont's monitors load a solid ball into a 15-inch Dahlgren smoothbore during the April 1863 attack on Fort Sumter.

95

A 200-pound 8-inch Parrott rifle at Fort Gregg on Morris Island commands the southern water approaches to Charleston harbor in 1865. A similar Union gun there, known as the "Swamp Angel," shelled the city – 7,900 yards distant – in late August 1863, but blew up before causing much damage.

ASSAULT ON FORT WAGNER

(immortalized in the 1989 motion picture *Glory*)   July 18, 1863

by **Captain L.F. Emilio**, 54th Massachusetts Infantry (Colored)

Upon that memorable 18th of July, 1863 [after several hours of shelling] ... at 6 p.m. a single regiment marched toward the front, along the road. ... While passing over the low ground to the left of our artillery line the long blue column drew from James Island several ineffective shots. The only response of the 54th Mass. (Colored) was to double-quick, that it might the sooner close with the foe. On every side the killed and wounded were falling; still the survivors pressed on, stumbling over the prostrate forms of comrades, or into the pits made by the great shells of our navy and batteries. Darkness had gathered. ... Every cannon flash lit up the scene and disclosed the ground strewn with victims. Over the sanguinary field, the indomitable [Colonel Robert G.] Shaw had led the stormers; then down into and through the ditch, and up the parapet of the curtain [wall]. There he stood a moment shouting to his followers, and then fell dead. Both of the regimental colors were planted on the work, the national flag carried and maintained there by the brave Sergt. William H. Carney of Co. C.

As the 54th mounted the parapet..., for a few minutes a hand-to-hand struggle went on. ... The weakened ranks of the 54th soon gave way to superior numbers, and they fell back upon the slopes of the work. Hardly a shot had been fired by the 54th up to this time; but now were heard revolvers, and the louder reports of musket shots. ... Still, by encouraging the men to remain, it was hoped help would be afforded the other troops as they came up. While engaged in this, many brave men fell. Capts. Cabot J. Russell and William H. Simpkins were killed. ... The enemy supplemented their musketry with hand-grenades or shells, which they threw down the slopes into the mass of men in the ditch below. ...

The writer went into the assault as the junior captain of the 54th, and by the casualties of the field [3 officers, 62 men killed; 11 officers, 145 men wounded; some 40 others captured] came out in command of the regiment.

In contrast to the disfigured walls, the inside of Sumter's sally-ports remained unscathed. A sally-port was an opening through which defending gunners of the 1st South Carolina Artillery might "sally forth" against assaulting infantry - never necessary at Sumter.

Though its walls were battered and mauled by the Union navy, Fort Sumter managed to hold out for nearly four years of war. The view is of Battery B on the interior; the battle flag of a white field and the crossed bars in the corner was adopted during 1863.

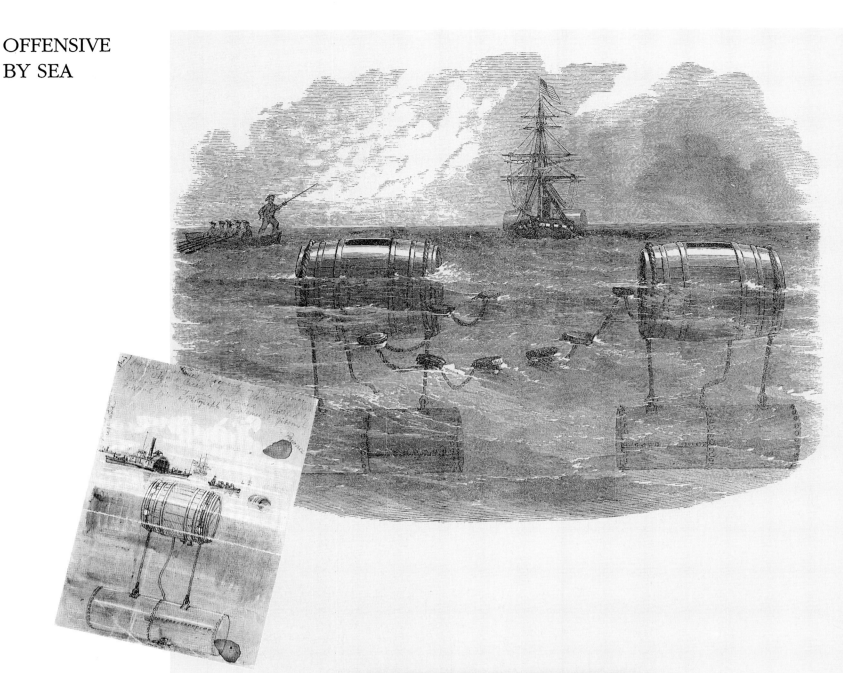

A longboat of crewmen from the Union sidewheel gunboat Thomas Freeborn *(above) prepares to dispose of floating rebel "infernal machines" – powder charges suspended from barrels – near Aquia Creek Landing on the Potomac in June 1861. The gunboats kept open the sea route between Washington and the Chesapeake Bay. Sketch by Waud.*

Charles Wilkes (left), fiery captain of the screw frigate San Jacinto, *was sixty-three years of age when he seized the rebel diplomats Mason and Slidell from the British packet* Trent *in 1861, causing an international crisis. Promoted to commodore of the West India Squadron, he violated British territory there during 1862-63 and was relieved of his command.*

A tiny sailing sloop flying the Stars and Bars tries to evade a Union blockader to run goods into the South.

Above: the official seal of the Confederate States Navy.

Left: David G. Farragut. Falsely suspected of disloyalty because of his Southern birth, wife and residence, Farragut was not given an active command until January 1862. As flag officer, he brilliantly captured New Orleans and also, eventually, Mobile to become the Navy's first rear admiral (1862), vice admiral (1864) and full admiral (1866).

OFFENSIVE BY SEA

First as flag officer then as rear admiral, the superb Samuel F. DuPont served on the strategy board that devised the blockade. Heading the South Atlantic Blockading Squadron, he captured coastal Port Royal, South Carolina, and Fort Pulaski, Georgia, in 1861-62 but failed to take Charleston in 1863.

Traditional seagoing swabs of the line of battle sailing ships show their disdain for the new steam engines and coastal monitors ("Can't see it" says the spyglass) in this cartoon with its convoluted, ungrammatical caption.

A sectional view of a coastal monitor.

Left: iron against wood. The CSS Virginia *rams and sinks the Union sailing frigate* Cumberland *in Hampton Roads, Virginia, March 8, 1962. The* Virginia's *skipper, Flag Officer Franklin Buchanan, then turned on and sank the frigate* Congress, *whose officers included his brother.*

Below: as Flag Officer Buchanan was wounded by Union during the sinking of the Congress, *the next day his executive officer, Lieutenant Catesby ap R. Jones, led the* Virginia *against the Union frigate* Minnesota, *only to be confronted by the equally revolutionary ironclad, USS* Monitor.

During this furious battle, the first ever fought between ironclads, the Monitor *and the* Merrimac *slugged it out in a virtual stalemate, although a Southern shell exploded near the peephole of the* Monitor's *captain, Lieutenant John L. Worden, partially blinding him. His executive officer, Lieutenant S. Dana Greene, carried on the fight.*

John Ericsson was canonized for his invention of the Monitor, *several more of which were then constructed by the Union. Their flat trajectory of fire, however, compromised their effectiveness against Confederate coastal forts, particularly at Charleston.*

A July 1862 photograph (right) shows the only structural damage inflicted on the Monitor'*s turret by the* Merrimac *during their epic battle. This tactical draw between mutually indestructible weapons anticipated the stalemate of modern weapons technology. Similarly, Civil War siege trenches foreshadowed those of World War I.*

Officers of the Monitor *(above) pose while riding at anchor on the James River, July 9, 1862. The straw hat (on the right) probably belongs to the photographer, James Gibson.*

Resigning as a veteran U.S. Navy commander, Raphael Semmes (left) served as captain of the Confederate commerce raiders Sumter, during 1861-62, and Alabama, during 1862-64, capturing 100 Yankee merchant ships. By the end of the war he was the only rear admiral in the rebel navy.

Unseaworthy beyond inshore waters, the Monitor foundered in a storm off North Carolina's treacherous Cape Hatteras on December 30, 1862. When her wreckage was discovered over a century later, one of the first items to be salvaged, in 1979, was a brass lantern base (below left).

Commerce raiders such as the Alabama were designed to sink merchant ships, not men-of-war such as the Union steam sloop Kearsarge. Thus the latter, under Captain John A. Winslow, used its two 11-inch Dahlgren guns to sink the Alabama, seen afire (below) off Cherbourg, France, June 19, 1864.

Of several expeditions which destroyed Confederate ironclads, none was more dramatic than that against the ram Albemarle *(right) in the Roanoke River, North Carolina, which was carried out by fifteen men in a small launch, using a spar torpedo.*

Below: two ladies pose on the gun deck of the rebel ram Albemarle.

The monitor Weehawken *(right), under Captain John Rodgers, pounds the Confederate ironclad ram* Atlanta *as she runs aground trying to effect a sortie from Wassaw Sound near Savannah, June 17, 1863. The rebel vessel surrendered after taking five hits in fifteen minutes, thus frustrating the one major Southern attempt to break the tight blockade of Savannah.*

Inventor John A.B. Dahlgren (left) armed the Navy as head of the Washington Navy Yard and Bureau of Ordnance. As rear admiral, he then commanded the South Atlantic Blockading Squadron off Charleston and Savannah during the final two years of the war.

The two-man Confederate submarine Pioneer (below), built at New Orleans during 1861-1862, was to have operated as a privateer. Before she could be deployed, however, the city fell to Farragut's attack, and the submarine had to be scuttled.

A religious service is held on the deck of the monitor Passaic (left) off Charleston in 1864.

A two-man Southern "infernal machine" (left) maneuvers to attack the blockading steam frigate Minnesota. No such attack actually occurred, although the torpedo boat Squib did succeed in damaging the Minnesota with a spar torpedo off Newport News, Below: another sketch of a Hunley-type submersible.

Left: a Confederate sub is portrayed exploding a "torpedo" (mine) against the hull of a twin-turreted monitor on blockade station.

Right: a Confederate "David" submerged torpedo boat. The original David exploded a 70-pound charge against the casemated ironclad New Ironsides, October 5, 1863, inflicting heavy damage.

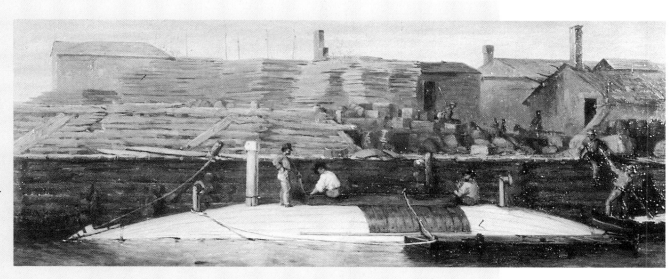

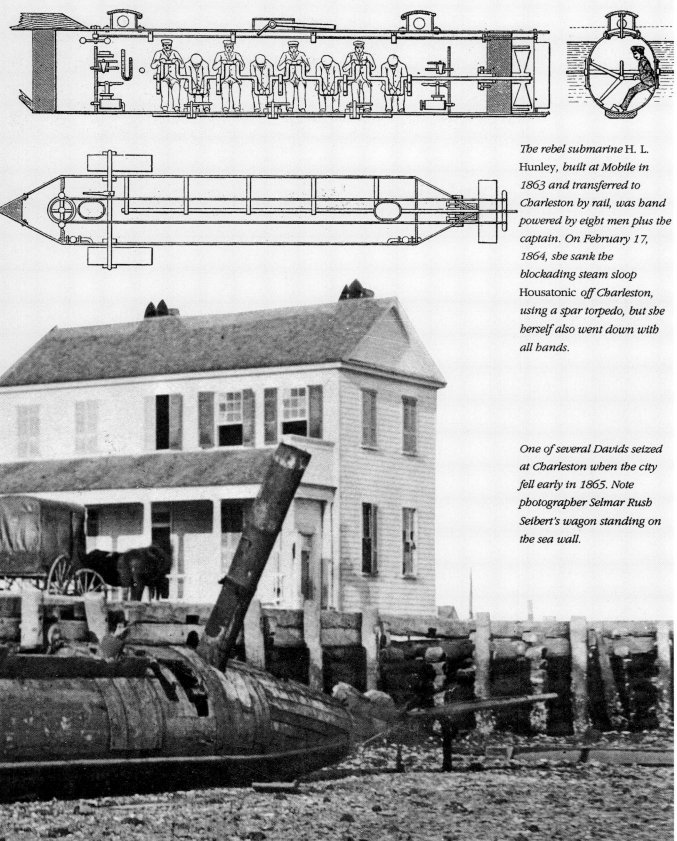

The rebel submarine H. L. Hunley, built at Mobile in 1863 and transferred to Charleston by rail, was hand powered by eight men plus the captain. On February 17, 1864, she sank the blockading steam sloop Housatonic off Charleston, using a spar torpedo, but she herself also went down with all hands.

One of several Davids seized at Charleston when the city fell early in 1865. Note photographer Selmar Rush Seibert's wagon standing on the sea wall.

OFFENSIVE BY SEA

Impressed by rebel torpedo boats, the U.S. Navy built the Spuyten Duyvil *(Dutch for "spitting devil"), the only wartime torpedo boat built as such from the keel up. The recessed spar torpedo exited from the bow. The vessel helped blockade the rebel squadron in the James River during the last winter of the war.*

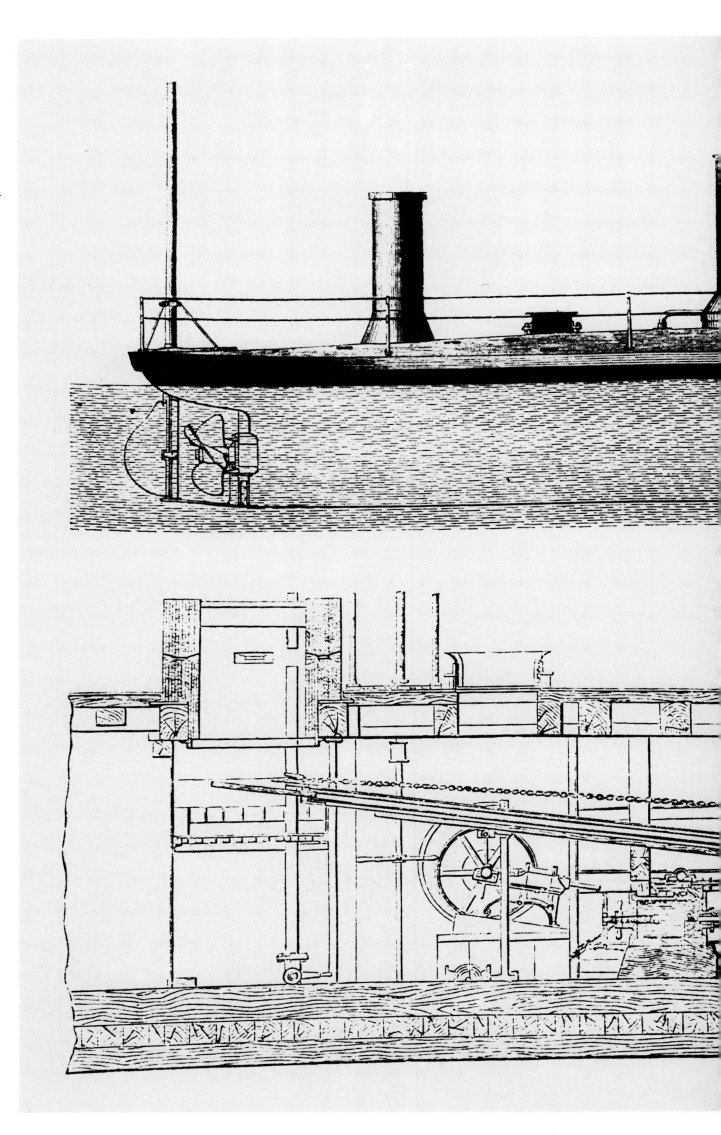

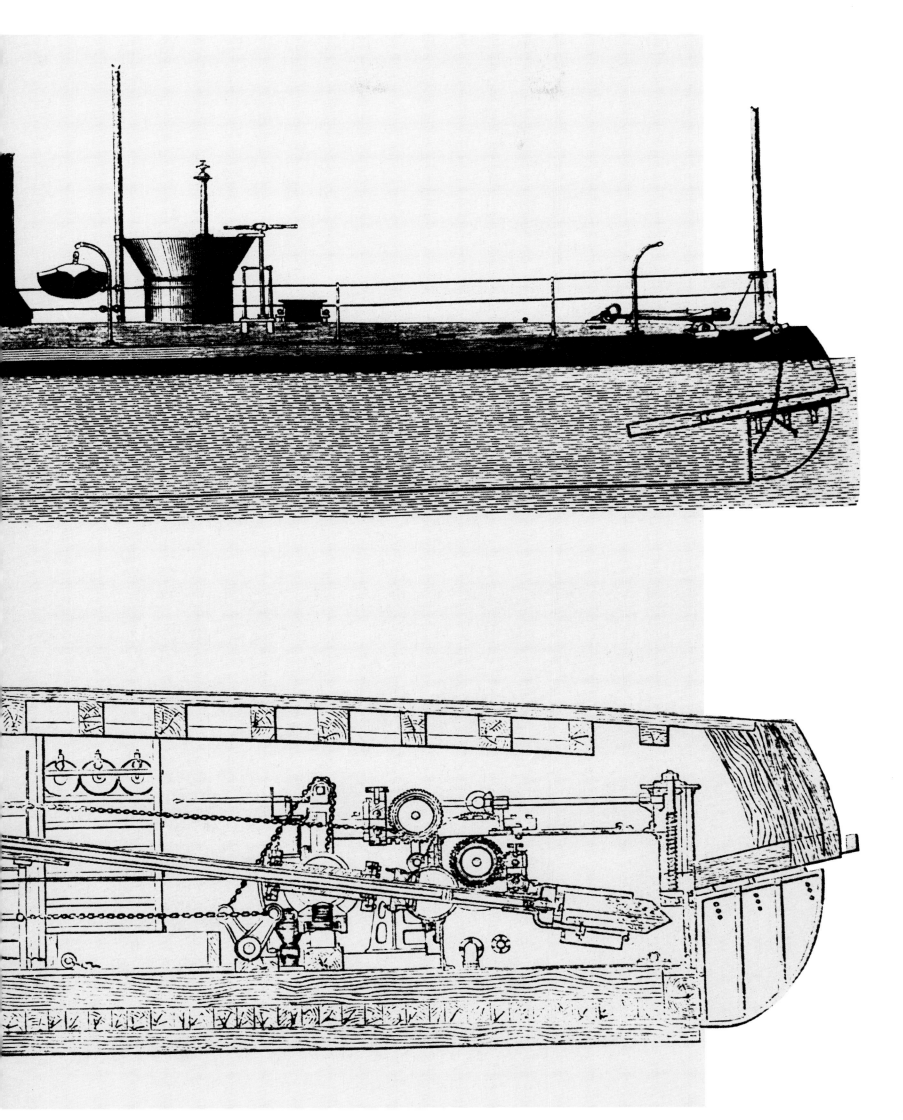

OFFENSIVE
BY SEA

Union naval construction produced the mammoth 16-gun ironclad screw frigate Dunderberg *(a Swedish word meaning "thundering mountain"). She is seen here under construction at the New York shipyard of William H. Webb. Not launched until July 1865, she was later sold to the French Navy.*

3
ARMIES OF THE RIVERS

The Western Forts, Shiloh, New Orleans – Early 1862

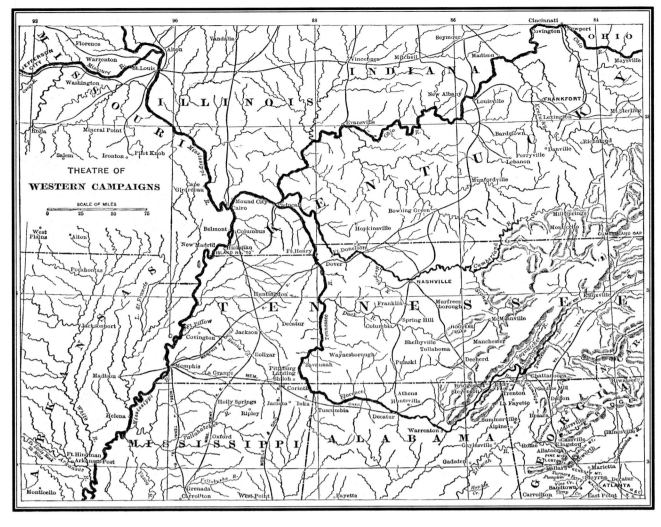

THEATRE OF
WESTERN CAMPAIGNS

SCALE OF MILES
0   25   50   75

*Commercial steamboats clog
the Cincinnati levee on the
eve of the Civil War. Such
vessels were easily converted
into Union army transports
and cargo ships to operate
down the Ohio River into the
Cumberland, Tennessee, and
Mississippi rivers.*

Like the fingers of a great hand, the five rivers from which the new Union armies of the Western theater took their names appear on the map to emanate from a common point – the site of Cairo (pronounced "Kay-roe") at the southern tip of Illinois. Thumb and forefinger – the Missouri and the Mississippi – form a separate joint 250 miles upriver from Cairo at St. Louis. The middle finger is the Ohio, flowing down from Cincinnati and Louisville. The fourth finger is the Cumberland, which reaches eastward past Nashville to the Appalachians. The pinkie is the Tennessee, dipping through that state into northern Alabama then up to Chattanooga and the hills. Union control of the first three fingers at the outbreak of war enabled ground and naval forces to be concentrated around Cairo both to secure the disputed border regions on both flanks – Missouri and Kentucky – and then to move against the two other fingers of the Cumberland and the Tennessee, followed by a drive down the long arm of the lower Mississippi toward the Gulf of Mexico.

During the hasty mobilization in the summer of 1861, both governments contested the environs of Cairo in minor campaigns which however set the stage for the dual Union advances into Tennessee and down the Mississippi. The Confederacy attempted to conquer Missouri with a force of over 11,000 men led by Brigadier General Ben McCulloch which attacked and defeated a force of half that size at Wilson's Creek in August. But since several rebel units had to be shifted east of the Mississippi, the issue for Missouri could not be settled. Over the winter Brigadier General Samuel R. Curtis led a Union army of 11,000 troops against a larger force of Confederates under Major General Earl Van Dorn, crossing into Arkansas where it defeated the Southern force at the Battle of Pea Ridge in early March. Missouri thereafter remained under Union control, although raids and guerrilla operations continually plagued the region.

The contending theater commanders in the Western theater made tentative moves in the Cairo region. From St. Louis, Major General John C. Frémont, a famous explorer but ineffective commander, in August 1861 ordered the slaves in the rebel areas freed in order to undermine Southern authority, only to have the order

The St. Louis waterfront bustles with merchant steamers serving Union forces in the Western theater. This busy river port on the Missouri River was both Army and Navy headquarters for the initial Federal offensives. The man in the rowboat is removing driftwood that would be dangerous to the shallow-draft paddlewheelers.

Workers "wooding up" the steamer Sultana by torchlight on the Mississippi River just before the war. The mammoth vessel was then engaged as a Union army transport.

I WISH I WAS IN DIXIE'S LAND

This catchy tune, which became the unofficial anthem of the Confederacy, was composed by an Ohioan, Daniel D. Emmett, for a minstrel show in 1859. It caught on so rapidly in the prewar South that it was performed at the inauguration of President Jefferson Davis in Montgomery, Alabama on February 4, 1861. Before long, the entire South adopted the nickname "Dixie."

I wish I was in de land ob cotton,
Old times dar am not forgotten;
Look away! Look away! Look away! Dixie Land.
In Dixie Land whar I was born in,
Early on one frosty mornin';
Look away! Look away! Look away! Dixie Land.

Chorus
Den I wish I was in Dixie,
Hooray! Hooray!
In Dixie Land, I'll take my stand,
To lib an' die in Dixie,
Away, away,
Away down south in Dixie.

Old Missus marry "Will-de-weaber,"
Willium was a gay deceaber;
Look away! Look away! Look away! Dixie Land.
But when he put his arm around 'er,
He smiled as fierce as a forty pounder.
Look away! Look away! Look away! Dixie Land.

(Chorus)

His face was sharp as a butcher's cleaber,
But dat did not seem to greab'er;
Look away! Look away! Look away! Dixie Land.
Old Missus acted de foolish part,
And died for a man dat broke her heart.
Look away! Look away! Look away! Dixie Land.

(Chorus)

Now here's a health to the next old Missus,
An all de gals dat want to kiss us;
Look away! Look away! Look away! Dixie Land.
But if you want to drive 'way sorrow,
Come and hear dis song to-morrow;
Look away! Look away! Look away! Dixie Land.

(Chorus)

revoked by President Lincoln as politically ill-advised, given the Union's limited war aims. But Frémont appointed Brigadier General Ulysses S. Grant to command at Cairo and assisted the senior naval commander, Captain Andrew H. Foote, in obtaining local shipping for use as gunboats and transports on the rivers. Meanwhile, Confederate Major General Leonidas Polk, former Episcopal bishop of Louisiana but like Grant a West Point graduate out of uniform for years, undertook establishing Confederate defenses of the upper Mississippi and occupied Columbus, Kentucky, 25 miles downriver from Cairo, on September 4. Two weeks later, the superb General Albert Sidney Johnston assumed overall command of the Confederacy's Western Department and quickly occupied Bowling Green in south central Kentucky. Frémont then ordered Grant to seize Paducah, Kentucky up the Ohio River from Cairo and situated at its confluence with the Tennessee River, which he did on October 6. Grant then moved down the Mississippi on river boats and occupied Belmont, Missouri on the shore opposite Columbus on November 7, despite being stung from a counterattack by Polk.

By mid-November 1861, then, the semblance of a military frontier had been established in the West.

Flag Officer Andrew H. Foote displayed the same sort of aggressiveness in supporting the army on the Western rivers during 1862 that he had in attacking warlord forts in China six years before. The wounds he received at Fort Donelson caused his untimely death in mid-1863 while en route to take command of the blockade off Charleston.

ARMIES OF THE RIVERS

U.S. Army sternwheelers such as the Bridgeport *provided mobility on the Western rivers, their open decks suitable for human or material cargo. An artillery piece at the bow provides a modicum of protection against enemy forces on the river banks. The crew includes several blacks, typical of Union vessels of war.*

Johnston's Confederate defense line ran across southern Kentucky, from Columbus on the Mississippi through Bowling Green in the center to lesser forces holding the eastern foothills of the state. His military engineers were building fortifications to defend the point where the two key rivers entered Kentucky from Tennessee – Fort Henry on the Tennessee and Fort Donelson on the Cumberland. The base of the western Confederate defenses was Nashville, further up the Cumberland. The South's only east-west railroad, which connected Memphis,

Tennessee with Charleston, South Carolina, ran along the Tennessee–Mississippi–Alabama border, well to the rear of Johnston's forts and was joined to Nashville by a feeder line. To deepen the defense of the Mississippi River, Johnston had forts constructed below Columbus at New Madrid, Missouri and Island No. 10 in mid-river. And early in the new year he welcomed Flag Officer George N. Hollins and a squadron of makeshift gunboats brought upriver from New Orleans to help defend Memphis. The key seaports of the Gulf coast – New Orleans, Mobile,

One of the first Confederate ten-dollar Treasury notes.

With her side paddle wheels and open decks boarded over for protection, the wooden former commercial river steamer Conestoga *(right) displays her tall smoke stack and broadside guns. As part of the Army's Western Gunboat Flotilla, she participated in the capture of forts Henry and Donelson in February 1862.*

The ironclad Army river gunboat Cairo *(below), built by the James Eads Company, served on the Mississippi. The Eads gunboats were transferred to the Navy in October 1862, when the latter finally gave full support to the Western theater, but the 13-gun* Cairo *was sunk by a torpedo (mine) above Vicksburg in December.*

and Pensacola – remained secure, although a Union garrison had managed to hold Fort Pickens controlling the approaches to Pensacola ever since the beginning of the war, and the blockade was beginning in the Gulf.

The Union strategy in the West passed to Major General Halleck in November when Lincoln sacked the incompetent Frémont. An able administrator and theorist nicknamed "Old Brains," Halleck at St. Louis commanded the Department of the Missouri, all Union forces west of the Cumberland River. Appointed to command the Department and Army of the Ohio east of the Cumberland in November was Brigadier General Don Carlos Buell at Louisville. Flag Officer Foote commanded the gunboats being assembled at Mound City, Illinois, near Cairo on the Ohio River. At the suggestion of Grant, Halleck decided to allow him, with the help of Foote's gunboats, to attack Forts Henry and Donelson. If successful, the Confederate line of defense in the West would be pierced, forcing Johnston to abandon western and central Kentucky. Buell, in the meantime, sent a force under Brigadier General George H. Thomas against the rebel forces in

eastern Kentucky. Thomas met and defeated Major General George B. Crittenden at the Battle of Mill Springs (or Logan's Cross Roads) on the banks of the Cumberland in January 1862. Simultaneously, a brigade under Colonel James A. Garfield drove a Confederate force from positions in the mountains, both actions clearing eastern Kentucky of Confederate troops.

The Union invasion of Tennessee got underway at the beginning of February 1862 as Foote's squadron of seven powerful gunboats and two of Grant's divisions moved up the Tennessee against the uncompleted Fort Henry. On the 6th Foote's naval cannon so bludgeoned the lightly-armed fort that it surrendered before Grant's troops arrived on the scene. Foote then steamed upriver across the entire state as far as northern Alabama, destroying rebel defenses and bridges. This unique naval raid into the interior of the Confederacy ended when the squadron retraced its course down the Tennessee to the Ohio where it rejoined Grant for the attack on Fort Donelson. The fall of Henry convinced the Confederate Johnston that he would soon be outflanked, and he immediately transferred two divisions from Bowling Green to reinforce the one at Donelson. All three were to protect Johnston's flank as his main force abandoned central Kentucky by falling back on Nashville.

Time being of the essence, Grant moved without delay and gave only general information to Halleck lest the initiative be lost through endless messages. On February 12 he marched his 27,000-man army overland from Fort Henry to Fort Donelson and formed his siege lines against the defending force of perhaps half that size. Bitter sub-freezing cold exacerbated the operation, and when on the 14th Foote's gunboats bombarded the fort from the river they were driven back, with Foote being seriously wounded. A Confederate infantry attack nearly succeeded next day, but sluggish leadership soon doomed the garrison. The two senior Southern generals managed to escape, and when their successor asked Grant for terms of surrender on the 16th, Grant replied that he could settle for nothing less than "unconditional and immediate surrender." The mortified Confederate officer had no

Confederate uniforms of (left to right) an artilleryman, infantry general, cavalry general, cavalry officer, and infantryman, with (rear) a black servant and mounted cavalryman.

Both armies followed French examples not only in infantry tactics and fortification designs, but also in military fashions. The standard head gear for infantry was the tilted flat-topped kepi – dark blue for the Union, light blue or gray for the Confederacy.

Because of the Confederate army's shortage of horses, most of which were owned by the individual cavalrymen and artillerymen, it occasionally relied on teams of oxen, such as this one (above right) pulling a mammoth Columbiad gun, which weighed nearly 50,000 pounds.

choice but to capitulate, and Grant's no-nonsense words thrilled the North. It also gave a hint at the total character the war was to assume, if men like Grant were to lead the Northern armies. His command was immediately upgraded to be what now became generally known as the Army of the Tennessee, and Grant was promoted to major general. But "Old Brains" Halleck, in spite of the victory, was miffed at what he regarded as precipitous action by Grant and suspended him from command for a week in early March.

The fall of Forts Henry and Donelson shattered the Confederate defense line in the West. Even as the latter battle raged, General Buell's Army of the Ohio occupied the abandoned Bowling Green, then pressed south toward Nashville. Johnston, lacking sufficient forces to defend that city, retreated through it and clean out of

Tennessee to regroup at Decatur in northern Alabama. Buell occupied Nashville on February 24 and deployed his divisions further south of it. General Polk, similarly outflanked on the Mississippi, evacuated Columbus, Kentucky in favor of defending the river forts at New Madrid and Island No. 10 on the Kentucky–Tennessee–Missouri border. Halleck concurrently authorized Brigadier General John Pope to organize major Union forces in Missouri as the Army of the Mississippi in order to capture these two posts. When Pope laid siege to New Madrid on the Missouri side of the river, the rebel garrison evacuated the place, crossing the river to the peninsula opposite formed by a bend in the river's course. Because the shore batteries of Island No. 10 prevented Union transports from supporting Pope for a river crossing below the fort to isolate it, he put engineers to work cutting

Overleaf: the camp of the 2nd Company of Massachusetts Light Artillery.

ARMIES OF
THE RIVERS

From November 1861 to July 1862, Major General Henry W. Halleck, known as "Old Brains" for his intellectual talents, directed Union forces in the Western theater, where his lack of personal and professional flair made him unpopular. He was, at best, an able administrator but was only a mediocre strategist.

a canal through a bayou direct to New Madrid above the island bastion.

On March 11, 1862 the U.S. War Department merged all the armies in the West into one overall Department of the Mississippi under Halleck. While Pope invested Island No. 10, Halleck had Grant move his six divisions south, up the Tennessee to Pittsburg Landing near the Tennessee–Mississippi state line, and ordered Buell to move south overland from Nashville to reinforce Grant. Such a combined force could drive a wedge through the western Confederacy and hopefully destroy Johnston's army in the process.

Johnston, however, prepared a masterstroke to disrupt the obvious Union strategy. Shifting his headquarters

from Decatur, Alabama to Corinth, Mississippi, just twenty miles south of Grant's advanced base of Pittsburg Landing, he began concentrating all available forces in the West for a surprise attack. General Beauregard arrived from Virginia to assemble the troops in western Tennessee and was made Johnston's second-in-command.

The coastal garrisons from Pensacola and Mobile were brought by rail to Corinth, while a force was transported by boat from New Orleans up the Mississippi to Memphis then by rail to Corinth. By the beginning of April this new Confederate Army of the Mississippi had quietly concentrated 40,000 troops at Corinth. Johnston planned to strike Grant's army of equal size before Buell's 25,000 men arrived to reinforce Grant.

THE FIRST DAY AT SHILOH

April 6, 1862

by **B.F. Sawyer**, Blythe's Mississippi Regiment

Ascending a little slope [at sunrise] we encountered General Beauregard and his staff. The general had a magnificent coach and four [horses]– a la Napoleon – drawn out on the hillside. Captain Dewberry … had supreme contempt for [this] obstruction, stretching the full front of his company. … That gaudy coach … flanked too by the general and his staff in all the glory of gold, lace, and feathers [in their hats], was more than his "tactics" had ever provided for. Without knowing how to flank it he marched his company squarely against it, when perforce the men halted and looked around in confusion. The regiment was aligning upon the colors, and of course the sudden halt of Co. C confused the entire line. "Move forward, Captain Dewberry," thundered Colonel [A.K.] Blythe, mortified at the ignoble confusion of his line under the very eyes of General Beauregard.. … At length [Dewberry] turned to one of the tinsel-bedecked aide-de-camps and roared out: "Take that damned old stage out o' the way or I'll tumble it down the hill!"

… [After clearing] an almost impenetrable thicket of brambles and briers … we were brought [up to the crest of a hill] face to face with the battle. Never shall I forget the grandeur of that sight. The enemy's camps lay before us, spreading far and wide … then came the order, thrilling every heart – "By the left of companies, forward into line; doublequick, march." No order was ever more handsomely executed. Each company filed into line as deliberately as if that long line of sullen blue that lay scarcely three hundred yards in front was a line of friends instead of foes. Co. A…. had scarcely attained position before the enemy opened fire; our line moved forward until within one hundred paces of the line of blue, and then we were lost in the blaze, the thunder, and frenzy of battle.

[Blythe, Dewberry, and five other officers and 80 of the regiment's 330 men were killed, 120 wounded.] A musket ball through the right knee tripped me up as the enemy's line was broken.

The first inkling Grant had of Johnston's scheme was when rebel troops suddenly burst through the woods against two Union divisions encamped about Shiloh Church on the morning of April 6. As the surprised Yankee troops broke and ran back toward the west bank of the Tennessee River, which formed the left side of the Union encampment, Union division commanders tried to form a makeshift line of battle. The Confederate attack was little more than a simple frontal assault, aimed at exploiting the element of surprise to achieve a quick victory. It nearly succeeded, but the forces on the Union left managed to stall that portion of the attack, enabling Grant to establish a line of defense fixed on Pittsburg Landing at the rear. This was covered by heavy artillery

Union troops, many of them German- and Hungarian-American immigrants who had fought in the abortive European revolutions of 1848, drive back Confederate forces at Pea Ridge, Arkansas, March 8, 1862. Indian regiments fought for the South in this action, and one Union scout was "Wild Bill" Hickok, future Western gunslinger.

ARMIES OF THE RIVERS

"Camp Punishments" reads the caption on this 1862 caricature of discipline in the Union Army of the Mississippi. "Too Fond of Whiskey" reads the barrel: the guilty soldier had forged a surgeon's signature on a requisition for alcohol. The man's mates tease him for resembling the ironclad Monitor.

formed up near the river bank and by naval guns on the *Lexington* and *Tyler.* Johnston personally directed the attack in this quarter, only to be mortally wounded during midafternoon. Beauregard took command but suspended the attack at nightfall, figuring his now-exhausted troops could finish Grant's army next day before Buell's army arrived. However, after being delayed by swollen rivers, the first division of Buell's army crossed over the Tennessee at Pittsburg Landing to reinforce Grant's left late in the day. And throughout the night, the rest of Buell's army arrived on the scene.

Now the tables were turned. Beauregard's tired fighters spent the night hoping for Earl Van Dorn's 20,000-man army to cross over the Mississippi from Arkansas to reinforce them, while Grant moved three fresh divisions into his line for a counterattack at dawn. The three division commanders reflected the hodge-podge backgrounds of volunteer officers: Lew Wallace, newspaperman-lawyer-politician who would later author *Ben Hur;* William "Bull" Nelson, a navy lieutenant on leave to rally fellow Kentuckians for the Union; and Thomas L. Crittenden, Kentucky businessman whose Confederate brother George had just lost eastern Kentucky to the Union. At dawn of April 7 their divisions drove Beauregard's troops back onto the scene of the previous day's fighting where bloody hand-to-hand combat now raged until Beauregard learned Van Dorn's reinforcements would not arrive. He then began his withdrawal, his enemy too worn out to pursue. Both armies at Shiloh suffered phenomenal casualties: the Union 20 percent,

Pope's engineering troops cut away the swampy undergrowth (left) of Wilson Bayou to create a canal to New Madrid on the Mississippi, enabling Union army transports such as the W. B. Terry to bypass rebel guns at Island No. 10. The canal was completed on April 4, 1862.

Overleaf: Zouaves in camp pitching quoits - a circle of iron or rope rather than a horseshoe. Painting by the young Winslow Homer, destined to dominate American painting later in the century.

Below: wounded soldiers photographed by Matthew Brady.

the Confederacy 25 and one of its best generals lost – Johnston (no relation to Joe Johnston in Virginia).

The very day that Beauregard broke off the action at Shiloh to fall back on Corinth, Island No. 10 surrendered to Pope after the canal had been completed and Pope had isolated the fort. Flag Officer Foote's gunboats then moved down the Mississippi as far as Fort Pillow, the batteries of which blocked the way to Memphis. Meanwhile, south of Nashville, one of Buell's divisions under Brigadier General Ormsby M. Mitchel marched due south from Shelbyville to cut the key Memphis and Charleston Railroad in northern Alabama. The aggressive Mitchel, an astronomer by profession but a West Point classmate of Robert E. Lee, marched his 7,000-man command 57 miles in 48 hours to capture Huntsville,

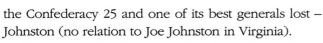

129

Home, Sweet Home *by*
Winslow Homer.

Alabama on April 11. He then took one brigade on board captured trains and moved 80 miles east to capture Bridgeport, Alabama at the approaches to Chattanooga. Another brigade under Colonel J.B. Turchin – a veteran Russian army colonel and Midwest railroad builder – took another train west to capture Decatur and Florence, Alabama, the rearward approach to Corinth, where Beauregard's army lay.

April 1862 spelled even more disaster for the Confederacy in the West. Johnston's strategy for Shiloh had stripped the Gulf ports of troops, and now Navy Secretary Mallory, convinced that the victorious Union

forces would advance down the Mississippi to capture the great seaport of New Orleans from the landward side, ordered Flag Officer Hollins to keep his naval squadron at Memphis rather than return to New Orleans. This was a strategic mistake, for Union Assistant Navy Secretary Fox arranged for an attack on the city from the sea. Tennessee-born Flag Officer David G. Farragut, commanding the West Gulf Blockading Squadron, undertook the operation. While Major General Benjamin F. Butler – a Massachusetts politician by trade – gathered 15,000 troops at Ship Island off the delta of the Mississippi, Farragut used a fleet of 37 warships to bombard Forts

A view of Farragut's foray against the great seaport of New Orleans.

Known to his men as "Old Stars" for his distinguished career as an astronomer, the diminutive Brigadier General Ormsby M. Mitchel constructed the defenses of hometown Cincinnati during the autumn of 1861 and proved to be an aggressive division commander in Tennessee. An untimely death from disease ended his promising career.

Overleaf: as Farragut's fleet passes up the Mississippi toward New Orleans in the pre-dawn darkness of April 24, 1862, it exchanges fire with Fort Jackson on the left bank and Fort St. Phillip on the right. At the cost of only one ship, the fleet destroyed the forts and sank the defending rebel squadron.

FARRAGUT APRIL 24ᵗʰ 18

ARMIES OF
THE RIVERS

R. G. Skerrett
1904

Political connections led to Benjamin F. Butler receiving a commission as a major general of volunteers in May 1861, a commission he kept throughout the war despite his military ineptness. He became notorious while military governor of New Orleans for labeling haughty local women as strumpets, causing the Lincoln Administration considerable embarrassment.

Jackson and St. Phillip, commanding the entrance to the river, throughout the week beginning April 18. Then he moved past them, annihilated the few rebel warships there, and occupied New Orleans on the 25th. Butler landed separately and marched overland to begin the occupation of this great prize, and Farragut steamed upriver as far as Vicksburg, Mississippi where rebel shore batteries stopped him. Early in May, the Confederates abandoned Pensacola, Florida, as strategically unimportant, except that its fine anchorage now became Farragut's base for concentrating on the blockade of Mobile.

Thus, even before McClellan's Peninsular Campaign had barely begun, aggressive Union commanders stood on the verge of destroying Confederate defenses in the West. Unfortunately, General Halleck was not equal to seizing the opportunity. Still miffed at Grant's initiatives, Halleck took personal command of the victorious armies

Eng'd by A H Ritchie

The ironclad ram Manassas *embodied a radical design for deflecting enemy cannon balls off its low, convex, armored deck. She rammed and damaged the blockading Union steam sloop Richmond off Head of Passes, on the Mississippi River, in October 1861, but was sunk by Farragut's fleet before New Orleans in the following April.*

TAPS

Reflecting on the stillness that fell over the Virginia battlefield – and over the Union offensive everywhere – Brigadier General Daniel Butterfield of the Army of the Potomac spent the night of July 1, 1862 meditating on musical ideas with which to capture the serenity of evenfall. Next morning, the 30-year-old peacetime New York City businessman summoned Oliver W. Norton, bugler of the brigade Butterfield commanded, and whistled some notes. That evening Norton played the beautiful, sad strain for the brigade. As other units heard it, they took it up. Several days later, it was used at the funeral of an artilleryman in place of the customary three rifle volleys, lest these provoke the nearby encamped enemy to open fire.

"Taps" was adopted by the Army of the Potomac, by every unit in which Dan Butterfield served, and finally by the U.S. Army in 1874. And so, with lyrics added later, it has remained the bugle call by which Americans bid farewell to each day and to the nation's war dead.

Day is done,
Gone the sun,
From the lakes, from the hills, from the skies.
All is well,
Safely rest,
God is nigh.

Flag Officer Charles Henry Davis uses five ironclad gunboats and two rams to sink eight of nine rebel gunboats at the naval battle of Memphis (left), June 6, 1862. The captain of the ram Queen of the West, Army Colonel Charles Ellet, Jr., was mortally wounded while leading the Union attack.

RUNNING FORTS JACKSON AND ST. PHILIP AT NEW ORLEANS

April 24, 1862

by **Major General Benjamin F. Butler**, Commanding Union Army Expeditionary Force

The fire of Fort Jackson [two hours past midnight, April 24, 1862] is incessantly kept up with precision, so that it seemed impossible that the Hartford [Farragut's flagship], a wooden ship, could live while passing through that volcano of fire. See! The heavens light up with something different from the flashing red of artillery. A new danger threatens the daring Farragut. A fire-raft comes sweeping along the current at four miles an hour– a flatboat some 200 feet long by 60 wide filled high with cotton picked open, saturated with rosin, pitch, and turpentine, intermingled so as to burn more hotly, and interlaced with cross-piled sticks of light wood, all ablaze, burning fiercely, fanned by the light wind. Such a fire-raft is sent broadside upon the Hartford, so well directed that it engages her bow and the hot flames set fire to her fore-rigging and are burning the foremost sails of the flagship. ... While the crew of the port [left side] guns ply their batteries upon the foe, the rest of the men, organized as a fire brigade, fight the fire. ... Boats are lowered and manned, grapnels thrown on board the burning raft, which is towed away to float harmless down the river, as the Hartford passes up beyond the range of fire of the forts....

[Then] a new peril met the Federal fleet. The ironclad ram Manassas came tearing down from above, forced by current and steam, upon the fleet. She is nearest the [sidewheel steam frigate] Mississippi, for whose side she is making with her fearful prow. The Yankee commander, Melancthon Smith [whose executive officer was Lieutenant George Dewey], was equal to the occasion. He calls out: "Flag officer, I can ram as well as she; shall I ram her?" "Go for her," is the answer, and the stem of the Mississippi struck the ironclad ...; the ram is disabled, and a few shot crash through her armor and set her on fire and she drifts down a useless hulk.

AN actual sketch, made on the spot by one of the Special Artists of Frank Leslie's Illustrated Newspaper.

Mr. Leslie holds the copyright and reserves the exclusive right of publication.

at Shiloh, reduced Grant to the ignominious role of second-in-command, and on April 29 began a slow, methodical advance toward Corinth with 90,000 men, eventually gaining 20,000 reinforcements en route. Whenever he encountered rebel forces, he had his troops dig in, enabling Beauregard to strengthen his army at Corinth to 66,000 men. In short, Halleck was plodding along in the same manner as McClellan in Virginia, covering only 20 miles by the end of May when an outnumbered Beauregard elected to evacuate Corinth and fall back into Alabama. Halleck, who had not been particularly impressed with Mitchel's gains in northern Alabama, now sent Buell's Army of the Ohio to join Mitchel for a possible advance on Chattanooga. But when Halleck learned of a possible Confederate advance

from Knoxville against Nashville, he decided to look to Nashville's defenses rather than attack Chattanooga or seek out Beauregard's army. The energetic Mitchel, promoted major general for his capture of Huntsville, irritated Halleck sufficiently for Halleck to have him transferred to command of the blockading base at Port Royal, South Carolina, where Mitchel soon contracted yellow fever and died.

Meanwhile, aggressive naval action improved the Union position on the Mississippi River. In May, Flag Officer Charles Henry Davis relieved Foote, whose

General Butler's forces arrested many citizens of New Orleans suspected of actively supporting the Confederates. Note the saddle bolster for a pistol on the gray horse in the foreground.

One of Butler's rowboat patrols on Lake Pontchartrain near New Orleans captures a smuggler of contraband – vital war materials – to rebel forces. Butler had earlier labeled slaves as "contraband of war," i.e. enemy property to be liberated, which made "contraband" a synonym for slave. Drawing for Leslie's by Frank H. Schell.

ARMIES OF THE RIVERS

The ironclad Confederate ram Arkansas, hastily completed on Mississippi's Yazoo River, pounded two Yankee gunboats there, using her ten guns, on July 15, 1862, and is seen thereafter running through Farragut's fleet to the defenses of Vicksburg. Badly damaged, she had to be scuttled three weeks later.

wounds from Fort Donelson had undermined his health and would lead to his death a year later. With his own gunboats and a flotilla of rams built and commanded by Colonel Charles Ellet, Jr., Davis bombarded the Confederate positions at Fort Pillow throughout May, forcing its evacuation on June 4, after which he pressed on to Memphis. There, on the 6th, Davis' fleet destroyed the small rebel squadron in the hour-long naval battle of Memphis. The victorious Yankee ships pressed downriver to Vicksburg, where the shore batteries prevented them from going on. Later in the month, Farragut's fleet ran the Vicksburg batteries from the south to the north side of the city but, having no troops to land there, had to withdraw back to Louisiana.

West of the great river lay the Trans-Mississippi Department of the Confederacy – Texas, Arkansas, Missouri, western Louisiana, and Indian Territory, by June 1862 linked to the southeastern states only along the 125-mile strip of the Mississippi between Vicksburg and Port Hudson near Baton Rouge, Louisiana. Most of the fighting by the troops of this district was done along the Missouri-Arkansas line plus skirmishes further west. Colonel Stand Watie, a Cherokee Indian chief, led the elements of that tribe which sided with the Confederacy and later became a brigadier general. At the beginning of the year, Brigadier General H.H. Sibley left El Paso (Fort Bliss) and moved up the Rio Grande with a 2,600-man brigade to claim the territories of New Mexico and Arizona for the Confederacy. Although Union garrisons abandoned Albuquerque and Santa Fe to him, Brigadier General Edward R.S. Canby concentrated enough troops to defeat Sibley in two small actions in late March and convince him to fall back downriver to El Paso. Whatever

hopes Sibley had for opening the way to California were dashed when a Union army column from that state crossed the rugged Indian country to Santa Fe over the summer, forcing Sibley to abandon El Paso and retire 700 miles to San Antonio. Generally speaking, the Trans-Mississippi remained a strategic backwater of the war.

By the beginning of July 1862, the war had been in progress for more than a year, and the idea by both sides for a short war had evaporated. The Union had exploited its sea power to gain control of the rivers and adjacent lands of Kentucky and Tennessee and the ports of New Orleans and Pensacola; begin the blockade with coaling stations along the coasts of Georgia and the Carolinas; and support McClellan on the Virginia peninsula. With the U.S. Navy growing daily, Congress in July created the rank of rear admiral and conferred it first upon Farragut

for his success at New Orleans. The Union army, however, had failed to take Richmond or destroy rebel forces in the West, now reforming into another new army in Mississippi and threatening Nashville. Lincoln needed a general with administrative talents to coordinate the immense Union military machine and in July transferred Halleck to Washington to take the post of general-in-chief, vacant since McClellan's removal from it four months before. No one could dispute Halleck's abilities as a manager, but his lack of strategic genius and of patience with aggressive commanders like Grant and Mitchel made him a less-than-perfect choice for the top Army job. Furthermore, Lincoln's limited war aims had become unrealistic. If the Union was to switch to a policy of total war – and to defeat the battlefield genius of Robert E. Lee – it would need very aggressive generals indeed.

4
FROM LIMITED TO TOTAL WAR

2nd Bull Run, Antietam,
Emancipation – Late 1862

FROM LIMITED TO TOTAL WAR

The American Civil War, like any organized conflict, developed a momentum that could not be interrupted in order to assess lessons being learned and to solve problems. Generals trained in the Napoleonic style of warfare knew no other formula for fighting battles, which meant that when flanks could not be turned because of the deadly massed firepower, frontal assaults became the only alternative. This had led to bloodbaths at Malvern Hill and Shiloh, resulting in public criticism and doubts about the generals' abilities. By July 1862, with a long war in view, the presidents of both nations therefore began to consider drastic changes by which to break the will of their enemies. Jefferson Davis planned to mount invasions of Maryland and Kentucky, not to conquer the Union but to force it to accept defeat and Confederate independence. Abraham Lincoln wanted to proclaim the freedom of all slaves in the rebelling states, thereby undermining the Southern socio-economic base and forcing the C.S.A. to collapse. This meant a shift in Union war aims from the limited goal of restoring the South intact to destroying the very fabric of Southern society – a fundamental change.

Lincoln's shift was tentative, for such a radical attempt

Forceful, direct, efficient, and honest, Edwin M. Stanton (left) brought considerable executive talent to the office of Secretary of War when he was appointed in January 1862. He prevailed upon Lincoln to seize control of the railroads and telegraphs, checked war profiteering, and was the major voice in having McClellan replaced. Stanton also ardently supported U.S. Grant's promotions.

A sharpshooter (above) of the Army of the Potomac using a telescopic sight to pick off selected targets, such as high-ranking enemy officers or cannoneers. Although they used breechloading rifles invented by Christian Sharps, sharpshooters took their name from their accuracy, usually as skirmishers, but also as snipers as in this case; note his canteen.

A Yankee drummer boy (right) writes a letter in the field, using his drum as a desk.

Overleaf: Going into bivouac at night is artist Edwin Forbes' title for this sketch of the Army of the Potomac. Note the Zouave and the mascot dog by the campfire.

FROM LIMITED TO TOTAL WAR

at social experimentation in the midst of wartime was risky indeed. Once proclaimed there could be no turning back. Lincoln had revoked Frémont's order of emancipation the previous year, and he did the same in May 1862 when Major General David Hunter tried to free and arm slaves liberated by Hunter's capture of Ft. Pulaski on the Georgia coast. The fact that the Confederate government put a price on Hunter's head for his bold act demonstrated that the South would fight to the bitter end to preserve its institutions. Lincoln, long an opponent of slavery, mulled over the implications of such a measure and in July presented the draft of an emancipation proclamation to his cabinet. Secretary of State Seward counselled him not to issue it, however, until a major Union victory in the field could give it teeth. Lincoln accepted this sage advice and waited for his generals to produce results.

The problem for both Lincoln and Davis and their generals was largely one of tactics. The advent of improved weapons was drastically altering the battlefield. The old inaccurate smooth-bore muskets and bronze

cannon that had enabled Napoleonic generals to maneuver at 300 yards from each other and then drive in an enemy's flank with a bayonet charge just did not work as the new rifled muskets and iron or steel artillery pieces not only extended ranges, the rifles to 400 yards, but increased rates of fire. The old 12-pounder smoothbore flat-trajectory "gun" or the high angle howitzer could blast 300 yards flat and up to 1,600 at a 5-degree elevation but without the accuracy of the new 2,500-yard rifled field pieces. No general could figure out how to adopt new infantry tactics to accommodate such longer-range missilry, so that heavy casualties were the invariable result. And the bayonet lost its importance with the longer small arms ranges. Neither could cavalry enjoy decisive mobility, due to the dearth of open ground and new rapidly- and breech-loaded carbines; the horsemen served best as mounted infantry, dismounting to fight on foot. One entire Pennsylvania regiment even entered the war equipped with lances – hand-held spears for jabbing! Transportation was greatly facilitated by river steamers, railroads, and improved plank road and bridge

HE SLEW HIS OWN BROTHER

by **J. Esten Cooke**, Confederate

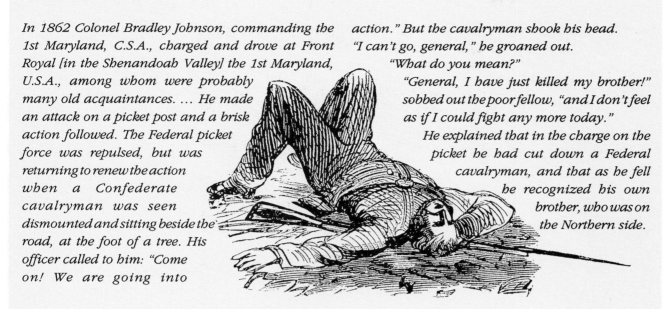

In 1862 Colonel Bradley Johnson, commanding the 1st Maryland, C.S.A., charged and drove at Front Royal [in the Shenandoah Valley] the 1st Maryland, U.S.A., among whom were probably many old acquaintances. ... He made an attack on a picket post and a brisk action followed. The Federal picket force was repulsed, but was returning to renew the action when a Confederate cavalryman was seen dismounted and sitting beside the road, at the foot of a tree. His officer called to him: "Come on! We are going into action." But the cavalryman shook his head. "I can't go, general," he groaned out.

"What do you mean?"

"General, I have just killed my brother!" sobbed out the poor fellow, "and I don't feel as if I could fight any more today."

He explained that in the charge on the picket he had cut down a Federal cavalryman, and that as he fell he recognized his own brother, who was on the Northern side.

Two gamblers, whose punishment is to wear a sign labeling them as such, nevertheless continue to gamble in camp. Such punishments were meted out at the command of the authoritarian Brigadier General Marsena R. Patrick, provost marshal general of the Army of the Potomac from Antietam to Appomattox. Pencil drawing by Waud.

FROM LIMITED TO TOTAL WAR

construction, but the horse-drawn wagon on dirt roads remained the customary way to move supplies as well as cannon in four- and six-horse teams. By the Atlanta campaign of 1864, the Union army required 60,000 horses and 6,000 wagons for supplies, cavalry, and the artillery. Combining the old with the new simply exacerbated generalship, which could only be learned by trial and error.

Technological progress also held out the hope of possible miracle weapons and the naïve notion that they would revolutionize warfare. The ironclad *Merrimac-*

Virginia was a good example, as well as the *Monitor*, which sufficiently dazzled Assistant Secretary Fox to divert too much of the Union navy's resources to similar craft. So did the rebel Mallory push development of submarines and mines, both sides using torpedo boats which, however, rarely proved decisive. Improved siege guns and mortars became so effective that they would create absolute stalemates as in the long siege of Petersburg late in the war (which would recur in World War I). Both sides tinkered with machine guns, rockets, and manned,

A Union pontoon bridge constructed to cross a ford at Bull Run creek, the scene of two major battles.

150

tethered observation balloons but with minimal effect. Most promising at the start of the war was the telegraph, which enabled despatches to be instantaneously transmitted over long distances. Secretary of War Stanton brought the Western Union company into the War Department to perform this invaluable service and using its own ciphers and codes, unknown even to the generals lest security be breached. But telegraph lines had to be guarded against guerrillas and cavalry raiders. Battlefield signaling, however, had not changed since Napoleonic times. Signal flags, mounted couriers, and word of mouth still had to suffice, leaving no effective means for transmitting tactical intelligence or maintaining tactical control. Once the battle started, in effect, contact with the generals was lost. No wonder Civil War battles were usually melees like Shiloh.

If tactics could not decide the issue, then superior strategy would, but only if executed through a well-run military organization. Since the beginning of recorded history and down to the 1860s, strategic and tactical

A map of northern Virginia, showing the battlefield of Second Bull Run near Manassas Junction, August 29-30, 1862.

FROM LIMITED
TO TOTAL WAR

Major General Philip Kearny (pronounced CAR-nee), who had lost an arm in the Mexican War, was a brilliant and popular division commander under McClellan and Pope. After he fell at Chantilly, a medal was struck in his honor and a town in New Jersey later named for him.

command had been centralized in one person, the "great captain," of which Napoleon was the epitome. The appointment of McClellan in 1861 to command the Union armies followed the precedent so closely that his troops dubbed him the "Little Napoleon." He did develop a sound organization but did not prove to be a great captain in the field. By the time Lincoln brought Halleck to Washington to be general-in-chief in July 1862, Lincoln wanted Halleck only for his organizational talents. The armies were getting so large that no one man seemed able to handle both the strategic and tactical dimensions, not to mention logistics. Halleck's task therefore was to develop an ad hoc staff of experts to do all the thinking, planning, and coordinating of the several armies, thus releasing their commanders to do the fighting. The Prussians of Europe had already seen the future by creating a general staff of experts which would help create and lead the modern German Army, but the small peacetime U.S. Army had recognized no such need – nor did its leaders in the Civil War.

The Union high command in the summer of 1862

therefore consisted of a loosely coordinated warmaking organization with no dynamic leader dictating strategy, other than Lincoln, who was a military amateur. With Secretary Stanton equipping the Army and Secretary Welles the Navy, General Halleck administered the armies and Gustavus Fox the naval squadrons. Lincoln, wanting a general with a winning record to capture Richmond, personally selected Major General John Pope – victor at Island No. 10 on the Mississippi – to command a new Army of Virginia. With 50,000 troops made up from the forces which had been operating in the Shenandoah Valley, Pope was to advance on Richmond from the environs of Washington, much as McDowell had done during the Bull Run campaign one year before. This time, however, the 80,000-man rebel army under Lee would be caught in a pincers action between Pope's 50,000 in northern Virginia and McClellan's 90,000 men still on the Peninsula. With such high Northern hopes placed on this operation, the Union armies in the West remained in place across Tennessee to watch rebel movements there. Lacking any overall theater commander, they were, west

Near a wrecked bridge, on the eve of the Second Battle of Bull Run, two photographers share their lunch from a large wicker picnic basket. Because camera shutter speeds were so slow, only posed or absolutely still scenes could be photographed.

FROM LIMITED TO TOTAL WAR

to east, the Army of the Mississippi under Major General William S. Rosecrans, Grant's Army of the Tennessee, and Buell's Army of the Ohio. Ben Butler held New Orleans.

The Confederate high command similarly had no great captain at the helm, save in the person of President Davis. Given his own military background, Davis actively played the role of commander-in-chief, going through no fewer than five different secretaries of war during his tenure in office but generally giving Secretary Mallory a free hand with the Navy. To administer his armies, Davis relied upon the 64-year-old General Samuel Cooper as adjutant and inspector general and senior officer in the army. General Robert E. Lee commanded the Army of Northern Virginia defending Richmond. In the West, Davis appointed General Braxton Bragg, who had led the right wing at Shiloh, as commander of the Army of Mississippi, which he moved from that state to Chattanooga, Tennessee in July for the invasion of Kentucky. A man of questionable ability, Bragg however enjoyed the confidence of the Confederate president. Two other sizeable armies existed in the West. Major

General Edmund Kirby Smith's Army of Kentucky, then at Knoxville, Tennessee, was to spearhead Bragg's invasion. Major General Sterling Price commanded the Army of the West, holding Vicksburg, the vital link with the Trans-Mississippi region.

Before any Confederate forces could move northward, the South had to meet the threat posed by Pope's advance into northern Virginia in mid-July 1862. If Pope and McClellan closely coordinated simultaneous drives against Richmond – from the exterior position – they should have had no difficulty in overwhelming Lee. But Lee, a master tactician, adroitly exploited his interior position by shifting forces between the two threats. With strong batteries at Drewry's Bluff checking any movement up the James River on Richmond by McClellan's Army of the Potomac and supporting gunboats, Lee rushed Stonewall Jackson with 24,000 men to attack the vanguard of Pope's army, which Jackson did in a fierce fire-fight at Cedar Mountain on August 9. Now Halleck ordered McClellan, instead of advancing on Richmond, to embark his forces on transports for passage up the Chesapeake to reinforce

In an 1862 photograph, a well-armed Yankee infantryman, complete with bedroll and knapsack, poses in front of a Napoleon 12-
pounder of Captain George W. Cothran's Battery M, 1st New York Artillery, recently posted at Harper's Ferry.

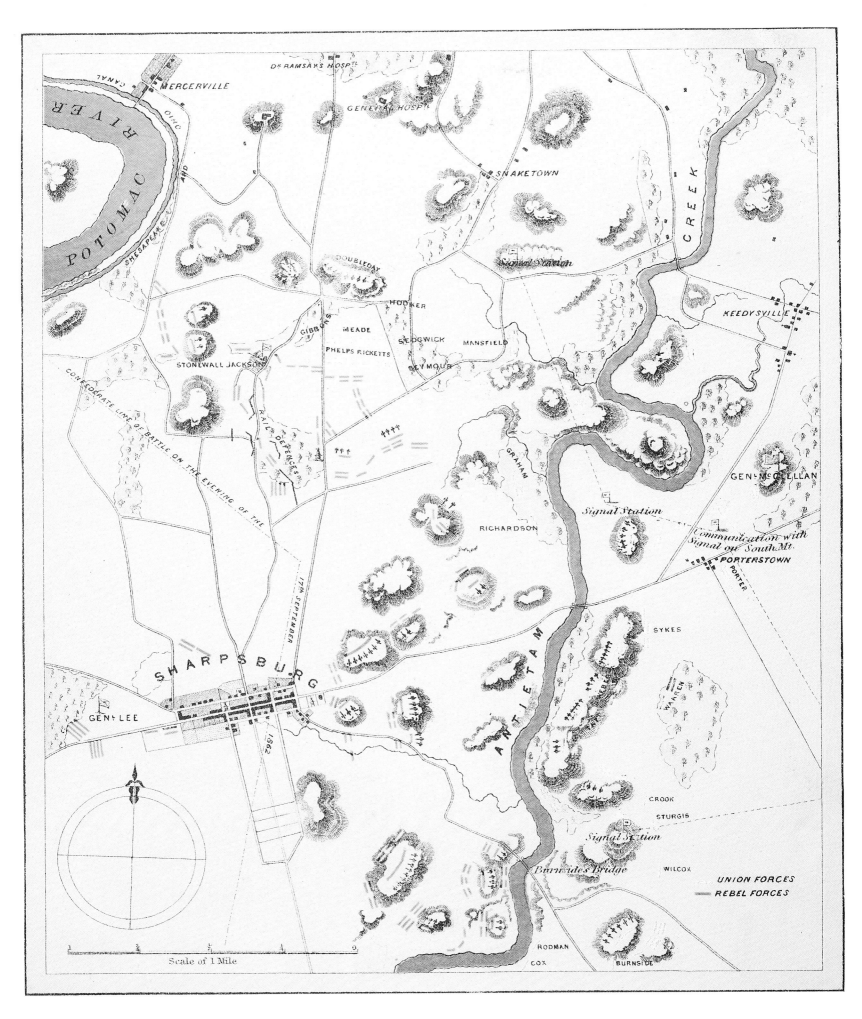

A post-battle map showing Union and Confederate units as deployed on September 16 and 17, 1862. Note the use made of the terrain, particularly Antietam Creek, and the location of the Potomac River.

A GLIMPSE OF STONEWALL JACKSON

by **George J. Stannard**, Colonel, 9th Vermont Infantry

When Harpers Ferry surrendered to "Stonewall" Jackson, in September 1862, General Jackson halted his horse in front of the 9th Vermont, and, taking off his hat, solemnly said, "Boys, don't feel bad; you could not help it; it was just as God willed it."

One of Jackson's staff asked me if I had anything to drink. I handed him my flask, and the young Confederate captain poured out a horn [drink] and arrogantly said, "Colonel, here is to the health of the Southern Confederacy."

I answered, "To ask and accept a courtesy of a prisoner and then insult him is an act that an honorable soldier would scorn."

Jackson turned on his staff officer and gave him a severe scolding, saying the repetition of such an insult to a prisoner would cost him his place. Then turning to me, General Jackson apologized for the conduct of his officer, saying that it was an exceptional act of insolence on the part of a young and reckless man; and, bowing gravely, the famous Confederate captain rode away. (A militia officer and merchant by trade, Stannard was exchanged and promoted brigadier general then wounded no less than four times – at Gettysburg, Cold Harbor, and twice at Petersburg, where he lost an arm.)

Burnside's 9th Corps crosses the hotly disputed bridge and fords of the creek against the rebel right flank during the midafternoon of the second day – only to be driven back by the arrival of A. P. Hill's division.

Pope. When Lee saw this happening, he took Major General James Longstreet's corps overland to join Jackson for a concerted attack on Pope before all of McClellan's army arrived. Lee boldly determined to employ the Napoleonic technique of using Jackson's wing to sweep around Pope's right flank to cut his communications with Washington. He had little respect for Pope's abilities and even mortified the Union commander, who had boasted that his headquarters were "in the saddle," by capturing Pope's actual headquarters in a cavalry raid led by his nephew, Brigadier General Fitzhugh Lee, on the 22nd.

The Second Battle of Bull Run ensued. When Jackson suddenly reached Manassas Junction, Pope fell back to a position between Jackson's 24,000 and Longstreet's 30,000 and was thus able to use his 75,000 troops, including elements of McClellan's army, to crush Jackson. Jackson kept maneuvering his divisions so much, however, that he kept Pope off-balance, enabling Longstreet to join up. The main action began on August 29 when Pope moved to drive in Jackson's well-entrenched position on the Confederate left. Longstreet came up at midday but

A highly-stylized Currier & Ives print captures some of the ferocity of the Battle of Antietam, notably Alfred Pleasonton's Union cavalry attacking the rebel center on the second day. The retreating Southern troops would hardly have kept their rifles on their shoulders.

157

FROM LIMITED TO TOTAL WAR

failed to attack through a gap in the Federal line, while Major General Fitz-John Porter, McClellan's 5th Corps commander, refused to obey a late afternoon order to launch an attack on Jackson which might well have been counterproductive and wasteful of human life. Pope subsequently had Porter kicked out of the army for this, and the controversy lingered for over two decades until Porter was reinstated. But Pope was no tactical genius. Misinterpreting Jackson's withdrawal to a stronger position as a retreat, Pope launched fruitless frontal assaults next morning, only to have Longstreet turn his left flank. Defeated, Pope managed to cover his withdrawal toward Washington. Lee pressed on for a furious skirmish at Chantilly on September 1 in which two of McClellan's best generals were killed. Both sides averaged about 20 percent casualties or over 17,000 men in all.

Despite lost opportunities at Second Bull Run, the battle demonstrated Lee's superior generalship and the woeful qualities of the Union's. Lincoln immediately restored McClellan, whose cooperation in the campaign had been less than enthusiastic, to command in the East by having him absorb the short-lived Army of Virginia into the Army of the Potomac, now being repositioned in northern Virginia. With the Federal forces in temporary disarray, Lee obtained President Davis' approval to keep up the momentum by invading Maryland. Such a bold move might weaken public support for the war in the North, strengthen the Confederacy's case for recognition by Britain and France, and enlist the support of more Marylanders. Significantly, Lee displayed acute strategic awareness of Union naval power by planning to cross the Potomac River well above the Great Falls, beyond which Federal gunboats could not reach. Indeed, as at Second Bull Run, he would henceforth attempt to fight all his battles west of the fall line not only of the Potomac but of the Rappahannock River in northern Virginia as well. If he could not prevent McClellan from shifting his army by bay and rivers to protect Washington, Lee could at least keep his own army away from the U.S. Navy and force Yankee ground commanders to fight on his own terms.

For the invasion of Maryland, Lee planned also to protect his own supply lines by capturing Harpers Ferry and utilizing the Shenandoah Valley behind the Blue Ridge mountains. On September 9 he ordered the Army of Northern Virginia again to split into two wings under Jackson and Longstreet, the former to capture Harpers Ferry, the latter Hagerstown, Maryland. Unfortunately, on the 13th the copy of this order to division commander Major General Daniel Harvey Hill was found wrapped around three cigars by a Union soldier at Frederick, Maryland. With this information, McClellan immediately

Burnside's troops hold their position against A. P. Hill's rebel counterattack at Antietam, September 17, 1862.

Sketch of a dead Confederate soldier on the field at Antietam.

Overleaf: enraged onlookers try to attack Confederate prisoners being marched up Pennsylvania Avenue in Washington.

THE ARTILLERY DUEL AT ANTIETAM

by **H.H. Bowles**, September 17, 1862 , Private, Co. C,
6th Maine Infantry

*Cannon shot and shell were flying in all directions. …
Our brigade formed quickly into line and advanced to
the edge of the cornfield. … As we came out of [it] we
passed Captain [John D.] Frank's N.Y. battery …
"bellowing like mad." They were [six] inch Napoleon
guns [smoothbore cannon developed by Napoleon III's
army in the 1850s]. The cannoneers. . .were working*

marched due west from Frederick toward Sharpsburg to drive a wedge between Jackson and Longstreet. The van of his force, led by Major General Ambrose E. Burnside, was met short of Sharpsburg at South Mountain next day by Hill's division, which yielded the ground only after a spirited battle. Lee, discovering that McClellan knew his plan, recalled Longstreet's wing from Hagerstown to Sharpsburg. Meanwhile, Jackson captured Harpers Ferry on the 15th but not before two Yankee cavalry regiments fought their way out without losing a man and even capturing a 97-wagon rebel ammunition caravan. Lee now decided to concentrate his army at Sharpsburg for a major engagement with McClellan, whose well-known caution led Lee to discount his own considerably inferior strength of 40,000 against McClellan's 75,000 men.

By dawn, September 17, 1862, most of Lee's army was positioned in and around Sharpsburg, McClellan's along Antietam Creek east of town. McClellan, perhaps thinking he could simply overwhelm Lee, simply ordered frontal assaults. Supported by a thunderous artillery barrage, the Federal 1st Corps of Major General Joseph Hooker led a dawn assault against the Confederate left under Jackson, followed at midmorning by the 2nd Corps under Major General Edwin V. Sumner attacking Harvey Hill's division in the center. Because Burnside's 9th Corps delayed moving against the right, held by Longstreet, Lee shifted some of Longstreet's troops to reinforce Jackson and hold the left and center. At 4:30 in the afternoon, Burnside finally moved, crossing the hotly-contested bridge which thereafter bore his name. Just as he began to drive in Longstreet's lines, Major General A. P. Hill's division suddenly arrived from Harpers Ferry to fall on Burnside's flank and drive him back. The day ended with Lee holding the field of

with their sleeves rolled up, and some of them bare to the skin to their waist, and were black and grim with powder and smoke. The guns were vomiting forth grape and canister, double shotted at every discharge, and fairly leaped from their position at every shot. They were making a perfect hell of every inch of ground in front and on either flank. ...

In our immediate front the ground was literally covered with dead and dying. The gray coats of the Confederates were thickly mingled with the blue of the Union dead. The green coats of the U.S. sharpshooters and the red trousers and embroidered jackets of the 14th Brooklyn [or New York] lay thickly among the corn hills, and along by the rail fence were whole windows of dead. ... The sunken road was filled with dead and dying. ... The rebel sharpshooters were posted in the tree-tops in the west woods, and were picking off our men one by one. Little Charlie King – a bright eyed, dark-haired drummer boy of the 49th Penn., about twelve years of age, and the favorite of his regiment – was standing behind me, when a minie ball [rifle bullet] pierced his breast and he fell into my arms calling the name of his mother. ...

The deep booming of cannon went on, and hill answered hilltop with thunder, flame and smoke.

Don Carlos Buell's army repulses Bragg's invasion of Kentucky at the Battle of Perryville, October 8, 1862.

FROM LIMITED TO TOTAL WAR

Antietam, but total casualties for both sides exceeded 36,000 men, the bloodiest battle yet.

Both armies, exhausted and reforming, remained in position another day before Lee accepted the advice of his two wing commanders and recrossed the Potomac into Virginia. He had won the battle but failed in his mission. Not only did Maryland not rally to the Confederacy, but the European powers refused to recognize the Southern republic, and Yankee resolve only stiffened. For now, on September 22, Abe Lincoln used Lee's withdrawal to proclaim a Union victory and issue the Emancipation Proclamation. Beginning January 1, 1863, it said, all Negroes held in bondage in the rebellious states would be "henceforth, and forever, free." Transformed into a moral crusade, Union war aims electrified the civilized world, most of which had already abolished slavery and which therefore supported the North. The people of the Union were already singing Julia Ward Howe's new lyric "Battle Hymn of the Republic" to the popular melody "Glory, Hallelujah" – evidence of their acceptance of the moral issue. Though the proclamation was a war measure to undermine the South, Lincoln knew very well that this singular act was breathing new life into what had been regarded as the "American experiment in democracy."

But that was the rub – winning the war. Even though

The loading of a Union 32-pounder (right) is demonstrated by its crew in one of Washington's forts: while one man rams a ball into the muzzle, another covers the touch hole to prevent oxygen from entering. In the right foreground are two "canisters," one open, the other still in its tin sheathing.

This Confederate $100 note (below), issued three years after the appointment of Christopher G. Memminger (lower right) as Secretary of the Treasury, would yield on demand two years after the ratification of peace between the C.S.A. and the U.S.A. Memminger was replaced four months later by fellow Charlestonian, George A. Trenholm.

total war had now been announced, the Emancipation Proclamation would only remain little more than high-sounding words unless Lincoln could find a general to crush the rebellion. George B. McClellan was obviously not that man. With fresh troops at his disposal the day after Antietam, he refused to renew the attack and prevent Lee's escape across the Potomac. Lincoln decided to get rid of him, and finally in November Burnside reluctantly agreed to replace McClellan at the helm of the Army of the Potomac. No more dynamic than McClellan, Burnside – whose long facial whiskers gave us the term "sideburns" – would not prove equal to the task.

There was also the matter of saving the substantial

Foreign observers – possibly symbolizing Britain and France – show astonishment at the size of the Union ordnance.

FROM LIMITED TO TOTAL WAR

Union gains made in the West, jeopardized by a Confederate counteroffensive even as the Second Bull Run and Antietam campaigns raged in the East. The Union successes at Shiloh, Memphis, and Corinth had deprived the South of the western portion of the Memphis and Charleston railroad, connecting the Atlantic seaboard with the Mississippi River. General Braxton Bragg's Army of the Mississippi had fallen back on Tupelo, Mississippi, fifty miles below Corinth. But since Mississippi had no east-west rail link to the coast, Bragg had shifted his army to Chattanooga, the rail center connected by lines through Knoxville to Virginia and through Atlanta to Mobile on the Gulf. From this new base, Bragg planned to invade central Tennessee and Kentucky and perhaps bring the latter state into the Confederacy or at least get more recruits. In his way stood Buell with the Army of the Ohio, its advanced position at Bridgeport, Alabama, near Chattanooga, with new divisions being raised to defend Kentucky and middle Tennessee. During July, Bragg sent Colonel John H. Morgan on a successful cavalry raid through Kentucky and another under Brigadier General Nathan Bedford Forrest through central Tennessee which

alarmed Buell.

Though Bragg's overall strategy was somewhat vague, he initiated the campaign by having Kirby Smith's Army of Kentucky start first from Knoxville to cover his eastward flank against a Union force holding the vital Cumberland Gap through the Appalachians. Kirby Smith left Knoxville in mid-August, detaching a division to threaten the Gap while Morgan raided all the way west to Gallatin, above Nashville, burning the railroad bridge which linked Nashville with Louisville on the Ohio River. The rebel army attacked and captured Richmond in

northeastern Kentucky on August 30 and two days later pressed on to occupy Lexington. Meanwhile, Bragg's main army moved north from Chattanooga, forcing Buell to fall back on Nashville. Bragg then bypassed Nashville to attack and capture Munfordville, Kentucky, due south of Louisville, on September 17. Since he had outflanked the Cumberland Gap and Nashville, Federal forces evacuated the Gap, and Buell hastened north from Nashville after Bragg. Bragg moved on to Bardstown, only 35 miles from Louisville, making contact with Kirby Smith's army around Lexington and Frankfort – giving

Spotlessly dressed Yankee gunners pose at an opened sally-port at Fort Slemmer, part of Washington's defenses. One soldier is actually smiling – a rarity in Civil War photographs.

him 32,500 troops in all. At the same time, Buell reached Louisville, where four new divisions under Bull Nelson reinforced Buell's own seven, giving him 60,000 men. Meanwhile, Bragg had ordered forces still in Mississippi to attack Rosecrans at Corinth, lest Rosecrans reinforce Buell, whereupon Rosecrans defeated Van Dorn's attack at Iuka and Corinth on September 19 and October 3-4 respectively.

On October 1, Buell moved out from Louisville to give battle at Bardstown and Frankfort, but the contending armies gradually maneuvered into combat at Perryville, east of Bardstown, on the 8th. The battle developed piecemeal, many units not even aware of the heaviest fighting because of unusual atmospheric conditions that masked the noise of the guns from them. In the seesaw action, Brigadier General Philip H. Sheridan adroitly handled his Yankee brigade to beat back a determined Confederate attack and then to counterattack, driving the rebels through Perryville. The victory by such a large concentration of Union forces caused Bragg to abandon the field in haste and leave Kentucky altogether. During the withdrawal, Colonel Morgan received permission to carry out another raid, recapturing Lexington on the 18th, then swinging southwest to Hopkinsville, Kentucky, destroying railroad bridges along the way. Bragg reoccupied the Cumberland Gap and took up positions around Murfreesboro in central Tennessee, southeast of Nashville, which he continued to threaten.

While the Confederate invasions of Maryland and Kentucky had been repulsed, the danger of Southern arms to the well-being of the Union was only temporarily checked. In November, Lincoln, in addition to replacing McClellan with Burnside as head of the Army of the Potomac, made command changes in the West as well, believing – with the public – that Buell should have destroyed Bragg's army. The Army of the Cumberland

Facing page: dapper War Department clerks in Washington peer out across the years, one on the left clutching a large, official-looking tome.

A Boston recruiting office (below) is adorned with posters offering a $100 bounty for three-year enlistees in 1861 and 1862 – as opposed to $10 and $50 respectively in the Confederate army. Charles W. Reed, who drew this sketch, enlisted in the 9th Massachusetts Artillery Battery in the summer of 1862.

WE ARE COMING, FATHER ABRA'AM

Lincoln's call for 300,000 fresh volunteers inspired New York banker and abolitionist John Sloan Gibbons to write this poem, published in the *New York Evening Post* on July 16, 1862 and immediately set to music by Luther O. Emerson. It became an instant favorite, although Lincoln's call only garnered 91,000 recruits. The first verse reflects the sacrifices of the people.

We are coming, Father Abra'am, three hundred
*   thousand more,*
From Mississippi's winding stream and from New
*   England's shore;*
We leave our plows and workshops, our wives and
*   children dear,*
With hearts too full for utterance, with but a silent
*   tear;*
We dare not look behind us, but steadfastly before -
We are coming, Father Abra'am - three hundred
*   thousand more!*

Chorus

We are coming, we are coming, our Union to
*   restore;*
We are coming, Father Abra'am, with three
*   hundred thousand more*
*   [and repeat].*

In spite of the Emancipation Proclamation, rioting victims of the first Union draft in 1863 focused their wrath on blacks and abolitionists alike, ravaging Gibbons' home and smearing it with symbolic tar. The resentment of Southern soldiers against Negroes in Yankee uniforms led to atrocities, the worst being the Ft. Pillow massacre in April 1864; Forrest's cavalry raiders captured the post and wantonly slaughtered dozens of black and white prisoners. Such were the social, ethnic, and racial dimensions of total war.

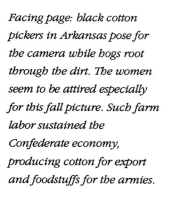

Facing page: black cotton pickers in Arkansas pose for the camera while hogs root through the dirt. The women seem to be attired especially for this fall picture. Such farm labor sustained the Confederate economy, producing cotton for export and foodstuffs for the armies.

was established under Rosecrans to replace the Army of the Ohio (although the names were often interchanged) and to deal with Bragg. The Confederate high command, similarly displeased with the failure in Kentucky, established an overall commander in the West, General Joe Johnston, finally recovered from his wounds received on the Peninsula. Bragg's force was renamed the Army of Tennessee, while Lieutenant General John C. Pemberton took command of the defenses around Vicksburg on the Mississippi.

All these armies required ever more men. By the spring and summer of 1862 both sides had begun to feel acute shortages of manpower through casualties, desertions, or general absenteeism. An obvious solution was the draft, which the Confederacy instituted in April 1862, calling up all able-bodied white males between the ages of eighteen and thirty-five to serve for three years.

When over one-third of Lee's entire force drifted away during the Antietam campaign, some opposed to fighting on Northern soil, the maximum age for Southern conscription was raised to forty-five, and in 1864 the range would be extended: seventeen to fifty. Lincoln tried to rely totally on volunteers, in July calling for 300,000 more. When this failed, the next month he ordered a draft of 300,000 militiamen to do nine months' service but had to call it off when anti-draft demonstrations erupted. But the payment of bounties of between $25 and $500 per enlistee, depending on length of enlistment, succeeded in filling the quota. (The Confederacy gave $50 bounties.) Still more men were needed, however, leading to the Federal government's first draft law in March 1863. A man could avoid service, however, by hiring a substitute to go in his place or by paying $300 – unfair but effective, except that it generated severe riots

FROM LIMITED TO TOTAL WAR

Facing page: plantation slaves on the Isle of Hope near Savannah pass under a giant, Spanish-moss-covered oak tree after having filled their buckets with water from the covered well. These coastal blacks welcomed the liberating Union troops even before emancipation became official.

Negro slave women (below) washing their laundry, and then leaving it to dry on the bushes, near Aiken, South Carolina. Many of their menfolk were absent, working as laborers for the Confederate army.

in New York City, especially by recent Irish immigrants, which had to be crushed by Federal troops.

Total war hit home as both governments began to realize that conscription had to be enforced rigorously if the necessary manpower was to be raised. The power of the state governments to resist such measures had to be checked. Lincoln, leading a federal union, could and did force his war governors to acquiesce, whereas Jeff Davis, heading a confederation of sovereign states, could not, and some Southern governors withheld troops and supplies until the end of the war. As in any war, the middle and upper classes could more easily escape duty in the ranks than could the lower classes, so that Irish and German immigrants were signed up even as they landed in New York. That life went on as usual for many Northern men is reflected in the fact that some thirty social-sporting baseball clubs continued to flourish in three states and Washington, D. C. (though down from fifty-four in five states in 1860). By contrast, the South, having no large middle class, drew its enlisted manpower from the poorer yeoman farming class, regarded by the planter aristocracy as "white trash." And as many of the latter deserted, disenchanted with the war, the Confederacy could not afford the manpower to round them up – or, as in the hills of North Carolina, government agents were driven off by the citizens. The North did better, simply because the vast majority of its troops were volunteers, only some 52,000 being actual draftees.

Total war reflected the moral dimensions of the conflict, which directly influenced the morale of the

FROM LIMITED TO TOTAL WAR

people. The struggle was not only patriotic but Romantic, reflected in literature and language by such common descriptive words as gallant, noble, honor, heroic, devotion, grand, stirring deeds, and desperate acts. Aristocratic Southern women rushed their menfolk off to war to perform chivalric acts for the honor of the South, except that by 1863 the brutal cost to home and hearth – lack of men, food, and other necessities – had awakened in a great many of them a deep resentment of the "noble cause." Middle- or even lower-class Northern women like Mother Bickerdyke, chief of Union nurses Dorothea Dix, and Red Cross founder Clara Barton played an active role for women frowned upon by Southern society but eventually tolerated. Part of the difference can be explained by the religious dimension of the struggle. The Union saw the moral justness of its war aims, especially after emancipation, leading churchmen and chaplains to preach this ethical message

MOTHER BICKERDYKE

by **Benjamin Woodward**, Surgeon, 22nd Illinois Infantry, Commanding Army Hospital, Cairo, Illinois in 1861-62

[At my request, Mrs. Mary Ann Bickerdyke, a widow] came to Cairo, bringing with her a good supply of hospital clothing and delicacies for the sick. … A large, heavy woman, about forty-five years of age, strong as a man, muscles of iron, nerves of finest steel – sensitive, but self-reliant, kind and tender, seeking all for others, for herself, nothing. … At first the men ridiculed her, but her cheerful temper took no offense, for she knew she was right; but woe to the man who insulted her. … She organized the nurses, saw that all

Contemporary lithograph of Negro slaves fleeing toward Union lines.

174

the sick were cleaned, and, as far as possible, given clean underclothes. A special diet-kitchen was established, and a great change for the better was soon seen in the patients.

As a rule she hated officers – "Them pesky ossifers," as she always called them – looking on them as natural enemies of the privates. … As she went with the army to New Madrid, Island No. 10, Fort Pillow, and up to Corinth, every man knew her and always hailed her as Mother Bickerdyke; and she was a mother to the men. Grant and Sherman highly esteemed her, and the latter gave her a large white mule, saddle and bridle, and as it was not a side-saddle she had it so altered that she could so ride on it. … Men of the Army of the Cumberland, or of the Tennessee, knew … that old sun-bonnet and the old white mule she rode, and when she rode into our camp or came into the dreaded field hospital, how the shouts went up, "Hurrah for Mother Bickerdyke!"

Her pertinacity was such that when, in Southern Tennessee, sanitary goods were needed at the front, but no quartermaster would give her transportation, she, in the night, loaded a car and had it pushed to a train. The quartermaster, seeing General Sherman, told him what she had done. "Well," said the general, "she ranks me. You will have to let it go, I guess." So this woman labored, month by month, and year by year [through nineteen battles] till peace came.

Cotton-field workers (above) worked the plantations under the loose reign of the woman of the house either until her husband was exempted from military duty and came home or until they themselves fled toward approaching Yankee forces.

No longer Southern "contraband," or war property, newly liberated blacks (overleaf) found gainful employment as dock workers for Northern military forces. White Yankees such as the man on the left labored alongside them in the common cause.

FROM LIMITED
TO TOTAL WAR

The first Negro troops (left) – unofficially organized into the 1st South Carolina (Union) Infantry by Major General David Hunter at Hilton Head, S.C. in May 1862 – are depicted clubbing and bayoneting bloodhounds with great alacrity. These were the beasts that had been used against them when they were slaves. The unit at this time belonged to Ormsby Mitchel's 10th Army Corps.

White officers (above) of "colored" Union infantry regiments relax at Fort Slocum, part of the defenses of northwest Washington, D.C. Guitar and zither provide music for drinkers and card players lying on the mud!

Black soldiers and a young white lad flank the "brass."

Right: "The Dis-United States – a Black Business" read the original caption to this satirical drawing.

and to cooperate with the government in the U.S. Christian and Sanitary commissions. The Confederacy did the reverse, avoiding the moral issue of slavery by encouraging preachers to stress only individual rather than national salvation. Moral superiority therefore contributed importantly to the will of the North to win, even in the face of repeated military setbacks.

The black American did not sit idly by while the war progressed. Freedmen North and South and Southern slaves contributed heavily to the separate war efforts. The Confederacy needed and depended upon Negro labor to provide the support services decimated by the departure of whites for the army. The black became the "invisible man" of the Southern war effort, the men building fortifications and ordnance and providing the bulk of railroad workers, men and women alike providing most nursing services in Confederate hospitals. In Virginia alone, over 37,000 Negroes worked in the labor force against only some 16,000 white civilians. Half of the 2,400 workers at Richmond's great Tredegar Iron Works were Negroes, slave and free; black iron workers made and installed the iron plate on the *Merrimac*. Plantations continued to be operated by slaves even after their masters had departed. In March 1863 the Confederate Congress passed a conscription law for slaves and eleven months later a second which made all free blacks between the ages of eighteen and fifty liable for drafting into military labor jobs. Blacks, however, could also be

FROM LIMITED TO TOTAL WAR

less than enthusiastic, subtly subverting the Confederate war effort and then going over to liberating Union armies.

The North had a smaller Negro population but one strong for abolition and which rushed to enlist as soon as permitted under the Emancipation Proclamation. Most had been farmers and servants but as soldiers were equal in every way to their white brethren. Secretary Stanton insisted they form separate regiments, officered by whites, and paid them only $10 a month, instead of the usual $13, so they refused their pay until this discrimination was rectified. Eventually 300,000 blacks served in the Union army, perhaps 30,000 in the navy, most of them

having come from Southern states.

So total war developed from the freeing of the Southern slaves, with emancipation of any Northern slaves being left to a general constitutional amendment after the war. The proclamation became one of the great documents in the history of democracy and went into force on January 1, 1863. "Upon this act," rang out Lincoln's final sentence in it, "sincerely believed to be an act of justice, warranted by the Constitution, upon military necessity, I invoke the considerate judgment of mankind, and the gracious favor of Almighty God."

Right: winter sport in a Confederate camp. The presence of battle flags suggests that the "combatants" belonged to rival regiments.

Anti-draft rioters (right) burn down a house on New York's Lexington Avenue.

Overleaf: Union troops encamped near Washington drill after a late fall snow shower.

5
LEE
Fredericksburg,
Chancellorsville, Gettysburg –
1862-mid 1863

LEE

Inventor both of a rifle and of the "sideburns" that he sported, Major General Ambrose E. Burnside (right) did not live up to his reputation as a decisive commander at Antietam, and then failed miserably while leading the Army of the Potomac at Fredericksburg. His performance continued to be erratic in lesser commands thereafter.

Robert Edward Lee epitomized the Old South, the dominant Virginia planter aristocracy, and the best generalship in the Western Hemisphere. Second in his class at West Point and eventually its progressive superintendent, he had excelled in many victorious actions in the Mexican War and had led the force which captured John Brown at Harpers Ferry in 1859. The peerless leader who had turned down command of the Union armies was revered by all who served under him, thus sustaining their high morale in adversity. His greatest strategic acumen was appreciating Union naval power, a knowledge which miscarried when he had lost coastal positions in the first year of the war but which eminently succeeded thereafter as he forced the Union army to fight away from naval support, west of the

north-south line from the Great Falls of the Potomac to Drewry's Bluff on the James. Lee had no equal as a battlefield tactician, audaciously shifting his outnumbered troops to defeat his opponents. Stonewall Jackson was his right arm, the cavalryman Jeb Stuart his eyes. His brother was a flag officer in the Confederate Navy, two of his sons and a nephew major generals. Nicknamed "Marse Robert," Lee was a tough fighter and chivalrous gentleman of the 18th century mold, his passion only to save Virginia and thus the Confederacy in a limited war of defense.

What Abraham Lincoln wanted to do was crush Lee's Army of Northern Virginia, capture Richmond, and bring the war to a speedy close. Given Confederate reverses in the West, such a victory over Lee might well have ended the hostilities but only if his army was absolutely destroyed. Unless Lee was eliminated, the mere capture of the rebel capital city would probably have been no more decisive than had the British capture of Philadelphia early in the Revolutionary War but leaving George Washington's Continental Army at large. Few Union leaders probably realized this, for the capture of Richmond had become an *idée fixe*, almost an end in itself, and was, incidentally but not too incidentally, proper Napoleonic strategy as espoused by Jomini and West Point textbooks.

With Lee's army split between Jackson's 2nd Corps in the Shenandoah Valley and Longstreet's 1st Corps west of Fredericksburg on the south side of the Rappahannock River, General Burnside moved the 122,000-man Army of the Potomac southward toward Fredericksburg on the way to Richmond in mid-

A Matthew Brady photograph of President Lincoln (above) in 1862, when the Commander in Chief was looking – in vain – for a valiant general to defeat Lee.

November 1862. Burnside not only failed to strike Lee's army but did not cross the Rappahannock for two weeks, giving Lee time to concentrate both his corps, 78,000 men, at Fredericksburg, well dug in on the heights commanding the south side of the river. Burnside, determined to cross over, had pontoon bridges erected and boats employed to effect the crossing on December 13. The Battle of Fredericksburg consisted of Burnside's three "grand divisions" – each comprising two army corps – making frontal assaults on Lee's positions after reaching the south bank. It was pure madness to attack infantry so well entrenched behind a stone wall on the high ground, from which a murderous fire poured down. The result was a slaughter, typified by the "Fighting 69th" New York Infantry of the Irish Brigade, carrying green flags for the old country and led by Irish emigré Brigadier General Thomas F. Meagher (pronounced "Marr"). Already decimated at Antietam, here the 69th lost 16 of its 18 officers, 112 of 210 enlisted men; the brigade had 545 casualties. Burnside's army suffered a total of 12,700 killed and wounded to less than half that for Lee, after which a deathly silence enveloped the scene.

Undaunted, incredibly, Burnside decided to try again to dislodge Lee's army. Attempting to envelop Lee's flank by crossing the Rappahannock upriver on January 20, 1863, the Army of the Potomac was struck by a two-day torrential rainstorm that swelled creeks and turned the Virginia soil into such a quagmire that the movement came to be known as the "Mud March." On the 23rd Burnside had no choice

Below: a column of Army of the Potomac cavalry has just crossed the Rappahannock River in Virginia via a pontoon bridge; the troops were preceded by supply wagons.

Following a heavy artillery bombardment on December 11, 1862, Union troops (left) enter Fredericksburg at night and proceed to sack the Southern town. Drawing by Arthur Lumley.

NIGHT ON THE FIELD OF FREDERICKSBURG

December 13, 1862

by **Joshua L. Chamberlain,** Lieutenant Colonel, 20th Maine Infantry (in peacetime, professor at Bowdoin College)

But out of that silence from the battle's crash and roar rose new sounds more appalling still; rose or fell, you knew not which, or whether from the earth or air; a strange ventriloquism, of which you could not locate the source, a smothered moan that seemed to come from distances beyond reach of the natural sense, a wail so far and deep and wide, as of a thousand discords were flowing together into a key-note weird, unearthly, terrible to hear and bear, yet startling with its nearness; the writhing concord broken by cries for help, pierced by shrieks of paroxysm; some begging for a drop of water; some calling on God for pity; and some on friendly hands to finish what the enemy had so horribly begun; some with delirious, dreamy voices murmuring loved names, as if the dearest were bending over them; some gathering their last strength to fire a musket to call attention to them where they lay helpless and deserted: and underneath, all the time, that deep bass note from closed lips too hopeless or too heroic to articulate their agony. ...

[The next night we finished burying the dead.] Splinters of boards torn by shot and shell from the fences we had crossed served as headstones, each name hurriedly carved under brief match lights, anxiously hidden from the foe. It was a strange scene around that silent and shadowy sepulture. "We will give them a starlight burial," it was said; but heaven ordained a more sublime illumination. As we bore them in dark and sad procession, their own loved North took up the escort, and lifting all her glorious lights led the triumphal march over the bridge that spans the worlds – an aurora borealis of marvelous majesty! Fiery lances and banners of blood and flame, columns of pearly light, garlands and wreaths of gold, all pointing upward and beckoning on. Who would not pass on as they did, dead for their country's life, and lighted to burial by the meteor splendors of their native sky?

Alexander Gardner photographed these scouts and guides (previous pages), who worked for the Army of the Potomac, while they were encamped at Berlin, Maryland, in October 1862. Lack of uniform dress enabled them to travel incognito.

The Beardslee telegraph machine (below) was an 1862 Union portable field communicator which transmitted each letter at which the pointer was aimed on the dial. It was slow, its range only ten miles, and it was outperformed by civilian telegraphs under army control.

A Yankee telegrapher (left) uses the Beardslee to great effect at Fredericksburg by keeping Burnside informed when river fog from the Rappahannock obscured visual signals. The Beardslee was scrapped a year later when the Signal Corps turned over all telegraphy to the Federal Military Telegraph System. Drawing by Waud.

but to call off the operation. And, with the morale of the army finally shattered, Lincoln had no choice but to relieve Burnside of command. An able enough professional soldier and inventor of an excellent carbine widely used by the army, Burnside by his own admission lacked the ability to lead the main Union army, but he was perfectly willing to serve in lesser commands, whereupon he was transferred to the Western theater. Part of his problem had been the rain, a common enemy of all soldiers who campaigned in the wooded morass of the Virginia Wilderness.

So the onset of winter halted further operations in Virginia while the Confederacy looked desperately for fresh ways to undermine the Union war effort. Lee was doing so well defending Richmond that some thought was given to using part of Lee's army in the West. Grant was threatening Vicksburg and Rosecrans Chattanooga; a major effort into Tennessee might cause the Union army to transfer forces to the West, thereby relieving the pressure on Lee. As long as Vicksburg held, supplies would continue to flow from the Trans-Mississippi area to the Southeastern states. Despite the U.S. Navy's increased vigilance, its blockade was simply not choking off most oceanic trade by runners into Charleston, Wilmington, Savannah, Mobile, Galveston, and several Florida inlets. Furthermore, the Davis government continued to use its purchasing agents in Europe not only to obtain commerce raiders but two powerful ironclad rams from the British Laird company, warships that could cross the Atlantic and perhaps attack the Union blockade or penetrate up the Mississippi.

Confederate naval efforts plagued the Union merchant marine. Depredations by the *Alabama*, *Florida*, and now also *Georgia* convinced more owners to transfer their registry to foreign flags. One of the *Florida's* captures, the coffee-carrying sailing brig

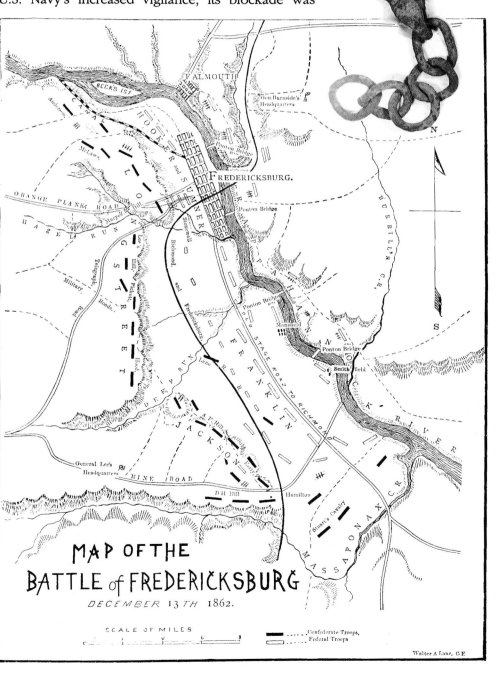

Manacles and handcuffs used on prisoners and found on the bleak battlefields around Fredericksburg.

MAP OF THE
BATTLE of FREDERICKSBURG
DECEMBER 13TH 1862.

SCALE OF MILES

Confederate Troops,
Federal Troops

Walter A Lane, C.E

Facing page: drawing depicting the suicidal assault of Major General Darius N. Couch's 2nd Corps through the town of Fredericksburg, and against impregnable Confederate positions on Marye's Heights, situated behind the town, December 13, 1862. Many of the attackers pinned notes on their uniforms with their names for notifying next of kin.

Overleaf: the return of the "Fighting 69th" New York to its home city after suffering heavy losses at Fredericksburg. These immigrants from Ireland had entered the battle wearing sprigs of green in their hats. Painting by Louis Lang.

196

197

Probably the only illustrated wartime newspaper in the South presents a ten-year-old likeness of Lee to its readers in January 1863. Not only had he aged and grayed considerably in real life, but his middle name was actually Edward, and he commanded only the Army of Northern Virginia, not all the Confederate forces.

SOLDIER LIFE

by **Carlton McCarthy**, Private, 2nd Company, Richmond Howitzers

Rain was the greatest discomfort a soldier could have; it was more uncomfortable than the severest cold with clear weather. Wet clothes, shoes and blankets; wet meat and bread; wet feet and wet ground; wet wood to burn, or rather not to burn; wet arms and ammunition; wet ground to sleep on, and mud to wade through, swollen creeks to ford, muddy springs and a thousand other discomforts attended the rain. There was no comfort on a rainy day or night, except in "bed," that is, under your blanket and oil cloth. Cold winds, blowing the rain in the faces of the men, increased the discomfort. Mud was often so deep as to submerge the horses and mules, and, at times, it was necessary for one man or more to extricate another from the mud holes in the road.

Night marching was attended with additional discomforts and dangers, such as falling off bridges, stumbling into ditches, tearing the face and injuring the eyes against the bushes and projecting limbs of trees, and getting separated from your own company and hopelessly lost in the multitude. Of course, a man lost had no sympathy. If he dared to ask a question, every man in hearing would answer, each differently, and then the whole multitude would roar with laughter at the lost man, and ask him if his mother knew he was out?

Very few men … had comfortable or fitting shoes, and fewer had socks, and, as a consequence, the suffering from bruised and inflamed feet was terrible. It was a common practice, on long marches, for the men to take off their shoes and carry them in their hands or swung over their shoulder. Bloody footprints in the snow were not unknown to the soldiers of the Army of Northern Virginia.

THE Southern Illustrated NEWS.

RICHMOND, SATURDAY, JANUARY 17, 1863.

Vol. I.

No. 19.

ROBERT EDMUND LEE,

COMMANDER-IN-CHIEF OF THE CONFEDERATE FORCES.

[FROM A PHOTOGRAPH BY REES, TAKEN TEN YEARS AGO.]

[W. B. CAMPBELL, Engraver.]

Winter weather made campaigning in Virginia impossible. Even standing on simple picket duty at an artillery post was a miserable occupation.

Cavalrymen (left) escort a long line of Union stragglers and deserters to Confederate headquarters on February 2, 1863, following Burnside's lamentable Mud March the week before. Since the men are still carrying their arms, they are only going to be returned to their units rather than punished. Drawing by Edwin Forbes.

Overleaf: heavy rains have made the Rappahannock River virtually impassable during Burnside's attempt to use the Army of the Potomac to turn Lee's flank, January 20-22, 1863. Burnside had no choice but to abandon what came to be known, accurately, as the "Mud March."

Under cover of morning fog, on April 29, 1863, the New York and Pennsylvania regiments of Sedgwick's 6th Corps cross the Rappahannock River in pontoon boats in order to threaten the town of Fredericksburg, and thus enable Hooker to move upriver against Lee's left flank.

Clarence, was turned over to Lieutenant Charles W. Read, fitted with a cannon, and turned loose as a raider off the Chesapeake Bay. Read succeeded in capturing six merchant ships, to one of which, the faster sailing bark *Tacony*, he transferred his crew and gun, burning the rest. He sent the captured crews ashore where they alerted the Union navy. As *Florida No. 2*, this new raider captured no fewer than fifteen prizes off the New England coast in mid-June 1863. To elude his pursuers, Read shifted again to one of his captures, the fishing schooner *Archer*, and burned the others. Making their way into the harbor of Portland, Maine, Read and his crew boldly seized the U.S. Treasury Department's revenue cutter *Caleb Cushing* after midnight on June 17. Before they could destroy the shipping there, they had to clear the harbor after daybreak and burn the cutter before they were captured by Union warships closing

in on them. Schemes to outfit raiders in Canada to attack Great Lakes shipping were also underfoot, though never realized.

While the South did not lack for arms or munitions, food for its armies and citizens was becoming a pressing need. The able Confederate Secretary of State Judah P. Benjamin pressed the British for recognition, so that the blockade could be lifted and Britain import more Southern cotton, thereby bolstering the Southern economy. But what both England and the Confederacy needed was grain, the former because of crop failures in 1861, the latter because its annual supply of ten million bushels of Western wheat had been cut off by the war. Britain could get cotton from India and Egypt, but it imported over 40 percent of its grain from the North between 1861 and 1863. Yankee wheat farmers, aided by new production in California, harvested 187 million bushels in 1862, with even a larger amount due

by the end of 1863. So Benjamin's entreaties for cotton exports carried less weight with the British than did Union grain. By contrast, bread riots broke out in cities and towns throughout the South during 1863, including Richmond, where irate women joined together to pilfer grocery stores and individually resorted to shoplifting to prevent their families from starving. Even Lee's army was so undernourished that with the coming of spring Lee detached Longstreet with two divisions to scour the southeastern Virginia countryside for foodstuffs for the 60,000 men of the army and its horses.

At this inauspicious moment for Lee, the Army of the Potomac – now an enormous 134,000 strong – launched its spring offensive. Its commander, appointed immediately after the Mud March, was Major General Joseph Hooker, veteran of all the army's battles since the Peninsular Campaign at the head of a division, a

Left: "Fighting Joe" Hooker. His able leadership of the 1st Corps at Antietam led to a brigadier generalcy in the regular army along with his position as major general of volunteers. Although he failed utterly when leading the Army of the Potomac at Chancellorsville, Hooker redeemed himself with the 20th Corps in the West.

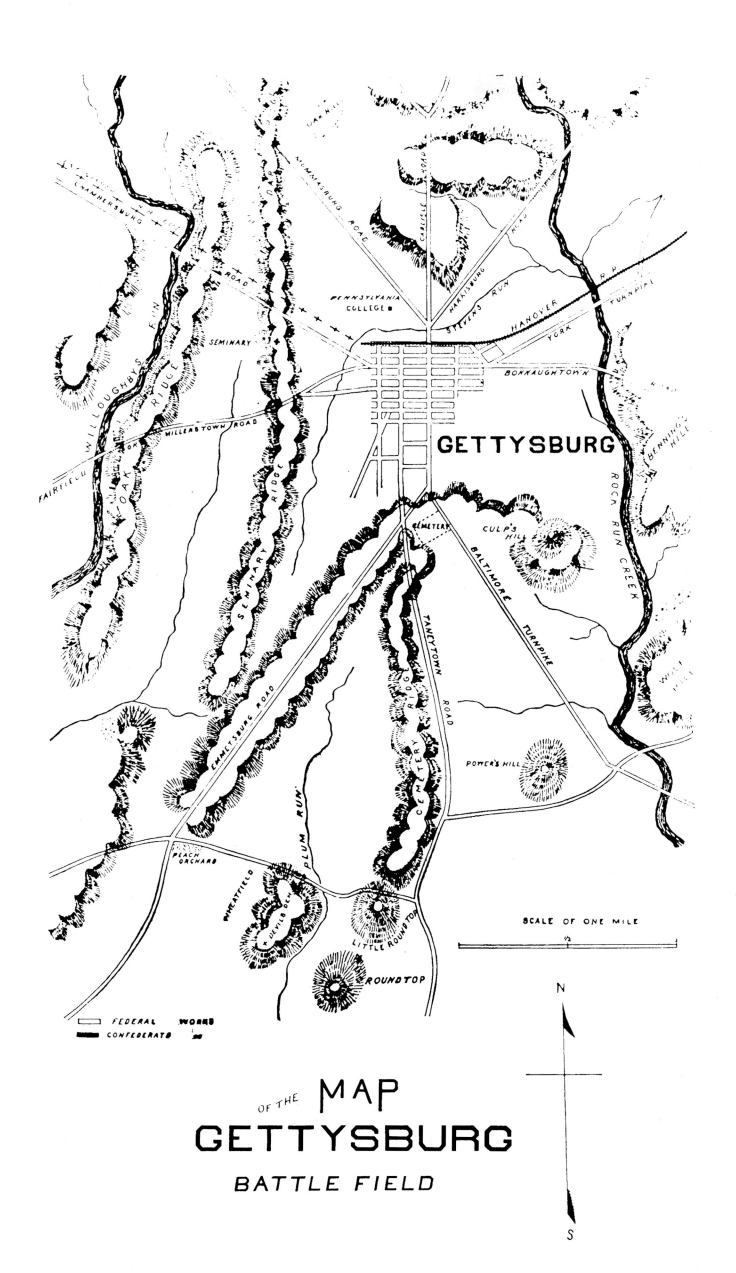

GETTYSBURG

FEDERAL WORKS
CONFEDERATE

MAP
OF THE
GETTYSBURG
BATTLE FIELD

SCALE OF ONE MILE

N

S

209

LEE

Always either a corps or wing commander in the Army of Northern Virginia, Lieutenant General James "Pete" Longstreet retained Lee's trust for his steady leadership, in spite of several missed opportunities, disagreements, and unimaginative performances when Longstreet led independent operations, especially during the Knoxville campaign.

Captain Charles A. Phillips of the 5th Massachusetts Battery uses a prolonge rope (designed to fix a gun to its limber carriage) to drag a cannon off the field while simultaneously supporting Dan Sickles' endangered salient on the Union left, July 2. Drawing by Charles Reed.

Union artillery on Little Round Top fires down on Lee's right flank on the second day of Gettysburg, July 2, 1863. Painting by Forbes.

reorganized into three infantry and one cavalry corps. Hooker still had an impressive 122,000, and Union militia and garrison forces in the North could be expected to concentrate against Lee's invading army. But Lee had just whipped Hooker's big army with only half the men and stood an excellent chance of doing it again with more forces at his disposal. He no longer had Jackson for advice and leadership, but a defeat would surely end any further opportunity to invade the North. So the timing was right; he must move now or never.

Leaving A. P. Hill's 3rd Corps at Fredericksburg to deceive Hooker on the opposite side of the Rappahannock, Lee moved Longstreet's 1st and Dick Ewell's 2nd Corps westward to Culpeper, screened by Stuart's cavalry, the first week in June. Hooker, to ascertain the extent of such maneuvers, ordered Alfred Pleasonton's cavalry to reconnoiter upriver in force. With unprecedented aggressiveness for Union cavalry, now armed with rapid-firing breech loaded Spencer carbines, Pleasonton launched a surprise attack across the river on the 9th and fought the biggest cavalry action of the war near Brandy Station, punishing Stuart's cavalry and confirming the westward movement of Lee's army. Ewell then marched into the Shenandoah Valley, repelling or capturing Union garrison forces, followed by Hill into the Valley and Longstreet east of the Blue Ridge. Cavalry clashes continued apace as Ewell's advance elements crossed into Pennsylvania.

The alarm rang out across the North. Militia forces skirmished with the Confederate advance, Hooker marched the Army of the Potomac into Maryland to keep it between Lee and Washington, and Jeb Stuart mounted a raid across Hooker's rear, pestering Union garrisons in northern Virginia, Maryland, and southern Pennsylvania and capturing a supply column – all the last week of June. Stuart's customary audacity failed in

Captain Greenleaf T. Stevens' battery of the 5th Maine Artillery defends Cemetery Hill in the Union center at 6:00 p.m. on July 2 as the "Louisiana Tigers" brigade attacks from Gettysburg (left background). The Tigers gained a toehold before being driven back by sundown. Wash drawing by Waud.

The hotly-contested Trostle's House on the Union left center was where 2nd Corps commander Dan Sickles was wounded in the late afternoon of the second day at Gettysburg. His leg had to be amputated, ending his military career. Sketch by Reed.

Gettysburg on left
Battery

Lee's own communications by attacking Lee's rear near Harpers Ferry. General-in-Chief Halleck in Washington however refused permission, sensitive to Lee's progress northward. Hooker, stunned, asked to be relieved of command. The Lincoln administration, disillusioned with Hooker since Chancellorsville, granted the request that very day, the 28th. Major General George G. Meade, a veteran brigade, division, and now 5th Corps commander, got the job, a very risky change given the imminence of a major battle.

As Meade pressed north to prevent Lee from crossing the Susquehanna, Lee finally realized the situation and ordered his army to turn about and concentrate near the hamlet of Gettysburg, Pennsylvania. The battle for the nation – and the world – was about to begin. It was governed by the usual Napoleonic style of warfare. Both armies were organized much like Napoleon's had been, the staffs of Lee and Meade as well, except that Lee's staff was much smaller and of lower ranking officers, a feature of all Confederate staffs which tended to overwork the commanding general. Both commanders were determined to cut the communications of the other, Meade to prevent Lee's return to Virginia, Lee to turn one of Meade's flanks and prevent him from falling back on Washington. If either succeeded, the war was sure to take a dramatic change of direction. But Lee still had one tactical problem – ignorance of Stuart's whereabouts. In fact, the rebel cavalryman had reached the environs of Carlisle on the approaches to Harrisburg and was about to attack a Union infantry division dug in there. When Stuart learned of Lee's movement toward Gettysburg on July 1, he abandoned his plans and hastened to rejoin Lee. He would not make it in time to alter the course of battle.

That very morning, July 1, a Union cavalry division bumped into a rebel infantry brigade trying to find shoes just west of Gettysburg. Dismounting, the horsemen used their carbines to fight a delaying action at Seminary Ridge while the 1st and 11th Corps hastened into the town from the south to support them, and Hill's 3rd Confederate Corps attacked in strength from the west. General Reynolds of the 1st Corps assumed command of the hard-fought Union defense of the town but was picked off by a sharpshooter. As the Yankee troops tried to hold Seminary Ridge against Hill's relentless attacks – with heavy losses on both sides – Lee's 2nd Corps under Ewell began arriving from the north and drove into Gettysburg. The Union 1st and 11th Corps could not withstand the onslaughts and fell back through the town to a sound defensive position on high ground called Cemetery Hill where they dug in while the rest

one elementary respect: he lost touch with Lee, who badly needed the cavalry to keep him informed of enemy movements. Lee nevertheless turned northeast and east through the southern Pennsylvania countryside, receiving the surrender of undefended towns along the way and paying with Confederate money to obtain badly-needed shoes, beef, and corn. Ever the gentleman and sensitive to Northern and foreign opinion, he forbade any looting or pillaging; he was not waging total war.

On June 28, Lee ordered Ewell's corps forward to the Susquehanna River and to seize Harrisburg, capital of Pennsylvania. Beyond lay the Schuylkill River and the Reading-to-Philadelphia railroad, both of which carried vital anthracite coal necessary to maintain Union blockading squadrons. The same day Hooker, with the Army of the Potomac about Frederick, Maryland, saw an opportunity to cut

COMMANDS AND STAFFS AT GETTYSBURG

Army of the Potomac

Major General George G. Meade (U.S. Military Academy 1835)

Staff

Major General Daniel Butterfield, Chief of Staff (merchant)

Brigadier General Gouverneur K. Warren, Chief Engineer (USMA 1850)

Brigadier General Henry J. Hunt, Chief of Artillery (USMA 1839)

Provost Marshall-General – a brigadier general

Adjutant-General – a brigadier general

Inspector-General – a brigadier general

Quartermaster-General – a brigadier general

Chief Commissary of Subsistence – a colonel

Chief of Medical Department – a major and surgeon

Chief Ordnance Officer – a major

Chief Signal Officer – a captain

1st Corps

Major General John F. Reynolds (USMA 1841) 3 divisions of 2 or 3 brigades each; artillery brigade

2nd Corps

Major General Winfield Scott Hancock (USMA 1840) 3 divisions of 3 or 4 brigades each; artillery brigade

3rd Corps

Major General Daniel E. Sickles (lawyer; politician) 2 divisions of 3 brigades each; artillery brigade

5th Corps

Major General George Sykes (USMA 1842) 3 divisions of 2 or 3 brigades each; artillery brigade

6th Corps

Major General John Sedgwick (USMA 1837) 3 divisions of 3 brigades each; artillery brigade

11th Corps

Major General Oliver O. Howard (USMA 1854) 3 divisions of 2 brigades each; artillery brigade

12th Corps

Major General Henry W. Slocum (USMA 1852; lawyer)
2 divisions of 3 brigades each; artillery brigade

Cavalry Corps

Major General Alfred Pleasonton (USMA 1844) 3 divisions of 2 or 3 brigades each; horse artillery

Artillery Reserve

Brigadier General R. O. Tyler (USMA 1853) 5 artillery brigades

Army of Northern Virginia

General Robert E. Lee (USMA 1829)

Staff

Chief of Artillery – Brigadier General William N. Pendleton (USMA 1830)
Adjutant-General – a colonel
2 aides-de-camp – both colonels
Chief Quartermaster – a colonel
Chief Commissary – a colonel
Chief of Ordnance – a colonel
2 Assistant Inspectors-General – one a colonel, one a major
Chief Engineer – a colonel
Medical Director – a doctor
Assistant Adjutant-General – a major

1st Corps

Lieutenant General James Longstreet (USMA 1842) 3 divisions of 3 or 4 brigades each; 5 artillery battalions

2nd Corps

Lieutenant General Richard S. Ewell (USMA 1840) 3 divisions of 4 or 5 brigades each; 5 artillery battalions

3rd Corps

Lieutenant General Ambrose P. Hill (USMA 1847) 3 divisions of 4 or 5 brigades each; 5 artillery battalions

Cavalry Corps

Major General J.E.B. Stuart (USMA 1854) 6 brigades; horse artillery

Edwin Forbes' panoramic sketch portrays Union reinforcements moving up the Taneytown Road from the south to reinforce the Union center at Cemetery Hill (on the horizon, in the center) at 10:00 a.m., July 3, 1863. Culp's Hill is on the right.

215

of the Army of the Potomac came up from the south. Meade sent ahead the superb Hancock of the 2nd Corps, seasoned leader in all the Army's battles over the preceding year, to organize the forces at Cemetery Hill. Hancock extended the line eastward to Culp's Hill, lest the rebels turn his right flank and cut the Army's communications. The day ended with Lee waiting for Longstreet's 1st Corps to come up from the southwest.

By the time Meade arrived on the field during the night, his army held a solid defensive position in a fishhook of high ground south of Gettysburg. On the right (east) Slocum, with the 12th Corps and part of the 1st, held Culp's Hill and the flank and with the 11th Cemetery Hill facing Ewell. In the center, curving southward, Hancock had the 2nd and rest of the 1st holding Cemetery Ridge facing Hill, posted on Seminary Ridge. Sickles' 3rd Corps formed the left all the way to the hillock called Little Round Top, facing Longstreet as he came up. The adjacent Big Round Top was unoccupied, and Sykes' 5th and Sedgwick's 6th Corps were still approaching from the southeast. Lee was determined to attack, certainly with Longstreet, if possible with Ewell, to envelop either flank, although Longstreet counselled Lee to assume the defensive posture so successful in past battles. The aggressive Jackson was missed already.

Little happened early on July 2 except that an overzealous Dan Sickles positioned his 3rd Corps too far forward on the Union left, which encouraged Longstreet to launch John B. Hood's Texas division against the round tops in midafternoon. Meade's engineer Warren happened to be standing atop Little Round Top, saw them coming, and hurried down the back slope to order up arriving elements of the 5th Corps. These arrived just in the nick of time to drive Hood back with severe losses. Meanwhile, Sickles' 3rd Corps yielded its forward salient but was reinforced by Meade, who exploited his interior position to shift troops quickly. Now Ewell decided to assault Cemetery

Dead Confederate sharpshooters at the foot of Little Round Top, after the battle. Photograph by Matthew Brady.

Having crossed the open field that stretches for a half mile behind them, Pickett's division, together with Pettigrew's and Trimble's, strike Hancock's 2nd Corps behind the stone walls of the Union center at Gettysburg; this was the high water mark of the Confederacy, July 3, 1863.

The damaged caisson and dead horses of a 2nd Corps battery – victims of the rebel artillery barrage which preceded Pickett's charge – as sketched by Forbes the following day, July 4.

PICKETT'S CHARGE

July 3, 1863

A Confederate View

by **William Miller Owen**, 1st Lieutenant and Adjutant, Reserve Artillery, 1st Corps

For forty minutes the dreadful din [of the artillery duel] continued, until the cannoneers, exhausted with their work, and fainting from the heat on that July day, slackened the fire. ... Then Pickett's brave Virginians formed for the assault, their gallant commander riding up and down his lines, talking calmly to officers and men. Longstreet could not bear to give the order to throw these men against the breastworks of the enemy, and when at last Pickett said, "Shall I go forward, sir?" Longstreet turned away his head. Pickett, proudly and impetuously said, with the air of an old crusader, "Sir, I shall lead my division forward."

Orders from the officers now rang out, "Attention!" and the brave fellows could be heard calling out to friends and comrades a few files from them, "Good-bye, boys! Good-bye!" The final order came from Pickett himself, who, superbly mounted, seemed the very incarnation of war. "Column forward! guide center!" and the brigades of [James L.] Kemper, [Lewis A.] Armistead, and [Richard B.] Garnett moved forward in common time, their battle flags fluttering as they passed over the greensward. ...

Heth's division, under [Brigadier] General [J. Johnston] Pettigrew, emerged from the timber and followed Pickett on his left flank and in echelon. [The brigade of Cadmus M.] Wilcox moved out upon his right. Pickett's lines were seen to halt, and under a tremendous fire he changed direction by an oblique movement, beautifully, coolly, and deliberately made. ... [When they reached Cemetery Ridge] the blue line rose and poured a deadly fire into the Confederate ranks. The Confederates responded with a wild yell and pushed on unfalteringly. ...

Lee's retreat along the rain-soaked roads of Maryland after his defeat at Gettysburg, as depicted by Forbes.

A Union View

by **Charles E. Troutman**, Lieutenant, Company G, 12th New Jersey Infantry, 2nd Brigade, 3rd Division, 2nd Army Corps

[About 4:00 p.m. the cannons stopped.] Then the sputtering fire along the skirmish line told us of an infantry advance. A gentle breeze rolled away the curtain [of cannon smoke] and opened to our view a magnificent array; Pickett's Virginians and Pettigrew's North Carolinians were moving over the intervening valley in two compact lines of battle. [Our division commander, Brigadier General Alexander] Hays rode down the line, sternly bidding every man to keep hidden from view. One man, in his eagerness to watch the approaching enemy, rose to his feet. "Lie down!"

roared Hays, "lie down like that man," pointing to a figure at his feet. "That man is dead, general." "I wish you were. Be quiet." Then turning to his orderly, the division color bearer, he spoke: "Orderly! When we are attacked I expect to ride where danger is thickest. Do you think you will keep up with that [2nd Corps] flag, even if I ride to hell?" Touching his cap visor, "With pleasure," said the orderly, "General, if you reach hell, just look out the window and you'll see the little blue trefoil [triangular clover Corps emblem] fluttering behind you."

On came the enemy, pecked by the little skirmish line retreating before it. The bugle now sounded the recall, and the skirmishers came dashing to our lines. Then [Captain William A.] Arnold's [1st R. I.] and other batteries opened with grape and canister [shot] upon the advancing line. Men were literally blown into the air, but the gaps were closed; no hurry, no wavering, but steadily moving onward, the movement eliciting admiration from those who were soon to mow them down.... With a roar and a yell the enemy now rushed toward our position ..., just lapping the Emmittsburg road when we heard the order, "Fire!" A sheet of flame, a clash of muskets, and the first line melted. On came the second... in isolated groups.... The shouts of combatants, surging lines, and roar of artillery made a picture that cannot be imagined, much less described. ...

Mortals could not stand the terrific fire that swept the valley. Pettigrew broke and ran.... Pickett... swept on ... and then went reeling back over the valley into the woods.

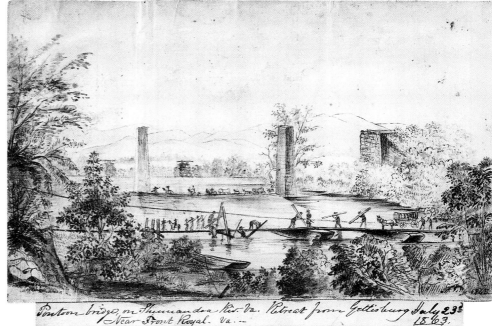

With the regular bridge spanning the Shenandoah River destroyed, Lee's retreating troops lay a pontoon bridge near Front Royal, Virginia, July 23, 1863.

This was the image transmitted to the people of the North through their newspapers of one of the two powerful 1,800-ton armored steam rams being built for the South by John Laird and Sons of Liverpool, England. Each ram was to have had four, mounted, 9-inch rifled guns, but the Battle of Gettysburg caused the termination of the project.

Hill and Culp's Hill to turn the Union right but only succeeded in occupying the base of the latter position by the end of the day. Although the right had been weakened from Meade's moving over forces to Sickles and the round tops, these troops remaining on the right were sufficiently entrenched to hold the high ground.

Lee, having failed to envelop either Union flank in Napoleonic fashion, now resolved to make a frontal assault on the Union center – Cemetery Ridge held by Hancock's 2nd Corps. If he could break it, Meade's army would be cut in half, and he had a freshly- arrived division of Longstreet's corps under Major General George E. Pickett to form the nucleus of the assault. It was risky in the extreme, but Lee had supreme confidence in his troops and overruled Longstreet's objections. Ewell's forces were driven away from Culp's Hill on the Union right early on July 3 anyway, so Lee ordered Pickett to attack the center, along with two divisions of Hill's corps, in the early afternoon.

Preceded by an artillery barrage, Pickett's charge of 15,000 men steadily advanced across the half-mile of open ground, only to come under a withering cannonade by the Union guns. They steadily closed ranks, however, and marched on, crossing the Emmittsburg road. Only when the rebel infantry was at point-blank range did the Yankee riflemen open fire. The blue and the gray clashed in hand-to-hand fighting at the stone wall and grove of trees held by Hancock. Two of Pickett's brigadiers fell, the other was wounded and captured, and all but 2,000 of the attackers died or were wounded

at this so-called "high water mark of the Confederacy," but making the Federals pay dearly; the 1st Minnesota Infantry alone suffered 82 percent casualties. The surviving attackers fled, and only the Southern cannon prevented a Union counterattack. Simultaneously, Jeb Stuart's cavalry finally arrived and attacked several miles to the east but was badly mauled by the carbine-wielding Union cavalry.

The Battle of Gettysburg was over; Lee had failed. Both armies lay exhausted next day, the 28,000 Southern casualties for the first time exceeding those of the Union, which had 23,000. Lee then withdrew under cover of heavy rains, and Meade's pursuit was too sluggish to prevent his escape into Virginia. Meade, because of his great victory, was not censured for this failure to finish off the Army of Northern Virginia. The strategic result was the resumption of the stalemate in Virginia between the two armies of the Eastern theater. The determination of the Union to destroy the Confederacy was stiffened by Gettysburg, and Union diplomats had little difficulty in forcing the British government to seize the Laird rams before they could be delivered to the Confederacy. Foreign recognition of the Southern nation henceforth became a fading vision. The British aristocracy favored the Confederacy, unlike the working classes who, long opposed to slavery, joined business and government in accepting the necessity of a Union victory.

That total war would be prosecuted against the South for the final reunification of the republic was

A sketch of a New York City riot in 1863 illustrates the sometimes horrific effects of mob violence: a Negro hanged and a building burned.

Lincoln's message when he journeyed to Gettysburg in November 1863 to dedicate the cemetery for the fallen Americans. From "these honored dead," he said in his humble but monumental address, "we take increased devotion to that cause for which they here gave the last full measure of devotion – that we here highly resolve that these dead shall not have died in vain; that this nation shall have a new birth of freedom; and that this government of the people, by the people, and for the people shall not perish from the earth."

Britain's "John Bull" and the Emperor of France give up any thought of extending official recognition to the Confederacy after the Battle of Gettysburg.

"RECOGNITION," or "NO."

J. BULL *to* NAPOLEON III. "Can you recognize that thing they call the C. S. A.?"
NAP. "Well, I think I could, if 'twere not for that Big Fellow who stands in front."

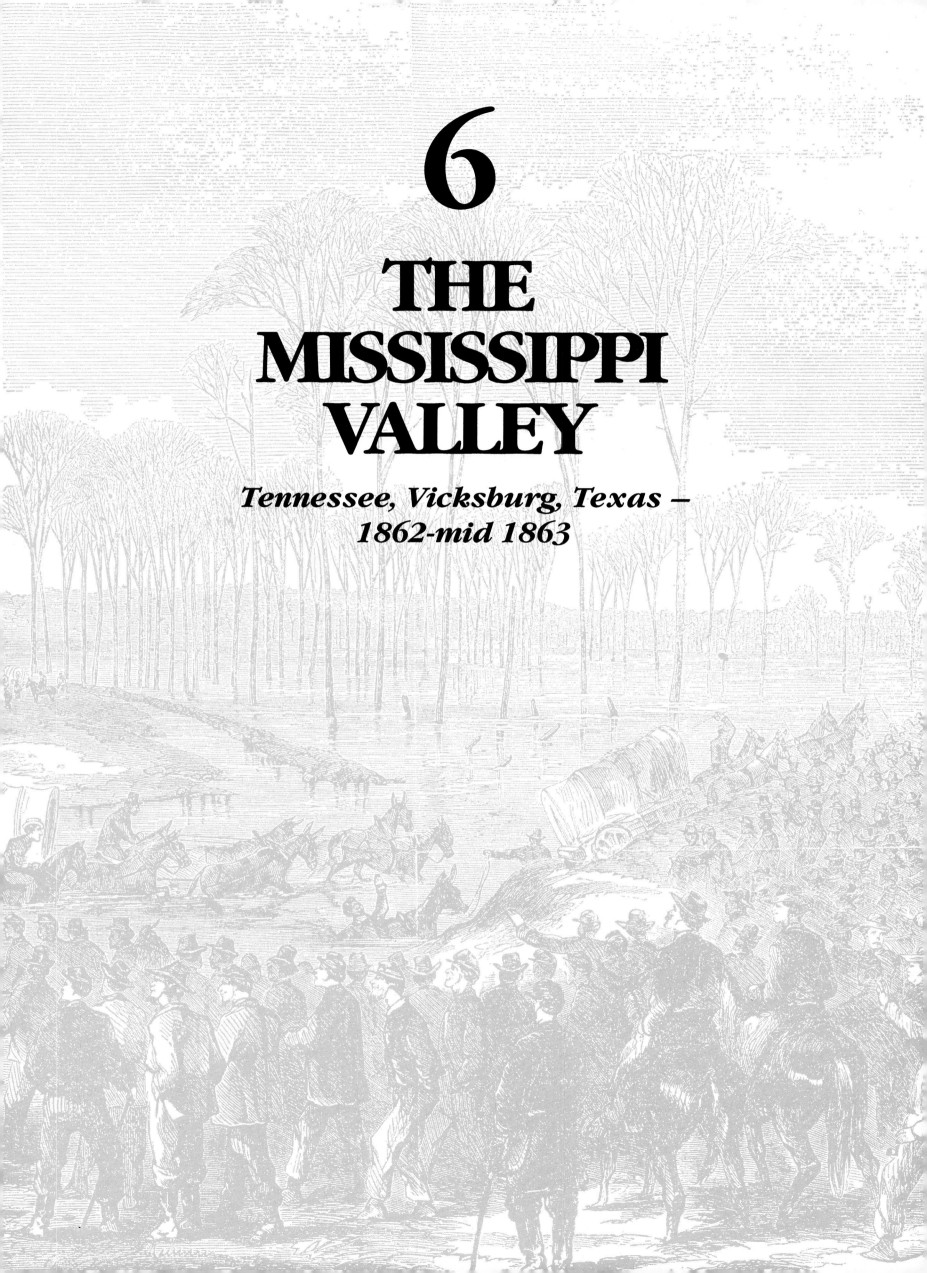

6
THE MISSISSIPPI VALLEY

Tennessee, Vicksburg, Texas —
1862-mid 1863

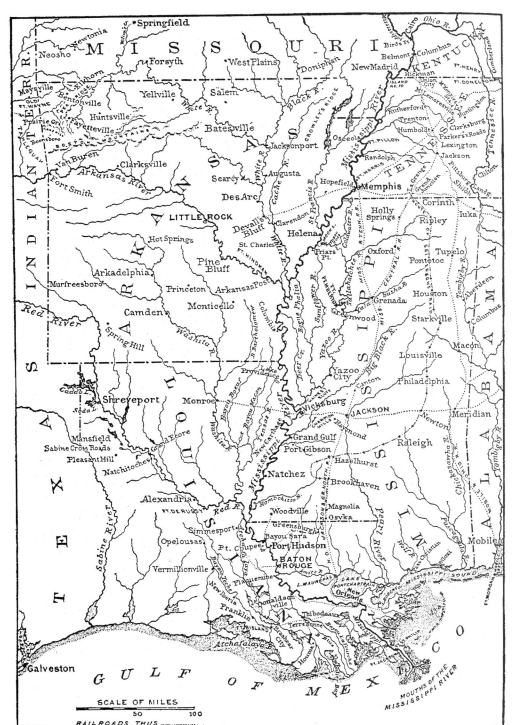

In strategy as in tactics the aim is to achieve concentration – the massing of one's major forces against a weak point of the enemy while holding the rest of the enemy's force at bay by feints and diversions. Lee's masterpiece at Chancellorsville was a classic example of concentration at the battlefield level. Strategically, the huge Union army had a golden opportunity to achieve concentration by holding down the main Confederate forces in one theater while striking its major blow in the other theater. For the South simply lacked the manpower and military resources to counter simultaneous advances in both the Eastern and Western theaters. With its fixation on the East, the Union – and the Confederacy in response – kept Virginia as the striking element of its strategy, leaving the Western armies in the valley of the Mississippi as the holding element.

In fact, however, Lee's string of successes against the Army of the Potomac was turning the Union strategy on

its head. By achieving and maintaining a stalemate in the East, the Army of Northern Virginia was converting the Army of the Potomac into the Union's holding element, creating the possibility for General-in-Chief Halleck to convert his armies in the West into the main hitting element. What was more, by operating from the exterior position, two simultaneous Union drives against Vicksburg and Chattanooga could split rebel forces in the West, unable to shift forces between the two cities quickly for lack of a connecting railroad. But Halleck lacked the strategic vision or verve to adopt such a strategy and continued to treat the West as the secondary theater.

In the event, the Federal armies in the West would eventually accomplish the feat of becoming the main striking force of Union strategy, but not before much fumbling and some tactical defeats at the hands of their opponents and never consciously by the Lincoln administration enamored with crushing Lee and taking Richmond. Instead, Rosecrans with the Army of the

A fanciful 1862 Yankee poster shows troops attired like Uncle Sam "marching into Dixie" with a patriotic zeal equal to the South's and overlain with the moral goal of ending slavery.

If the C.S.A. had any national anthem, it was "Dixie," but this 1862 song sheet cover for "God Save the South" clearly demonstrates the depth of Confederate patriotism.

Cumberland was charged with defeating Bragg's Army of Tennessee at Murfreesboro south of Nashville for an ultimate drive on the railhead at Chattanooga. Grant with the Army of the Tennessee was to advance the 400 miles down the Mississippi from Memphis to capture Vicksburg, although Lincoln allowed himself to be persuaded by a former Illinois politician, Major General John A. McClernand, for the latter to lead a separate expedition downriver as well. Unlike Rosecrans, whose campaign had to be conducted solely overland, Grant and McClernand could exploit the Mississippi Squadron of Rear Admiral David D. Porter to move downriver. From New Orleans, now commanded by Major General Nathaniel P. Banks, Union forces occupied Baton Rouge on the Lower Mississippi and put pressure on Port Hudson, Louisiana, a few miles upriver, supported by Admiral Farragut's naval forces.

Like Lincoln, Jefferson Davis remained wedded to the primacy of the Eastern theater but assigned

227

General Joe Johnston to coordinate the several armies in the West – Pemberton's in central Mississippi protecting Vicksburg, Bragg's at Murfreesville guarding Chattanooga, and Kirby Smith's at Knoxville. Johnston established his headquarters at Chattanooga in late November 1862 and immediately began urging the transfer of several thousand troops from Arkansas to reinforce Pemberton. This was sound defensive strategy utilizing the interior position by massing troops where they could repulse the main Union drive against Vicksburg. But as December began, Confederate Trans-Mississippi forces attacked Union forces south of Fayetteville, Arkansas but were defeated at Prairie Grove. With such forces useless in that sector, Johnston wanted them for the defense of Mississippi. President Davis refused and on a personal visit to Chattanooga ordered Bragg to transfer 8000 of his 40,000-man army from Tennessee to Mississippi. Johnston protested, for such a weakening of Bragg's army only encouraged General Rosecrans to move against Bragg from the environs of Nashville. Rosecrans' Army of the Cumberland numbered over 40,000 men, well-supplied from the North and well-fed from denuding the farmlands around Nashville.

So neither side had a well-coordinated strategy. Johnston's authority was compromised by Davis' meddling, and Bragg was left to deal as best he could with Rosecrans whenever the latter advanced against him at Murfreesboro. Grant's Army of the Tennessee in northern Mississippi – over 70,000 strong – was to make the main attack against Pemberton's 40,000 men defending the rest of that state. Grant intended to advance in two prongs – he to lead 40,000 overland along the north-south Mississippi Central Railroad, while Major General William T. Sherman – a trusted division commander ever since Shiloh – embarked 32,000 aboard transports at Memphis to descend the Mississippi for a landing just above Vicksburg. The only common strategic aspect of the Confederate defensive preparations was the mounting of three daring cavalry raids during December to cut Union communications. With a force of 2,500 Bedford Forrest rode into western Tennessee, destroying Grant's rail connections with his rear base of Columbus, Kentucky.

Previous pages: a Union regimental fife and drum unit in front of a blacksmith's tent.

*Previous pages: Stonewall
Jackson is depicted being
mortally wounded during the
Battle of Chancellorsville late
on May 2, 1863. The highly
imaginative artist has ignored
the fact that the revered
leader was hit by his own
men, under cover of
darkness, while inspecting his
lines at the end of the day.*

corps, and then a grand division. Dubbed by the press (to his dismay) "Fighting Joe," he developed a sound plan to "turn" Lee out of his position at Fredericksburg by crossing the upper Rappahannock at Kelly's Ford with a third of his army and moving against Lee's rear, forcing him to abandon Fredericksburg. Simultaneously, Major General John Sedgwick would maneuver against Lee by crossing the river below Fredericksburg with another third of the army. The remaining third would be held back until needed, while the bulk of the cavalry – for the first time concentrated into its own corps – destroyed Southern railroads in Lee's rear. The absence of the Union horsemen enabled Jeb Stuart's rebel cavalry to detect Hooker's advance after Hooker crossed the river on April 29 and moved into the Wilderness toward Chancellorsville. As at Second Bull Run and Antietam, Lee made the bold decision that, rather than fall back, he would split his own force and operate from the interior position, even though he had only Jackson's corps and half of Longstreet's, the rest still

absent foraging. Lee left Major General Jubal A. Early's division to watch Sedgwick and shifted the rest of his army to counter Hooker's turning movement. Hooker, shocked to learn of Lee's advance, dug in at Chancellorsville to make a defensive stand in the heavily wooded terrain. There Stuart's cavalry discovered Hooker's right flank to be completely exposed.

The Battle of Chancellorsville began on May 2, 1863 as Lee led 17,000 men against Hooker's front and sent Stonewall Jackson with 26,000 westward, delivering a crushing blow to Hooker's flank in the late afternoon. As night fell, Jackson personally inspected his advanced units to try to cut off the retreating Union forces in that sector when he was fired upon by his own men, unable to identify him, and was severely wounded. Stuart took over Jackson's corps and renewed the attack at dawn of the 3rd, forcing Hooker to order his forces back into a stronger position. Just then, a rebel shell struck the porch from which Hooker was directing the battle, and the overhang fell on him, knocking him senseless for

*As Howard's 11th Corps
retreats in the face of
Stonewall Jackson's late
afternoon attack at
Chancellorsville, May 2,
1863, Couch forms a battle
line with the 2nd Corps to
cover the retreat.*

After leading a brigade, a division, and a corps, Major General George G. Meade achieved fame as commander of the Army of the Potomac at the epic battle of Gettysburg. However, after failing to outflank Lee in the brief Mine Run campaign of late November 1863, Meade was placed under Grant's direct control.

This June 27, 1863 broadside (below) was General Cooper's response to the movement of 20,000 Union troops under Major General John A. Dix from the Peninsula to the South Anna River. Their threat to Richmond, simply a diversion to tie down troops and prevent them joining Lee's invasion of Pennsylvania, was easily repulsed by Harvey Hill's division.

TO THE CITIZENS
of
RICHMOND !

The President and the Governor of Virginia, deeply impressed with the necessity of a speedy organization of all able bodied and patriotic citizens, for local defence, in and around the City of Richmond, and throughout the State, urgently appeal to their fellow-citizens, to come forth in their militia organizations, and to commence and perfect at once, other organizations by companies, battallions and regiments. An imperious necessity for instant action exists, and they trust that this appeal will be all that is necessary to accomplish the result. No time is to be lost; danger threatens the City.

Therefore, with a view to secure the individual attention of all classes of the citizens of Richmond, and to impress upon them the full importance of the crisis, it is hereby ordered that all stores and places of business in this City, be closed to-day at three o'clock P. M., and daily thereafter, until further order, and the people be invited to meet and form organizations for local defence. They will be armed and equipped as fast as the companies are formed.

By command of Secretary of War,
S. COOPER,
Adjutant and Inspector General
By order of the Governor of Virginia,
JOHN G. MOSBY, Jr.,
A. A. A. General.

LEE

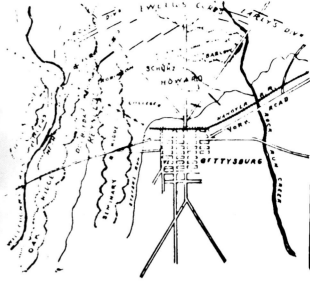

MAP SHOWING POSITION JULY 1st

a time. Over on the Union left, Sedgwick crossed the river and endured several setbacks by Early's troops at Marye's Heights but finally broke through them, then dug in to await a combined assault with Hooker early on the 4th. But Hooker remained entrenched, and during the night Lee moved 20,000 troops from Hooker's front the twelve miles to Fredericksburg and drove Sedgwick back across the river after daybreak. This masterstroke completely discouraged Hooker, who recrossed the Rappahannock on the 6th. Lee's stunning victory with only half the manpower of Hooker resulted in over 17,000 U.S. casualties, fewer than 13,000 C.S., the worst for Lee being Stonewall Jackson, who died of his wounds a week after the battle.

Lee's great victory of Chancellorsville left the Army of the Potomac as off-balance as it had been after Second Bull Run, like then a golden opportunity for Lee to strike another offensive blow as at Antietam. His army needed supplies. Longstreet returned to Fredericksburg with ample forage, but the men required shoes. When Lee complained to the chief quartermaster in Richmond, he was told he ought to go north to find such manufactured goods. Union pressure in the Western theater was acute, the South needed foreign recognition, and Northern pro-peace Copperheads and anti-draft protesters were eroding public resolve. Lee therefore recommended to President Davis that he be allowed to attempt another invasion of the North, this time to swing westward well beyond the Great Falls, cross the Potomac, and advance through Maryland into Pennsylvania. The Army of Northern Virginia could obtain supplies from the fertile farmlands and manufacturers in the region and force Hooker and the Army of the Potomac to quit Virginia in pursuit of him. If Lee could defeat Hooker on Yankee soil, the Union might then sue for peace. Davis accepted Lee's plan.

Lee probably realized that his army would never be stronger – by June 1863 totalling 89,000 men and

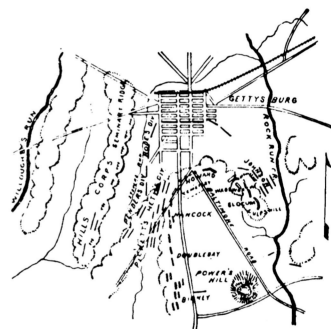

POSITION JULY 3d

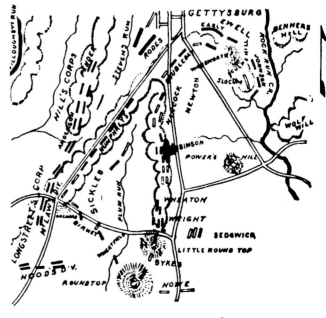

POSITION JULY 2nd

A federal observation post, complete with telescope, that has been set up in an abandoned attic, as sketched by A. R. Waud. Note the boots of a second soldier, whose legs dangle through the roof that he has mounted for a better view.

Winslow Homer's depiction of Confederate prisoners at the front. The Union officer resembles the "boy general," Francis Channing Barlow, one of the few clean-shaven generals of the war. Twenty-six years of age in 1861, Barlow only looked boyish; he was a Harvard graduate who rose to command the 2nd Corps by the war's end, having sustained severe wounds at Antietam and Gettysburg.

Woe unto any Southerner, such as this one, who expressed Union sentiments. Superpatriotism among the rank and file demonstrated the commitment of the South to the achievement of its independence, although many Confederate soldiers admitted to feelings of remorse whenever they fired on troops waving "Old Glory."

STRIPPING THE TENNESSEE COUNTRYSIDE

by **Calvin R. Zener**, Private, Company G, 15th Indiana Infantry (Zener was a direct forebear of the author of this book. His letters have been in the family ever since they were written. The punctuation and spelling are reproduced as in the original.)

Nashville, Nov 28th/62
Dear parents bro and ststers all

... *we are Camped within eighty rods of where we was Camped last Spring[.] things looks kind O familliar around here. I suppose that we will have to move South by degrees and build rail road bridges as we go [,] the same as we did last Spring. well, somebody has to suffer for it. if them that is in the rebbel army dont, them that is at home does, for we cannot get forage here no other way than to forage off of the country, and we make a clean sweep of every thing where ever we go. we stay in one place till forage gets scarce and move Camp. ...*

The forage train [of wagons] went out to a old rebs place [,] took all of his corn [,] six mules and the last horse – a Stallion be had valued at two thousand dollars. he came out and said it was to, DmB, bad to take all a man had. he said Mr Forest [the Confederate cavalry raider General N. B. Forrest] took six horses from him and now we had took the last one he had. The forage master told him if he would come to camp and prove his loyalty he could get his horse back and pay for his corn. he said it did not mak a, dmb bit of difference for says he [,] when you leave, here will come Mr Forest, says Mr. F[,] you have been swaring alegiance to the U S A [.] so he will take all I have left, so whats the difference[?]

The 15th [Indiana] went out with the forage train

A wartime drawing by Winslow Homer shows Yankee foragers at work, chasing down beef on foot. Another man waits in the background on his mount, carrying two bags stuffed with edibles.

yesterday. we went out about three miles and had a corn gathering [.] we pulled about forty acres of corn in about three hours. gathering corn pretty fast aint it. … That's the way we do it down here …

I am in hopes that this war will be carried on with a little more vigor than it has been. I believe if we had of had the write Gen in that this war would of been over, or nearer than it is. I believe that old Buel don more, or as mutch good for the rebbels as he done for the U.S.A. [.] you would think that we had an army large enoughf to whip the world if you could only visit Nashville[.] I could not begin to tell you how many there is here but there is a whole heap of them. …

Nashville Tenn Decem 15th/62
… We went out a Thursday on the Murfreesboro pike and had a little fight with the SeSh [Secesh, for secessionists] before we could get any forrage. We drove

them some three miles and then entertained them untill the wagons got loaded. …We go well prepared for them. There is two brigades and one batery of Artillery goes out with the train when it goes out side of our lines. … The country for ten or fifteen miles around Nashville is almost destitude of every thing. … farewell your Bro and Son Cal

(Letter of Cal Zener's sister Maggy to their brother, Private Melville C. Zener, 77th Indiana Infantry, at Louisville, February 28, 1863)

… Oh when will this wicked rebellion be crushed [?] there never was anything that I desire to see the end of so much as this war. … We want to know of a certainty if Father can get the body of Calvin. … [Cal Zener had been killed at the Battle of Stones River two months before.]

Logs, sandbags and earth protect these Union gunners and their 100-pound Parrott guns from the front, while the mound of dirt behind them can absorb the fragments and concussions of enemy shells exploding inside the fort.

THE MISSISSIPPI VALLEY

Awaiting the enemy's fire

Right: a montage of confederate uniforms, the Stars and Bars of the "Bonnie Blue Flag," the battle flag (to the rear) and generals Jackson, Lee, and Joe Johnston on medallions.

Awaiting the enemy's fire was the unknown artist's title for the sketch (left) of a Union cannon. The crew fired, swabbed out particles and possible embers, loaded powder and ball through the muzzle, aimed, and then refired.

A wounded rebel Zouave is offered water from the canteen of a conventionally uniformed Confederate soldier in an abandoned camp – perhaps captured from the enemy; the tent covers are gone and some of the framing broken.

Earl Van Dorn's 3,500 horsemen struck Grant's immediate rear base at Holly Springs in northern Mississippi. And John Hunt Morgan penetrated as far north as Bardstown, Kentucky with 4,000 to cut Rosecrans' rail connection with Louisville. These raids induced Grant to abandon his overland offensive and pull back his own forces over the Tennessee border to concentrate in and around Memphis. At Nashville, however, Rosecrans took advantage of Bragg's further reduced force from the absence of Forrest and Morgan to advance on Murfreesboro.

Rosecrans' 41,000 men clashed with Bragg's 35,000 at the Battle of Stones River (or Murfreesboro) on December 31, 1862. Rosecrans planned to concentrate his attack on Bragg's right flank. The latter, with no intention of fighting on the defensive, struck Rosecrans' right at sunrise, driving it back to a better defensive position by the end of the day. The fighting was savage as the rebel forces tried to dislodge the men of blue, but to no avail. The armies spent New Years Day in their lines, although Bragg's remaining cavalry hacked away at Rosecrans' supply lines, and Rosecrans posted Crittenden with three divisions on the high ground of the left flank north of the river. Bragg, against the advice of his generals, ordered Major General John C. Breckinridge's division to assault this strong position

THOMAS J. JACKSON 1824 1863

ROBERT E. LEE 1807 1870

JOSEPH E. JOHNSTON 1807 1891

I. Steeple Davis

on the afternoon of January 2. It succeeded, only to be bludgeoned and driven back by massed Union artillery beyond the hill. After another day of inaction, Bragg yielded the field. He had won the battle and inflicted casualties on one-third of Rosecrans' army, but he suffered an equal percentage, lost the campaign by withdrawing southward, and lost the confidence of his troops for uninspired leadership. Although Rosecrans did not pursue him, eastern Tennessee remained secure for the time being.

In the meantime, Sherman had moved down the Mississippi with 32,000 men in four divisions on army transports, covered by Admiral Porter's gunboats. The entire length of the river was flanked by low, marshy banks, except for Chickasaw Bluffs just north of Vicksburg where the Yazoo River enters the Mississippi from the northeast. Near here Sherman made his landing on December 26. Pemberton rushed reinforcements from

north-central Mississippi to Vicksburg after Grant's withdrawal to Memphis, and the addition of the troops from Bragg gave the defenders 14,000 men with which to meet Sherman. Most importantly, the Southern guns mounted on the Bluffs commanded the swampy bayous through which Sherman's men advanced and pinned them down during repeated Union assaults. Neither could Porter's naval guns from the lower Yazoo dislodge the defenders, forcing Sherman to abandon the entire enterprise on January 2. The first concerted Union attempt on Vicksburg ended a dismal failure.

General McClernand now arrived and assumed command over Sherman's force, but instead of trying to invest Vicksburg as he had promised Lincoln, he moved up the Arkansas River, which enters the Mississippi from Arkansas about midway between Memphis and Vicksburg. Rebel forces in southern Arkansas were building gunboats on the Arkansas River to contest Union activity on the Mississippi.

The mule-borne cacolet was invented as a means of transporting two wounded men still able to sit up; in all probability it was only rarely used.

236

McClernand decided on his own initiative to use his 30,000 troops and Porter's warships to capture Arkansas Post fifty miles up the Arkansas River. He landed his troops on both banks of the Arkansas to besiege Fort Hindman on January 9-10, 1863, and on the 11th Porter's vessels silenced the guns of the 4,500 defenders, which surrendered before the infantry attack matured. The small victory achieved little, however, for Grant immediately ordered McClernand to withdraw and rejoin the main effort against Vicksburg.

Unlike the other Union commanding generals in the West (Halleck, Buell, Rosecrans), Grant had no intention of remaining idle in the face of setbacks or interruptions. To maintain constant pressure against Vicksburg, he planned to exploit the advantage of his naval power by moving along the riverways and swamps of the Mississippi Valley rather than depend on railroads and long overland supply lines vulnerable to Confederate cavalry raids. In addition, he intended to cooperate

William S. Rosecrans (left), "Old Rosy," had an unrosy disposition but performed creditably in the West Virginia campaign of 1861 to become major general in charge of volunteers. Successive command of the armies of the Mississippi and the Cumberland proved him to be only a mediocre tactician; he defeated Bragg at Stones River, but was later routed at Chickamauga.

Confederate batteries at Vicksburg fire on the gunboat Indianola *as she speeds by just before midnight, February 16, 1863. Eight nights later, however, she was rammed and captured by two rebel vessels, which then scuttled her when a "river monitor" suddenly appeared – a bogus warship burning smudge pots and set adrift by ingenious Yankees.*

THE MISSISSIPPI VALLEY

Turning forty in 1862, Ulysses "Sam" Grant (right) became an aggressive major general, seizing Fort Donelson, repulsing the rebel army at Shiloh, and moving on Vicksburg. Rugged, unorthodox, and known to enjoy the odd whiskey, he rose to eminence first in the West and then as general in chief of all the Union armies.

with Banks, initiating operations against Port Hudson, Louisiana on the Mississippi from the south. Joe Johnston could do little to help Pemberton defend Vicksburg and central Mississippi without reinforcements. Bragg's understrength army could not spare them, but at least President Davis transferred Kirby Smith from Knoxville to command the Trans-Mississippi District and counter Banks' movements.

Grant tried several schemes to find a route for his army to bypass Vicksburg's batteries and bluffs for an attack from the south side of the river bastion during the winter months of early 1863 – just as Pope had done at Island No. 10 the year before. Porter's ships operated just north of Vicksburg supporting two attempts by the army to cut canals across the west banks – both frustrated by fluky winter river levels. Neither did two other attempts to make use of inland bayous, lakes, and smaller rivers bear fruit, one of them frustrated by hastily-constructed rebel defenses. A fifth attempt – at

Steele's Bayou, just north of Vicksburg – ended when several of Porter's vessels became mired in the heavy undergrowth of the swamp and had to be rescued by Sherman's troops. Then, at the end of March, with the swollen river finally receding, Grant landed his entire Army of the Tennessee at Milliken's Bend on the western bank of the Mississippi above Vicksburg and

Sherman's troops launch a diversionary attack at Haines' Bluff north of Vicksburg, April 30, 1863, drawing rebel attention away from Grant's movements westward and southward of the city.

*During the winter of 1863,
Grant's troops and hired
black labor gangs dig one of
two projected canals west of
Vicksburg, but without
success.*

THE MISSISSIPPI VALLEY

set about building a road across the neck of the peninsula on the western shore opposite Vicksburg to get below the city.

The investment of Vicksburg called for a sound strategic sense and resolute leadership, both of which Grant displayed. Pemberton's defenses were all arrayed on the east side of the river around Vicksburg, with 60,000 troops divided between these positions – at Haines' Bluff on the Yazoo eleven miles above the city, the bluff at Grand Gulf where the Big Black River enters the Mississippi 50 miles south of the city, and at Jackson, the state capital connected by rail 50 miles to the east. Using several diversions, Grant planned to cross the river below Grand Gulf, link up with the navy there, and, using tactical concentration, defeat Pemberton's forces piecemeal – first at Jackson then at Vicksburg.

The most distant distraction to confuse Pemberton was provided by General Banks, who with 15,000 troops during April cleared the west Louisiana region

along the Mississippi River opposite Port Hudson and up the Red River as far as Alexandria, which fell on May 7. North of Vicksburg, Grant had Sherman land several units at Haines' Bluff in a feint on April 30, then withdrew them the next day. The boldest and most successful lure was a cavalry raid across the entire state of Mississippi, the first major independent use of Union cavalry in the West. On April 17, Colonel Benjamin H. Grierson departed the environs of Memphis with 1,700 Illinois and Iowa cavalry and struck south, evading or skirmishing with local troops and sending his Iowa regiment on a successful diversion into eastern Mississippi. With his remaining two Illinois regiments and a six-gun battery, Grierson passed south to Newton Station, 50 miles due east of Jackson, forcing Pemberton to order several units to intercept him. But Grierson defeated one of them, eluded the others, and destroyed much railroad track and telegraph lines at a cost of only two dozen men before safely reaching Banks' base at

Baton Rouge on May 2. He had covered 600 miles – averaging 38 miles a day – to successfully divert much of Pemberton's attention from Vicksburg (Grierson's raid was dramatized in the 1959 motion picture *The Horse Soldiers*).

While Grant marched most of his army from Milliken's Bend to a point south of Vicksburg opposite Gulf Grant, Porter on the night of April 16 ran the Vicksburg batteries with a dozen ships, losing one in the terrific Confederate shelling, to link up with Grant. Porter then ran transports and supply barges through the maelstrom the night of the 29th, suffering some losses but bringing Grant ammunition and rations and covering his crossing of the river next day. On May 10 Grant defeated rebel forces at Port Gibson inland of Grand Gulf, which the Confederates then evacuated. Within a week Grant had 33,000 men concentrated below Vicksburg: Sherman's 15th Corps, McClernand's 13th, and Major General James B. McPherson's 17th. Pemberton, confused by Grant's several actions and diversions, unfortunately

Overleaf: while Union mortar boats shell rebel positions above Vicksburg at the end of April, Porter's ironclad gunboats run by to silence the batteries at Grand Gulf, below the city.

During Grierson's daring cavalry raid across Mississippi in late April 1863, a Yankee telegraph operator taps an enemy wire along the Mississippi Central Railroad near Egypt.

Supported by Admiral Porter's flotilla of transports and warships, Grant equips his army at Grand Gulf, below Vicksburg, preparatory to cutting his own communications and striking overland toward Jackson, Mississippi, early in May 1863.

withdrew his main forces inside Vicksburg instead of attacking Grant's precarious foothold. That it was shortsighted was shown also by the fact that Johnston was assembling reinforcements at Jackson, which Grant might now cut off. Grant's orders from Halleck were to move downriver to invest Port Hudson in cooperation with Banks, after which they could combine against Vicksburg. With Banks still on the Red River, however, Grant seized the initiative by driving toward Jackson. Furthermore, it meant cutting his communications with the navy on the river and living off the land, an unprecedented stratagem in the war. Ignoring his orders and the risks, however, Grant acted, taking with him only a wagon train of ammunition.

With 44,000 men, Grant abandoned Grand Gulf, struck eastward, brushed aside a rebel force at Raymond on May 12, and easily drove Johnston's 6,000 troops from Jackson on the 14th. Pemberton left Vicksburg next day to attack Grant with 22,000 troops, which he did at Champion's Hill – half way to Jackson – on the 16th. The heavy fighting seesawed as the Hill changed hands several times. Largely through the efforts of

McPherson's 17th Corps, the Union army defeated Pemberton there and followed up against his rear guard at the Big Black River next day. As Pemberton withdrew inside Vicksburg's formidable defenses, Grant launched three frontal assaults there between May 19 and 22, hoping to take the city before Johnston could organize a relief force from the east. But Pemberton's guns and 20,000 defenders repulsed these attacks, forcing Grant to institute a long and tedious siege.

A siege of Vicksburg had been desired by neither Grant nor Johnston. Johnston had advised Pemberton to abandon the city in favor of saving his army, but the stubborn Pennsylvanian – who had cast his lot with the South – refused. Johnston consequently set about collecting 30,000 troops in eastern Mississippi and Alabama with which to relieve Vicksburg, but they were too untrained and poorly armed to mount an attack on Grant's rear. Grant, for his part, relied upon the navy to transport reinforcements down from Memphis, doubling the size of his army to over 70,000 men. With half of them, he bombarded Vicksburg round the clock, with the rest he protected his rear.

GENERAL LOGAN'S ADVICE

May 16, 1863

by **J. B. Harris**, Private, 34th Indiana Infantry

At the battle of Champion Hills, Miss., May 16, 1863, the 34th Ind. was sorely pressed by the rebels, and, after losing one-third of the regiment in killed and wounded and being out of ammunition, were ordered to fall back. As this was our first fall back, many of the boys forgot and were falling back at will — some, in fact, were on the double-quick for the rear. While on the retreat we came across [Major] General [John A.] Logan [commander, 3rd Division, 17th Army Corps], who shouted that he had been wounded five times and had never turned his back to the foe yet. "What regiment is that?" he asked; and hearing that it was the 34th Ind., he said that Indiana should be disgraced and we must stop right there.

Of course we stopped, and as our adjutant came riding up the general said, "Adjutant, get your men together." "General, the rebels are awful thick up there," replied the adjutant. "Damn it, that's the place to kill them — where they are thick," shouted the general. The boys and the adjutant saw the point and said no more. While we were waiting irresolutely, some shouts arose and we knew that the Johnnies had started for Vicksburg. The general then left us for his command, which was on our right.

Pennsylvania troopers erect the building blocks of field fortifications: fascines — long stakes bound together — and gabions — open circular cages into which dirt could be poured to absorb enemy fire and shrapnel. Even when a gabion burned up, the dirt remained in place.

THE MISSISSIPPI VALLEY

Meanwhile, in Washington, Halleck appreciated Grant's success and urged Rosecrans to use his Army of the Cumberland to attack Bragg in eastern Tennessee lest Bragg detach more forces to Johnston. From Murfreesboro, Rosecrans finally moved with 65,000 men against Bragg's 44,000 on June 23 and successfully outmaneuvered him. Offering only skirmishes instead of a pitched battle, Bragg fell back on Tullahoma which he then abandoned on the 30th in favor of Chattanooga. Without reinforcements to go to Johnston, Vicksburg was doomed.

Despite the sacrifices of its defenders, including the civilian population, Vicksburg could not long endure the starvation, disease, and casualties inflicted by Grant's siege. Porter's gunboats joined in the shelling of the beleaguered bastion, and two mines tunneled under the ramparts were filled with explosives which when detonated inflicted more havoc. Buoyed by news of Lee's invasion of Pennsylvania, the defenders took to scavaging whatever edibles could be found in a vain effort to hold on. But it was hopeless, and on July 4 Pemberton surrendered the city. Coming the day after Lee's defeat at Gettysburg, the fall of Vicksburg was greeted with wild enthusiasm in the North, where fresh anti-draft riots in New York City were now suppressed. Grant's strategic and tactical genius had achieved a monumental victory.

Meanwhile, in late May, Banks had crossed the Mississippi from his Red River operation and assaulted the 7,000 defenders of Port Hudson from the landward side on the 27th. Lackluster execution of the attack led to its failure, whereupon Banks had instituted his own siege. Two more frontal assaults in mid-June miscarried, but the starvation of the garrison did not. With only 3,000 effectives left and Vicksburg lost, Port Hudson capitulated on July 9. Farragut's and Porter's warships now controlled the entire Mississippi, and Western wheat could be transported downriver to New Orleans for export abroad.

The Confederacy was now cut in two, leaving the Trans-Mississippi District as a virtually independent nation under its own generalissimo; his fiefdom came to be regarded as "Kirby Smithdom." But the mere opening of the Mississippi did not guarantee untrammeled passage by Union shipping. Confederate guerrillas and cavalry raiders had been plaguing the areas around the confluence of the Cumberland, Tennessee, and Mississippi rivers area ever since the

Union troops plant their colors on the Confederate works at Vicksburg during the general assault of May 22, 1863. However, the determined rebel defenders drove them off, forcing Grant to resort to a lengthier siege.

Main picture: with infantry posted on the hillocks to either side in front of them, a Union battery fires over the trees against the rebel fortifications at Vicksburg.

THE *VICKSBURG DAILY CITIZEN*

Excerpts

Thursday, July 2, 1863

We are indebted to Major Gillespie for a steak of Confederate beef, alias meat. We have tried it, and can assure our friends that if it is rendered necessary, they need have no scruples at eating the meat. It is sweet, savory and tender, and so long as we have a mule left, we are satisfied our soldiers will be content to subsist on it.

[Major General Martin Luther] Smith's impetuous division seems singularly unfortunate. He has lost many gallant men whose valor and worth the siege has fully developed.. ... [Colonel S. H.] Griffin, commanding the 31st Louisiana regiment, was killed on Saturday. He was a popular and efficient officer. Gifted by nature with undaunted courage, indomitable resolution and energy, he was also possessed of quick determination, keen glance and coolness in danger, which are the most essential qualities of an officer, while by his mingled firmness and clemency of his conduct, he won the confidence and good will of his men. May the soft south winds murmur sweet requiems o'er his manes, and the twilight dews fall gently like an angel's tear-drop, and moisten his turfy bed.

[Yankee Rear Admiral D. D.] Porter is enjoying a season of rest, and his men are doubtless obliged to him. ... On Tuesday he fired a few shells from his Parrots [naval cannon], and kept his men tolerably busy sharp-shooting across the river. ... Poor fool, he might as well give up the vain aspiration he entertains of capturing our city or extermination of our people, and return to his master to receive the reward such a gasconding dolt will meet at the hands of the unappreciating government at Washington.

TLE OF KEN'S BEND

The recently recruited "colored" Louisiana troops of Union Colonel Isaac F. Shepard's African Brigade defend Millikan's Bend on the river against an attack by 3,000 Trans-Mississippians, June 6, 1863. The following day, assisted by the 23rd Iowa and the ironclad ram Choctaw, *they drove back the rebels, inflicting 725 casualties against 492 of their own.*

Again we have reliable news from the gallant corps of Gen. Lee in Virginia. ... We lay before our readers in this issue an account of Lee's brilliant and successful onslaught upon the abolitionist hordes, and show even from their own record, how our gallant boys of the cavalry have fleshed their swords to the hilt with their vaunting foe, and now each musket of our infantry has told its fatal leaden tale. To-day Maryland is ours, *to-morrow Pennsylvania will be, and the next day Ohio – now midway, like Mohammed's coffin, will fall. Success and glory to our arms! God and right are with us.*

... the great Ulysses– the Yankee Generalissimo, surnamed Grant– has expressed his intention of dining in Vicksburg on Saturday next, and celebrating the 4th of July by a grand dinner, and so forth. When asked if he would invite Gen. Jo. Johnston to join he said: "No! for fear there would be a row at the table." Ulysses must get into the city before he dines in it. The way to cook a rabbit is, "first catch the rabbit," &c.

NOTE   July 4th, 1863
Two days bring about great changes. The banner of the Union floats over Vicksburg. Gen. Grant has "caught the rabbit". ...

249

THE MISSISSIPPI VALLEY

McPherson's 17th Corps uses saps – rolled wooden wickers – to protect the infantry edging toward the Confederate fortifications during the siege of Vicksburg in June 1863. Corps engineer Andrew Hickenlooper directed these siege operations.

capture of Fort Donelson early in 1862. Since this remained a key Union rear area for shipping, telegraph lines, and supplies, Yankee forces had been posted there, policing the region and being moved by transports to counter irregular rebel forces. By the spring of 1863 no fewer than 23 gunboats operated on the Tennessee, carrying the "Marine Brigade" of special army troops to land and pacify the countryside. Shifted to the Mississippi, this brigade under Brigadier General Alfred W. Ellet on May 23, 1863 landed, defeated a force of rebel cavalry, and burned the town of Austin, Mississippi for harboring and assisting the enemy forces. With guerrilla activity increasing, the Mississippi Marine Brigade was formally constituted in November 1863 to mount antiguerrilla operations along the river. On specially constructed transports, the mounted marines were brought to each trouble spot, whereupon ramps were dropped over the side and the horsemen charged ashore. Ellet's Brigade so effectively pacified the banks of the Mississippi that the unit was phased out the

Her great paddle boxes armored against fatal shellfire, the ram Lafayette, *under Captain Henry Walke, operates on the Mississippi. After passing below Vicksburg in May 1863, this and several of Porter's other vessels pressed south, rendezvoused with Farragut's fleet, patrolled the lower Mississippi, and fought in the Red River campaign of 1864.*

Colonel Hickenlooper had a mine dug under one of the rebel forts and 2,200 pounds of powder placed beneath the enemy works. The detonation (above) took place on June 25, 1863. However, the Confederates were prepared for such a device and quickly drove back the assault that followed.

following August. Also, lookout towers and cleared land around them gave a full view of the flat Mississippi bottomlands from which guerrillas might attack.

Flamboyant Southern raiders relentlessly attacked Union outposts in the Western theater for the rest of the war. During July 1863, Morgan again left Bragg's army with 2,500 picked cavalry to raid Yankee communications in Kentucky for the fourth time. After reaching Bardstown, however, he exceeded his orders by crossing the Ohio River into Indiana. Brushing aside local militia, Morgan entered Ohio and skirted Cincinnati before Union forces converged on his exhausted and depleted command. Regular troops, militia, and gunboats finally defeated him at Buffington, Ohio on July 19 and captured him and his last 364 men a week later. There were others to replace him, however, notably Forrest and Bragg's cavalry leader, Major General "Fighting Joe" Wheeler. Despite Gettysburg and Vicksburg, the Confederacy had plenty of fight left, even along the rivers.

The victorious Grant, with over 70,000 troops at his disposal, stood ready to move eastward against Johnston and Bragg, but nothing happened. As usual, Halleck and Secretary of War Stanton in Washington failed to exploit his great victory and instead began to disperse parts of his Army of the Tennessee to other points. Neither did they find reason to send the Army of the Potomac against the badly beaten Lee in Virginia. The Union high command squandered the summer of 1863 by resting on its laurels.

An artillery shell from a rebel army raiding force bursts in the ladies' social hall of the commercial steamer Welcome, *below Vicksburg, November 22, 1863. The explosion was followed by a hail of bullets. Only when Brigadier General William P. Benton, riding as a passenger, seized control did the ship avoid capture. The Mississippi Marine Brigade was formed to frustrate such attacks.*

Pemberton's defenders of Vicksburg march out of their fortifications to stack arms in surrender, July 4, 1863. Union troops, situated behind protective saps, await them in the siege trenches.

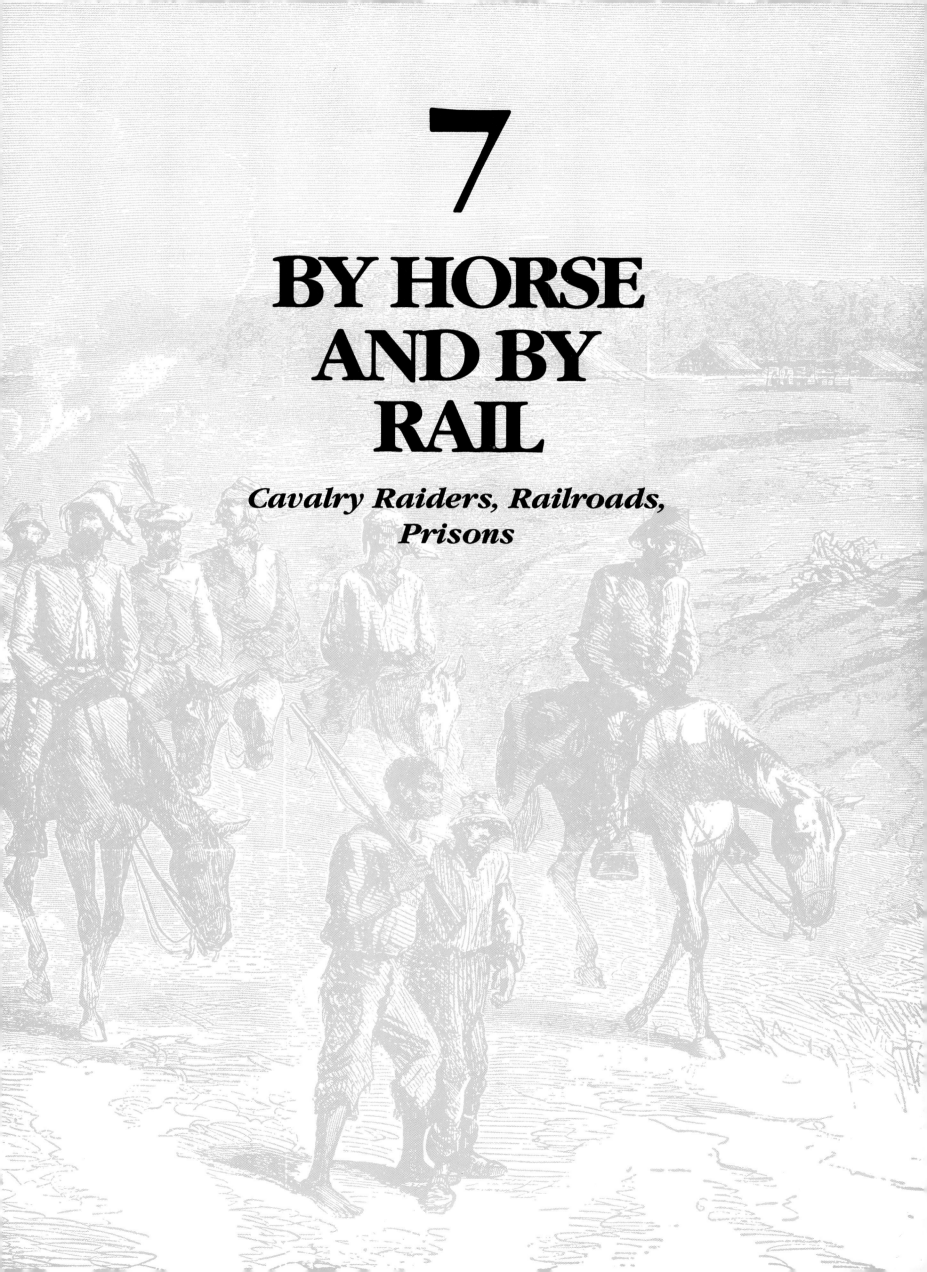

7
BY HORSE AND BY RAIL

Cavalry Raiders, Railroads, Prisons

BY HORSE
AND BY RAIL

A Union cavalryman with his great coat, saber, and scabbard. The saber had a carved blade with a thick backing, in contrast to the straight sword carried by infantry and artillery officers. The former was designed to deal a slashing blow, the latter was largely ceremonial and symbolic.

The war for communications – military supply routes – favored the side which could protect its own lines of communications while disrupting those of the enemy. The armies which could move by water had the greatest security from attack, a special advantage for the Union. But beyond the coasts and rivers lay the vast hinterland of the Confederacy, through which armies and supplies had to be moved overland. Traditionally, the bulk of men and horse-drawn supply wagons and artillery had travelled over dirt roads, the softer surfaces sometimes overlaid with tree trunks and branches as corduroy roads or the heavy-wood plank roads – bumpy but practical. The introduction of the military railroad in the Civil War offered new prospects for speedy movement. This in turn provided a powerful stimulus for utilizing cavalry for independent raids to destroy rail beds and bridges along with supply "trains" of wagons. Thus Southern cavalry was pitted against Northern locomotives in the struggle for logistical supremacy.

At the start of the Civil War, Confederate cavalry had a clear edge over that of the Union. The dearth of decent roads in the prewar South and the need to ride

across its sprawling plantation lands had forced Southern men to master the art of horsemanship from an early age. Northerners could ride too, of course, but better roads and planked turnpikes had made wagons the preferred mode of transportation in cities and farms. On the other hand, both sides enlisted each cavalryman only on the condition that he provide his own horse and riding accouterments, insuring recruits who understood the handling and care of mounts, especially their own. As the war progressed, however, and losses increased, the Federal government took over supplying the horses and superior saddles and harnesses and in the summer of 1863 created the Cavalry Bureau under Major General George Stoneman. It established six depots across the land to collect and train horses and their riders for the armies which needed some 500 new horses a day. The major depot, at Giesboro in the District of Columbia, handled more than 170,000 cavalry mounts and over 12,000 artillery horses during 1864 alone. The Confederacy, by contrast, never changed its practice of personal ownership; the government compensated the owner for his horse if lost in battle but not for other causes like disease or just wearing out. In

A Confederate cavalryman, also dressed in a great coat, but with his saber sheathed.

When the cavalry did mount a charge, it was usually against infantry or artillery. Center left: a cavalry regiment charges an enemy battery, sabers held high. The heavy bladed weapons proved too unwieldy, however, to inflict many casualties. Drawing by Edwin Forbes.

257

Penetrating eyes and clenched hands capture the fervent personality of James Ewell Brown Stuart, who was passionately religious, flamboyantly vain, and a daring cavalryman. He grew the large beard to hide his youthful looks - he was only twenty-eight years old in 1861 - and also possibly a receded chin. As a major general, he led Lee's cavalry until killed in action in 1864.

HORSES — AND SOUTHERN WOMEN

by **Eugene Marshall**, Sergeant, 5th Iowa Cavalry

(Letter to sister Olive from camp on the Flint River, near Maysville, Alabama, October 23, 1863)

... The life of a Cavalry man in this department is one of continual hard work. When marching or camping with infantry his hours of duty are nearly twice as many as theirs. He must be able to eat and sleep in the saddle and must never be too tired to walk a mile if necessary to procure feed for his horse. [If] the enemy [is] reported to be in any particular locality, he must find out whether they are there or not, must go feeling and pushing around their lines to find out their strength like a man feeling with his fingers in a pile of ashes for coals. He must be ready to mount at the bugle call at any hour of the night or day whether he has eat[en] or slept or not. He must be competent, if his own horse gives out, to catch, mount, and manage the wildest horse or mule ... even though it were so dark he could not tell a horse from a mule. If his horse falls he must always manage to be on top at the risk in the night of being left behind with his horse on top of

Officer of the Dragoons *is the title of this caricature of a Union dandy at a barbershop. In the prewar army, a dragoon was a mounted infantryman who rode into battle but fought on foot, as most Civil War cavalry units did in reality. Note the freed black barber.*

him. … I … have known men to be left behind with a horse lying on him & nobody the wiser for it. … In our heavy forced marches many horses give out and fall down by the rodeside to die or get up again, as the case may be. …

The women, particularly the young ones, are the most bitter in their secession proclivities of any class of people we meet, & relying on their immunities as women give expression at times to the most insulting and abusive sentiments, but often times they are more than matched. I wish I could say that the women here were what the people of the south have always claimed them to be, but I cannot. To me, the greater part of them are unbearably bold and lack most of the qualities we admire in women. Most of them are pale and yellow, & express great contempt of Yankees, yet a half hour's conversation will bring almost any of them into a sociable frame of mind, even with a Yankee. Many of them have and will marry Yankee soldiers & not of the best class. …

We see no young or middle aged men anywhere in the country. They are all gone to the war either as conscripts or Volunteers. Old men, children, & women are all that are left, & if by chance you see an able bodied man, it is safe to ask him what regiment he belonged to.

BY HORSE AND BY RAIL

Although he commanded the 3rd Corps at Fredericksburg, Major General George Stonemen spent most of the war leading cavalry. Captured leading a raid around Atlanta, he was exchanged and led several more successful independent forays late in the war.

BATTLE OF BRANDY STATION

June 8, 1863

by **William F. Moyer**, Sergeant, Company D, 1st Pennsylvania Cavalry

… Our sudden appearance on the flank and rear of the enemy took him by surprise, and for some minutes the hills and plains beyond the railroad swarmed with galloping squadrons of Johnny Rebs hurrying to a new position to meet our attack.… A whole brigade of [Union] cavalry, in columns of regiments, was moving steadily forward to the attack on our side, while the enemy's cavalry in new formation stood in glittering lines awaiting the assault, and his artillery, stationed on every hill, with rapid flash and continuous roar belched forth a concentrated fire on our advancing columns.

Still, with undaunted firmness, the brigade moved forward—first at a walk, then quickening their pace to a trot; and then, as the space between the battle fronts rapidly shortened, the gallop was taken, and when scarce[ly] fifty paces intervened, the order to charge rang along our front. In an instant a thousand glittering sabers flashed in the sunlight, and from a thousand brave and confident spirits arose a shout of defiance which, caught up by rank after rank, formed one vast, strong, full-volumned battle-cry, and every trooper rising in his stirrups leaned forward to meet the shock, and dashed headlong upon the foe. First came the dead, heavy crash of the meeting columns, and next the clash of saber, the rattle of pistol and carbine …; wild shrieks that followed the death blow; the demand to surrender and the appeal for mercy—forming the din of battle. …

[In a second charge, there] occurred an incident which illustrates how utterly Southern chivalry detested the rough arguments of cold steel when wielded by Northern mechanics. Just as we were raising the hill on our charge, a bold and audacious rebel rode forward from their ranks and called out: "Put up your sabers! Put up you sabers! Draw your pistols, and fight like gentlemen." But the mechanics, farmers, and laborers of Pennsylvania placed too great confidence in their tried blades and the iron nerves of their right arms to accept this advice, and soon these kid-gloved gentry shrank from the weight of their sturdy strokes. Here we met the flower of Stuart's cavalry. …

260

time, large numbers of unmounted rebel cavalrymen were simply gathered into a hodge-podge "Company Q" of each regiment. Nor were Confederate cavalry side arms, saddles and bridles as fine as the Union's.

Scouting for the armies in the early campaigns, Southern horsemen knew how to travel light, unlike their antagonists who had to learn the hard way not to carry extra clothes, blankets, horseshoes, tools and even ten-pound bulletproof vests! Cavalry units drilled to fight mounted actions with their opposite numbers, but the only major cavalry clash was at Brandy Station during the Gettysburg campaign. No cavalryman relished the idea of frontally attacking massed infantry, whose collective firepower and bayonets found the horse if not the rider to be an easy target. And once, on the first day at Gettysburg, Confederate infantry with bayonets formed into a hollow square to meet Major General John Buford's threatened cavalry charge. By mid-1863 both armies in the Eastern theater had begun to see the advantages of large concentrations of cavalry into divisions and corps for raids, due largely to the successes of the rebel Jeb Stuart and such able lieutenants as Wade Hampton and Fitz Lee. Their mobility and firepower were enhanced by the horse artillery, in which the gunners rode atop the six horses pulling each gun, in contrast to the field artillery, where the gun crews walked or rode wagons at the slower pace of the infantry. In neither case did the artillery depend upon the more difficult mules which pulled the hundreds of supply wagons and ambulances.

This Union cavalry charge against Stuart's horse and guns near Culpeper Court House, Virginia, September 13, 1863, is typical of many minor clashes. Fought near the post-Gettysburg encampments of the armies, the action caused 125 Confederate and forty-three Union casualties.

BY HORSE
AND BY RAIL

Naval Academy graduate
Samuel P. Carter left the
screw sloop Seminole in 1861
to become colonel of the 2nd
Tennessee (Union) Infantry
and later brigadier general in
the Army of the Ohio, leading
the first Union cavalry raid in
the West. He eventually
retired as a rear admiral, the
only flag and general officer
in U. S. history.

ARMY TEAMSTERS

by a Veteran

Army teamsters were never appreciated at their true value by soldiers in the field, for it was the general opinion that "any fool can drive mules." Those who tried the experiment found the teamster's office not a sinecure. The successful handling of six stubborn, pugnacious brutes required a degree of patience, skill, and will power only developed by long experience. When the roads were dry and even, wagon driving was a pastime, but when the trains reached the mountain passes, or the roads became seas of mud, then the task was no joke. Mud, three feet deep, as tenacious as stiff clay could make it, rendered the movement of wagons and artillery a difficult operation. The wheels were solid disks of mud, and the labor for both men and animals was multiplied four-fold.

Then the genius of the teamster was manifested.

With an inexhaustible vocabulary of oaths at command, and armed with a formidable snake whip, both were used with startling and telling effect. The air, blue with shocking profanity, and the huge whip whistling cruelly on the backs of the quivering brutes, gave them new strength, and the mired vehicle soon emerged from its muddy bed. It was a leading article of faith among teamsters that mules could only be driven by constant cursing, and they lived up to that belief with rare constancy. An attempt to drive a team of mules without indulgence in profanity invariably proved a failure, because the animals had become so accustomed to that method of persuasion that they would not move without it.

Teamsters, as a class, were brave and untiring in their peculiar sphere of duty, but they got very little credit from the rank and file.

The Union cavalry in the East matured under Stoneman and Pleasonton during 1863, bolstered by its rapid firing carbines and dashing division and brigade commanders like H. Judson Kilpatrick and George A. Custer. Kilpatrick concocted a wild scheme to lead a 3,600-man raid with Colonel Ulric Dahlgren around Lee's army into Richmond itself to free the 1,200 Yankee officers at Libby Prison and possibly even to kill Jefferson Davis. While Custer's division carried out a diversionary raid against Charlottesville, Kilpatrick and Dahlgren advanced to the defenses of the Confederate capital city at the end of February 1864. Losing the element of surprise, however, they split up and were unable to penetrate the city. Dahlgren was killed in an ambush, and Kilpatrick moved down the Peninsula to Union lines, from which he was sealifted back to the Army of the Potomac. Significantly, in addition to 340 men, the raid lost 583 horses and permanently wore out 480 other mounts, all of which, however, were quickly replaced with fresh steeds from the Giesboro Depot.

BY HORSE
AND BY RAIL

The Fort Pillow massacre of April 12, 1864, left perhaps the blackest mark on the Confederacy. Bedford Forrest's cavalry raiders mercilessly slaughter black and white troops after these have surrendered. "No quarter!" shout the rebels as they commit their atrocities.

The open countryside of the Western theater, however, provided the proper environment for raids against enemy communications, and it was here that Union cavalry leaders like Phil Sheridan, Benjamin Grierson, and James H. Wilson followed the examples of the rebels Morgan, Wheeler, and the greatest of them all, Nathan Bedford Forrest. Forrest's oft remembered dictum – "Hit the fustest with the mostest" – encapsulated tactical concentration and worked with telling success on virtually every raid he conducted. A self-made Memphis merchant without formal schooling in anything, much less the art of war, he was a physically powerful man who quickly established himself as the bane of Union armies in the West, rising to the rank of lieutenant general.

The far-ranging forays of the cavalry, even when they failed to inflict much physical damage, often provided a psychological boost to civilian morale. One example was the very first Union raid, by Brigadier General Samuel P. Carter – a professional navy lieutenant commander commissioned into the volunteer army to rally his native East Tennesseans to the Union. Raiding into that occupied region at the end of 1862, Carter's brigade of cavalry destroyed two rebel railroad bridges in the Cumberland Mountains and bolstered pro-Unionists in the region. The rebel Morgan's repeated movements into Kentucky encouraged that state's rebel sympathizers, but by exceeding his orders in invading Ohio in 1863 he discredited himself in the eyes of his superiors. Although he escaped from an Ohio prison later that year, Morgan was denied another place in the cavalry; he was killed in 1864. Most of these men became legends in their own time.

This sparkling wood-burning locomotive and tender is named for the first director of the U. S. Military Railroad, Brigadier General Herman Haupt. A West Point graduate, Haupt had gone into railroading and taught civil engineering at Gettysburg's Penn College. His expert initiatives made the Union's railroad triumph possible.

BY HORSE
AND BY RAIL

The depot of a Union military railroad on a waterfront in Virginia. Three wood-burning locomotives move supplies by flatcar, cattlecar, and boxcar to barges: early intermodal transportation for the army. The bewhiskered gentleman in the foreground is a naval officer.

A small trestle of the Orange and Alexandria Railroad in northern Virginia, typical of the hundreds of railroad bridges that had to be protected and maintained. Note the water tanks to the right and the roofless depot on the left.

FORREST'S TACTICS

by **William M. Towers**, Private, Gartrell's Company, Forrest's Personal Escort

I arrived on the battlefield [of Brice's Cross Roads, Mississippi, June 10, 1864] about 11 o'clock, just in time to bear General Forrest's orders to some troops that were lying on the ground for protection, while he and his staff and a portion of his escort were mounted. ... [He] on his nobel sorrel ... gave [the] command to charge. ... General Forrest adopted much the same tactics in all of his battles, that is to charge vigorously in the front, and at the same time to have a detachment often consisting of not over 100 picked men attack the rear around both the right and left flank with orders to make as much noise as possible, charging the

wagons and into the rear. For as all old soldiers know, there is nothing more demoralizing than to have the commissary department attacked.... After several hours of hard fighting, the fun began, and we had the enemy in full retreat. ...

We ... arrived at the outskirts of Memphis at three o'clock Sunday morning [August 21, 1864] having travelled 110 miles with a cavalry command of 1500, in a total time of 59 hours, ... a great feat, as the roads were very muddy ... and we had to build a bridge across the Cold Water River. ... When we arrived at the picket post, Capt. Bill Forrest [the general's brother] and his

The famous locomotive General, after receiving several shell hits during the Atlanta campaign of 1864. Two years before, she had been stolen by the Andrews' raiders in the celebrated Great Locomotive Chase across northern Georgia.

Overleaf: this 780-foot-long, four-tiered railroad trestle was built by Federal engineers across a ravine at Whiteside, Tennessee, just west of Chattanooga's Lookout Mountain. The year is 1864, by which time Union railroad bridges dotted the South.

company were in front. We heard the command "Halt!" given by the vedette, whereupon Capt. Forrest dismounted and approached to give the countersign, retaining in his right hand his "Colt Army" pistol. It was customary for a person giving the countersign to a sentinel to do so in a whisper, over the point of a bayonet. This Capt. Forrest was pretending to do and was in the act of leaning forward when he threw his pistol in the sentinel's face, the cap popped, and the pistol missed fire. ... Captain Forrest's men rushed forward and killed the vedette.

He remounted his horse, and we heard General Forrest's shrill voice call out to the bugler, Gaus (who, by the way, was a German and could come as near making a man's hair stand on end at the sound of his

bugle as any man on this earth could) to "BLOW! GAUS, BLOW!" and Gaus in his broken English was asking "VAT SHALL I BLOW, GINERAL?" And to this Gen. Forrest answered very quickly and shrilly "BLOW H—L AND G-D D—NATION!" At the sound of the bugle, the general and his men put spurs to their horses and rode at full speed toward the city [which they captured and held briefly, making off with 300 fresh horses and other booty]. (Billy Towers' father, Colonel John R. Towers, commanded the 8th Georgia Infantry in Lee's army most of the war. Billy's son, Admiral John H. Towers, born 21 years later and raised on tales of Forrest's exploits, led U.S. naval aviation before and during World War II.)

267

BY HORSE AND BY RAIL

The reason that the Southern cavalry had to make repeated raids into Union-occupied Tennessee and Kentucky, however, was that the railroad bridges they burned were quickly and efficiently replaced by Union engineering gangs. These forces became so proficient at it that they could actually build a completely new smaller bridge in a matter of hours, a longer one in less than a week. For example, the railroad trestle which bridged the Tennessee River at Bridgeport, Alabama near Chattanooga, was destroyed four times and rebuilt each time with great industry and efficiency. Similarly, wherever fixed bridges were down, or had never existed at all, Union engineers masterfully laid down low pontoon bridges over which the army could pass – flatboats lashed side by side and a timber and plank road stretched across them.

By 1864 each Union army corps in the West included

This old wood-burning locomotive is a victim of the fighting; its wooden cab and fittings have been burned away, leaving only the metal parts.

a bridging train of up to forty wagons loaded with bridging tools and pontoon boats. Confederate forces could perform similar tasks but never on such a scale or with the organizational efficiency and materials that the Union enjoyed.

The coming of the war had found the North with all the ingredients for forging what would a century later be known as a military-industrial complex. At its heart lay the burgeoning railroad industry, and Lincoln lost no time in giving himself war powers to bring private railroads under government control. He began to exercise these powers in 1862 when centralized planning and management became essential. The single track system meant that train schedules had to be tightly regulated via telegraph to avoid collisions and tieups, while coal-burning engines were increasingly employed to replace wood-burners – not possible in the Confederacy. As soon as Stanton, well versed in railroad operations, became Secretary of War early in

1862, he commissioned the general superintendent of the Erie Railroad, David C. McCallum, to direct Union military railroads in the West and in April 1862 brought in the chief engineer of the Pennsylvania Railroad, Herman Haupt, to direct all Union railroad construction and operations, with his headquarters in the East. The two colonels worked their railroading miracles and became brigadier generals, McCallum succeeding Haupt in September 1863. They standardized gauges – which the Confederacy was never able to do – and eventually had 23,500 personnel operating 365 locomotives on nearly 2,000 miles of military railroad track (connected to some 25,000 miles of commercial railroads across the North).

To build the ubiquitous bridges as well as forts and bases the Union enlarged its Corps of Engineers, which also in 1863 absorbed the Corps of Topographical Engineers, responsible for mapping the terrain across which the armies moved and fought. The Confederacy's small Corps of Engineers relied largely on makeshift

Union topographical engineers, protected from the elements by a large umbrella, map and survey the riverbank beneath a hilltop fort.

A Yankee Corps of Engineers road gang lays down a corduroy road of saplings freshly cut from the grove behind, to offset the mud into which the wagon tracks have disappeared. Their wagons are parked on the rise beyond.

"pioneer" units to provide similar services until 1863 when two engineering regiments were established.

Railroad communications in the South suffered a complete absence of genuine trunk lines in favor of short feeder-type railroads each less than 100 miles long. In spite of this, and different gauges of track, older locomotives, and declining maintenance due to scarcities of oil lubricants, the railroad remained vital to the Confederacy. Not only did the 9,000 miles of track in 1861 decline due to Union captures, but the C.S.A. could afford to relieve existing lines only with minimal new construction. The government in 1862 exerted priority controls over the private railroads and a year later gave itself the right to commandeer them if necessary, though it did not actually put them under Confederate authority until February 1865. By Herculean efforts, the Confederacy was able to keep its ever-constricted rail network operational, bringing supplies from the seaports and inland granaries to its main

armies and shifting military units between them. The main rail lines were four. The north-south road connected Charleston and Wilmington to Richmond for Lee's army, though its final link was not completed until May 1864. The east-west line ran from the same two ports to Augusta, Georgia, and thence to Atlanta and Bragg's army at Chattanooga. On the Gulf, supplies from Mobile could be carried by rail to Montgomery thence to Atlanta, while a new line in late 1862 ran from Mobile to Meridian, Mississippi, alongside steamers up the Alabama River to Selma, both for Johnston's army. A connection between Montgomery and Selma would have provided an east-west line across the Deep South, but it was never built. Finally, a vital military line ran between Chattanooga and Knoxville across the mountains to Richmond.

Although the Union did not have major Southern armies threatening its home rail network after Bragg's 1862 invasion of Kentucky, border operations by irregular enemy forces remained a constant menace to Union security. In addition to Confederate cavalry raids, guerrillas remained active in the border regions. In northern Virginia, beginning in January 1863, Major

(later Colonel) John S. Mosby used between 100 and 200 Partisan Rangers to plague the Union rear, even capturing a general asleep in bed and by 1864 turning much of northeastern Virginia into "Mosby's Confederacy" not unlike Robin Hood's Sherwood Forest. The most notorious rebel guerrilla in Missouri, Colonel William S. Quantrill, slaughtered over 150 civilians in a raid on Lawrence, Kansas in August 1863; his band of cutthroats included legendary postwar outlaws Jesse and Frank James. Even in the old Northwest, General John Pope countered an uprising by the Sioux Indians by sending expeditions under Brigadier General Alfred Sully into the Dakotas during the summers of 1863, 1864, and 1865; Sully's volunteer troops included Confederate prisoners in blue who preferred open air fighting to languishing in Federal prisons. The most bizarre, and distant, violation of Union territory occurred at St. Albans, Vermont, where a band of Confederate troops crossed over from Canada and raided the city's banks in October 1864; they were apprehended by Canadian authorities after making good their escape. In all such operations, Yankee railroads played key roles in shifting Union

Colonel William C. Quantrill's guerrillas bushwhack the citizens of Lawrence, Kansas, August 21, 1863, killing over 150 men, women, and children. Quantrill was mortally wounded in May 1865 while on a plundering expedition with a small band of men in Kentucky.

Lieutenant H. J. Segal (left) of the Confederate Army throws down his sword when trapped "like a raccoon in a tree" by Union infantry near Falls Church, Virginia. Pencil and watercolor drawing by Arthur Lumley.

Clement L. Vallandigham (below), former Ohio Congressman, is banished to the Confederacy, under a flag of truce, in 1863, for his anti-war activities as a Copperhead. When the Confederacy rejected him, he went first to Canada and then back to the North as a peace party Democrat. In 1864 he headed the pro-Southern Sons of Liberty.

Ambulance drill (left) by Zouaves of the Army of the Potomac at Brandy Station, Virginia. Several Northern and Southern volunteer regiments adopted the dress of French Algerian Zouaves, complete with turbans.

*Recuperating wounded,
including an amputee in a
wheelchair, enjoy a clean
Union hospital. The women
on the right may be relatives
or nurses, although the latter
were usually male. However,
more than 600 Roman
Catholic nuns worked for
both sides; most prominent of
the twelve serving orders were
the Holy Cross Sisters and
Daughters of Charity.*

*Previous pages: skilled
carpenters build ambulances
at a government shop in
Washington; several of them
sit in a finished product (left
rear). 1860s male fashion
dictates a hat, of which many
styles are seen here. Facial
hair comes in different
varieties, but is not
compulsory.*

forces to maintain the integrity of the homeland.

Railroads also figured in one marvelous espionage caper, the so-called great locomotive chase of April 1862. When General Ormsby Mitchel captured the Memphis and Charleston Railroad in northern Alabama, he concocted a plan with a civilian secret agent, J.J. Andrews, for the latter and 22 volunteers from the army to steal a rebel train in Georgia and race northward, burning the bridges below Chattanooga. Reaching the latter city incognito, they boarded a southbound train. Getting off at Big Shanty, Andrews and his men succeeded in stealing the engine *General* and raced northward, with another locomotive in such hot pursuit that they could not stop to burn bridges. The raiders were chased ninety miles before they ran out of wood for the engine. Most were captured as they tried to escape on foot, Andrews and seven others being tried and hanged as spies, the rest imprisoned. As for more traditional spies, both sides employed them aplenty, especially women, but none cut a more romantic image than Rose Greenhow, Washington socialite who provided intelligence to Beauregard vital to his victory at First Bull Run. Arrested and imprisoned, she was soon deported to the Confederacy, eventually going to Europe to enlist support for the South; she drowned trying to run back through the blockade at Wilmington in September 1864.

The movement of men by rail as well as river steamer included the wounded and prisoners. The state of medicine in the 1860s was such that field hospitals were primitive in the extreme, and the most successful if crippling remedy for a fresh limb wound was amputation. If a man survived such first-aid treatment, he was borne to the rear in severely-uncomfortable wagon ambulances and thence to regular hospitals by rail or steamer for regular treatment and convalescence. Male nurses, white and black, predominated there, gradually complemented by females and, for the Union, by the well-organized auxiliary U.S. Christian and Sanitary commissions.

Prisoners, whether or not they were wounded, faced the extreme trials of incarceration on both sides. Southern prison stockades, handicapped by lack of food and proper sanitation, were particularly squalid, the worst being at Andersonville, Georgia, where over a third of its 33,000 enlisted inmates perished during its existence in 1864. Such terrible conditions led Union

Medical personnel pose before a Federal field hospital, dreaded places where the wounded were treated and many amputations performed. Note the Medical Department armband. The title of this tableau could be "Pouring a Drink."

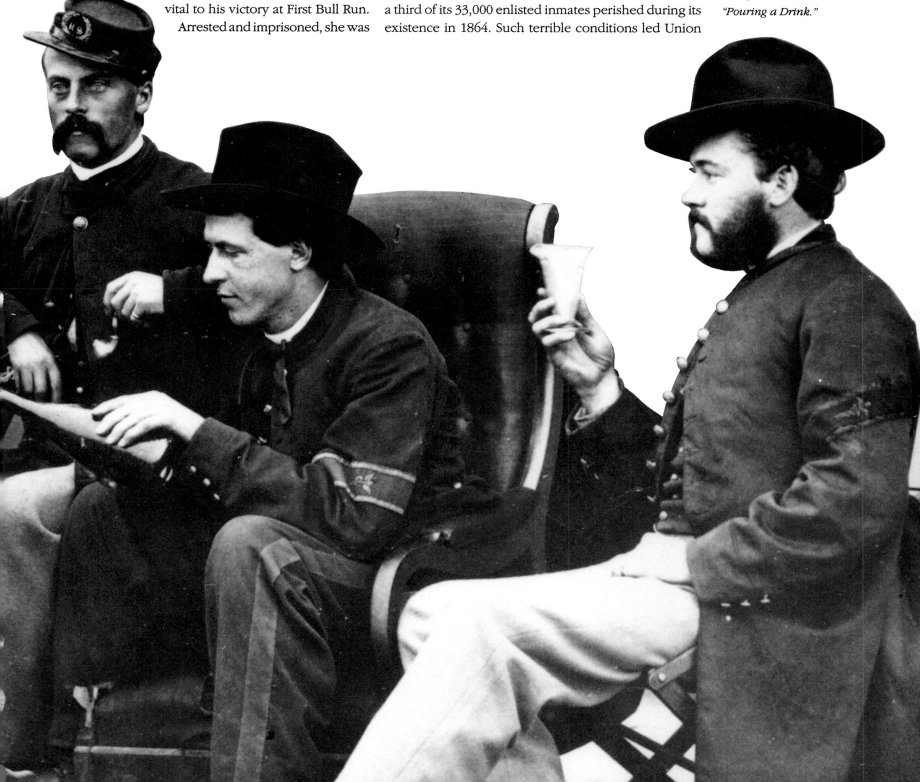

LIBBY PRISON'S TUNNEL

By **Frank E. Moran**, Captain, Company H, 73rd
New York Infantry and prisoner of war

[The night of February 8, 1864, a fellow officer] and I groped along the east wall and ... ran suddenly against a silent and densely packed crowd of men around the fireplace [of the prison kitchen]. Colonel [Thomas E.] Rose [of the 77th Pennsylvania Infantry] was the first man to go out, closely followed by the working party, who having completed their [four months of tunneling] work, placed the tunnel at the service of all.... [Waiting to enter it,] in my anxiety, I was magnifying minutes into hours; there seemed no perceptible reduction of the crowd in front, while the crowd behind had increased by hundreds and were pressing us to suffocation. The measured tread of the guard echoed on the sidewalk, within ten feet of where we were. Inquiries as to the reason of the delay were whispered from man to man; and fainting and weak men were begging for room and air.

At last all movement ceased. "A fat man was stuck in the tunnel and could not get either way." This news sent a chill of unutterable disgust through the crowd; muttered curses were rained thick and fast upon the unlucky victim's stomach. Meanwhile, the sensations of the luckless fat man in his appalling situation may be faintly conjectured.... At last, the corpulent comrade, with forty feet yet to go, made a supreme struggle for life and reached the open air in the stable yard; and I rejoice to add that he was one of the happy sixty-one who reached the Union lines. The escape of our fat comrade was a deplorable loss to the Confederates. They had been pointing him out to distinguished visitors as a stupendous refutation of the damaging charges that Union prisoners were being reduced to skeletons. ... (Moran also got through the tunnel, the streets of Richmond, and just beyond the city's outer defenses before he was recaptured next morning. So was the architect of the escape, Colonel Rose, "a brainy, cool, and intrepid man," along with 46 others of the 109 who had gotten clear of the tunnel.)

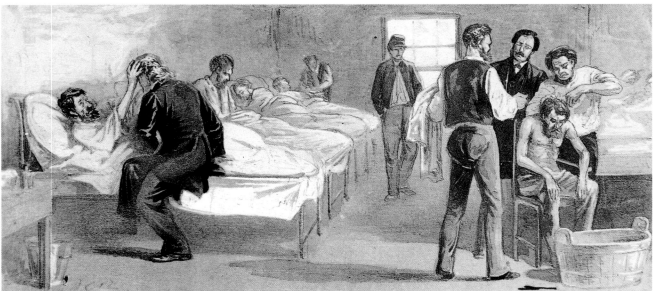

Yankee doctors dress a soldier's neck wound. Sketch by Allen C. Redwood.

authorities to try and to execute its commandant after the war as the conflict's only war criminal. Conditions in Richmond's Libby Prison for officers were only slightly better, and after the Kilpatrick-Dahlgren raid the prisoners were relocated to a stockade in Macon, Georgia. The situation in Northern prisons nearly equaled those in the South and for much the same reasons but also due to the severe winter cold. Chicago's Camp Douglas ultimately housed several thousand rebel prisoners; during February 1863 alone no fewer than 387 died, 10 percent of the total, the worst mortality rate for any wartime prison. The two governments agreed upon prisoner exchanges during 1862-63, especially of senior officers, but thereafter the demands of total war led the Union to cease the practice and thereby deprive the Confederacy of

replacement manpower. Forces on the move unable to be burdened with captives issued paroles – signed pledges that they would not bear arms again unless officially exchanged. The lot of prisoners being so grim, many attempted escape and occasionally succeeded.

Even waging total war through the use of military railroads and by turning Southern cavalry techniques against their formulators could not decisively shorten the war for the Union unless the Confederate armies could be deprived of fresh arms and equipment. This was the task of the Union blockade, and it was still not working by early 1863. To be sure, blockade-running steamers were being captured, especially by Rear Admiral Samuel P. Lee's (not of the Virginia Lees) North Atlantic Blockading Squadron off Wilmington; the

The U.S. Sanitary Commission, headquartered at Gettysburg, Pennsylvania, improved the diet and living conditions of the troops near railroad stations and of those at its convalescent home in Washington. A semi-official organization, it cared for the wounded on hospital ships and distributed private donations for army relief.

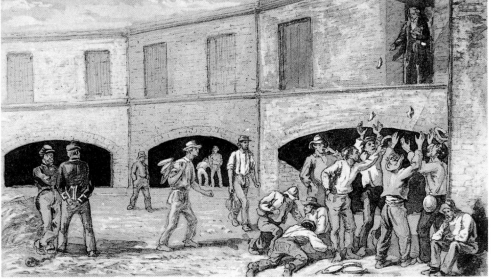

Artist Allen C. Redwood
depicts rebel prisoners in a
Union stockade, in reality a
converted fort, receiving
bread tossed down to them
from the upper story.

"The Reb That Never Saw a
Crab" gets his nose pinched
by a claw in this humorous
drawing of Confederate
prisoners in New England
being introduced to steamed
crabs.

A Union prisoner liberated from the notorious Andersonville prison in central Georgia in September 1864. The meager diet resulted in such living corpses; the official death count was nearly 13,000, though many more enlisted men probably perished there.

"Confederate Variety": a minstrel show (left) put on by black-faced rebel soldiers at a prison camp.

A steam engine (above) built by an enterprising rebel prisoner at Point Lookout, Maryland.

BY HORSE
AND BY RAIL

Matthew Brady photographs what in a later era would be regarded as refugees or displaced persons: a family evacuating the old homestead to escape the horrors of war. Note the pipe-smoking woman!

Paymasters of the Army of the Potomac hand out wages to some of their black teamsters. White or black, men who could handle mule teams were invaluable to all Civil War armies.

prize money from each capture was divided up among the captor's crew and Admiral Lee by admiralty courts. But more runners were getting through, especially to the major port of Charleston, to provide nearly two-thirds of the South's arms, three-fourths of the saltpeter needed for ammunition, vital shoe leather as well as finished footwear, and cloth for uniforms. And they were running out again with cotton for European buyers. The financial agent for the Confederacy in England was George A. Trenholm, leading figure of the merchant community in Charleston and head of Fraser, Trenholm and Company which carried out the most lucrative blockade-running enterprise.

Union amphibious operations against the islands abutting Charleston Harbor during the spring and summer of 1863, however, suddenly made Charleston too risky for runners, who thereafter shifted mainly to Wilmington. This seaport, whose approaches were difficult to blockade, mushroomed into the leading supplier of Southern arms, and Fort Fisher at its entrance was enlarged into the biggest fortification on either side. Simultaneously, in August 1863, the Davis administration began to seize private cotton and tobacco for export and commandeered half the space on runners to get these harvests abroad to increase Southern credit and to purchase war materials for replacing those lost at Gettysburg and Vicksburg. Government control over trade became absolute the following March, and the War Department took over fourteen runners from Fraser, Trenholm and another company to insure munitions imports. Then in July 1864, to guarantee the success of these measures, Trenholm himself was appointed Confederate Secretary of the Treasury. His ability to obtain foreign credit paid handsome dividends, and by September large quantities of guns, ammunition, vital metals, meats, cloth, blankets, and nearly 300,000 pairs of shoes had been run through the blockade.

So, in spite of Gettysburg and Vicksburg, with its imposed isolation of the Trans-Mississippi District, the Union armies and blockading squadrons were still fumbling toward a full application of total war. Lincoln's generals and admirals had yet to prosecute and maintain a relentless strategy by which to crush the Southern Confederacy. Even though Lee's tired Army of Northern Virginia began to suffer from increased desertions, the Army of the Potomac made no significant move against him during the autumn and winter of 1863-64, enabling him to send Longstreet's corps to Chattanooga to reinforce Bragg – a successful utilization of interior lines of communication. Such a long breather gave the Confederacy the chance to increase its imports. Unless and until the Union blockade effectively sealed off Wilmington, Charleston, and Mobile, the Northern armies would have to do the lion's share of the work. And unless the Union found a dynamic military leader to plan and execute a coherent strategy, the South might prolong the war indefinitely – not a pleasant prospect for Abraham Lincoln as the election of 1864 approached.

Eugene Marshall (left) belonged to a Minnesota company assigned to the 5th Iowa Cavalry, which guarded telegraph lines and fought rebel guerrillas in Tennessee during 1862-63. He went to the Dakotas as sergeant major of Brackett's Minnesota Battalion and was wounded by the Sioux at the Battle of Killdeer Mountain, July 28, 1864.

8
THE TENNESSEE VALLEY

Chickamauga, Chattanooga, Red River — Late 1863–Early 1864

THE MISSISSIPPI VALLEY

At the moment of the Confederacy's "high water mark" – July 1863 – Union forces in the Western theater were already preparing to mount a new offensive: Rosecrans' Army of the Cumberland against Bragg's Army of Tennessee at Chattanooga, and Burnside with a reconstituted Army of the Ohio against Knoxville. Once the North possessed these two cities as well as the Cumberland Gap, the Confederate rail connection between Tennessee and Virginia would be severed and the great granary of Georgia and Alabama left open to invasion. Stanton and Halleck therefore ordered Rosecrans to initiate the Tennessee Valley campaign in mid-August 1863. In response, the Confederate War Department decided to rush reinforcements to Bragg in order to protect the western approaches to Virginia – most of Longstreet's corps from Lee's army in Virginia and the bulk of a corps from Johnston's army in Mississippi.

Rosecrans, moving south from Tullahoma, Tennessee, crossed the Alabama line just west of Bridgeport and the Tennessee River to a position below Chattanooga early in September. As a result, Bragg recalled his forces holding Knoxville, which Burnside's army occupied on the 2nd, and one week later Burnside forced the surrender of a brigade holding the Cumberland Gap. This broke the Tennessee-Virginia rail line, forcing Longstreet's corps to take the circuitous route to join Bragg by way of Wilmington, Augusta, and Atlanta. On the 6th Bragg began to evacuate Chattanooga, not in desperation but to concentrate attacks against Rosecrans' separated forces as they approached from the southwest around Lookout Mountain just inside Georgia. Bragg's divisions repeatedly failed to mass against the divided Federal units before they supported one another, however, and Rosecrans' three corps concentrated near

A Virginian who stayed with the Union, George "Pap" Thomas (above) ably commanded a division in the Army of the Cumberland, as a major general. He saved that army as the head of the 14th Corps, earning them the nickname "the Rock of Chickamauga." His subsequent command of the whole Army of the Cumberland was nothing short of brilliant, and was capped by his triumph at Nashville.

The Army of the Ohio (right), under Burnside, reoccupies the Cumberland Gap in the Appalachian Mountains, September 8-10, 1863, capturing 2,500 troops and 36 cannon. With the gap in Union possession, Confederate troops could no longer move by rail between Virginia and Chattanooga.

Below: leggings and some unusually tall headgear adorn this unidentified Northern regiment in camp.

Overleaf: standing like a rock, and supported by batteries on Snodgrass Hill, Thomas' men repulse repeated attacks by Bragg's rebel army at Chickamauga, September 20, 1863. The man at left exchanges his empty rifle for a loaded one: it was common practice to defend infantry by allowing the best shots to deliver continuous fire.

THE TENNESSEE VALLEY

Chickamauga Creek in Georgia just south of the Tennessee line. The Union army occupied Chattanooga in the process, but Bragg believed he could drive it out again by crushing Rosecrans in battle.

After Yankee cavalry drove back a rebel attack on the 21st Corps on September 18, the two armies spent the night maneuvering into position for the Battle of Chickamauga, the name of the creek given by the Indians meaning "River of Death." And so it was to be. Next morning a Union probe toward the creek encountered and drove back Forrest's dismounted cavalry on the Confederate right flank. This brought on the general action all along the front, Bragg hoping to turn the Union left of Major General George H. Thomas and cut off Rosecrans' army from Chattanooga. The

Southern infantry pushed back its adversaries, only to be checked by devastating artillery fire. On Bragg's left, Hood's division – the first of Longstreet's corps to arrive – similarly pressed the Union right but with the same result. The day ended without a decision, but during the night Longstreet arrived with more of his corps and took command of the Confederate left. Polk commanded the right. Bragg now had 66,000 men, outnumbering Rosecrans by 6,000. The latter had Thomas in command of the 14th Corps on the left, Thomas Crittenden the 21st in the center, and Alexander M. McCook the 20th on the right. The ground was broken, hilly, and heavily wooded, which Thomas turned to advantage in the darkness by having his men dig breast works atop Snodgrass Hill.

Frolicking troopers play the French game of turnstile: trying to crawl across the device and grab a prize before falling off.

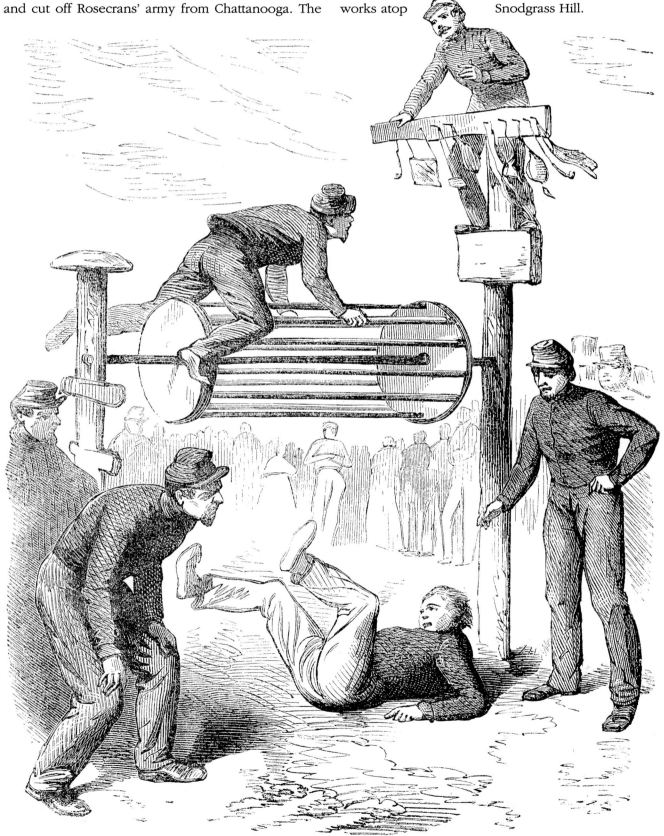

Bragg resumed the initiative on the morning of the 20th, again sending Polk against Thomas. With his breastworks on the high ground, Thomas withstood the determined attacks for two hours. A Virginian by birth and veteran campaigner of the Indian and Mexican wars, Thomas had stayed with the Union, commanding a division at Shiloh, Perryville, and Stones River. His preparations on Snodgrass Hill proved fortuitous, since Rosecrans, his commander, became confused over the proper location of his several units and gave orders which created a gap between Crittenden and McCook just before noon. Longstreet's troops rushed into the gap, splitting the Union army in half. While Crittenden's and McCook's troops broke and ran, taking Rosecrans with them, all the way back to Chattanooga, Longstreet

Too outspoken for his own good, Major General William "Baldy" Smith excelled as a division and corps commander in the East but was shunted to various lesser commands for criticizing the high command after Fredericksburg. His engineering skills helped save Grant at Chattanooga, but he failed as 18th Corps commander at Petersburg.

The mountains commanding Chattanooga.

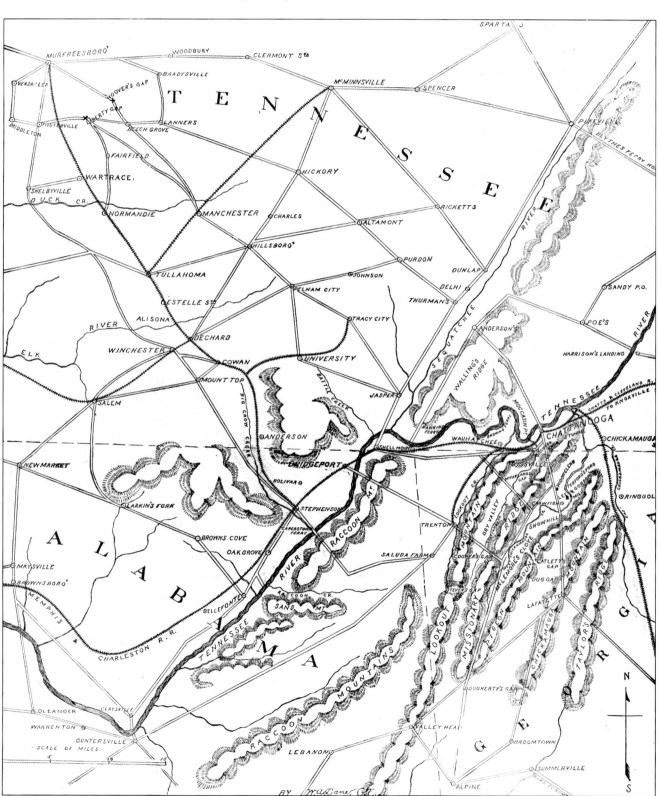

THE TENNESSEE VALLEY

wheeled to the right against Thomas, hoping to have the same effect. But Thomas formed a second line to face the onslaught and was saved by the initiative of Major General Gordon Granger who rushed forward his Reserve Corps. This force repulsed one of Longstreet's divisions in a bloody counterattack and held Thomas' right flank. Again and again, Bragg flung his army at Snodgrass Hill – six hours of butchery on both sides, but Thomas held his ground like a rock. At sunset, the fighting stopped, whereupon Rosecrans ordered Thomas back to Chattanooga.

The two-day bloodbath over the "River of Death" ended with 18 percent casualties for both armies: 18,500 for the South, over 16,000 for the North. Bragg had won the battle and quickly occupied Missionary Ridge, the heights commanding Chattanooga, inside which he besieged Rosecrans' beaten army. His heavy losses and the general confusion at Chickamauga, though, undermined what confidence his own generals had in him, some of whom he now relieved of command. The Union defeat finished Rosecrans, who had never been a particularly aggressive leader. The man who had saved the Army of the Cumberland from destruction was Thomas, henceforth appropriately nicknamed "the Rock of Chickamauga." To rescue Rosecrans' army, Halleck had already ordered Grant to redeploy part of his army by river steamer from Vicksburg to Memphis, thence by the Memphis and Charleston railroad to Chattanooga. And immediately after the Chickamauga disaster, Hooker was rushed by

rail and steamer from northern Virginia to Chattanooga with two corps from the Army of the Potomac, arriving at Bridgeport, Alabama in less than a week. Meanwhile, Burnside held Knoxville against a small rebel force, and Rosecrans' supply lines were decimated by Joe Wheeler's raiding cavalry throughout October.

Only one man had the reputation of being able to retrieve Union fortunes in the upper valley of the Tennessee River: the victor of Fort Donelson, Shiloh, and Vicksburg – U.S. Grant. In mid-October 1863 he was appointed to supreme command in the West. His new Military Division of the Mississippi comprised three armies plus Hooker's troops from the East: the Army of the Tennessee, now given to Sherman; the Army of the Cumberland, which passed to the heroic Thomas; and the Army of the Ohio under Burnside. He faced Bragg's Army of Tennessee, whose corps commanders were now William J. Hardee, John C. Breckinridge, and Longstreet. Although Johnston still had a force in eastern Mississippi, it was too weak to pose a serious threat to Grant's operations.

By the time Grant assumed command, Bragg had virtually sealed off the forces inside Chattanooga from outside supply. With the city nestled in a pocket on the south side of the twisting Tennessee, Bragg's army occupied the commanding heights – Missionary Ridge on the east, Lookout Mountain on the south, and Raccoon Mountain to the west, blocking river traffic trying to enter the city from the west. When Grant arrived, he found the Army of the Cumberland emaciated

293

THE TENNESSEE VALLEY

by food rationing, but he immediately accepted a plan by General William F. Smith to relieve the situation. "Baldy" Smith had a keen military sense and had led a division in the East, eventually ending up as chief engineer of the Army of the Cumberland. Grant so admired Smith's scheme that he let Smith take charge of it. Between October 26 and 30, 1863, Smith sent Hooker's troops across the river above Bridgeport, joined by others rafting down from Chattanooga under cover of darkness. This forced the rebels to abandon Raccoon Mountain and fail to dislodge Hooker's advance the following night near the hamlet of Wauhatchie. The first supply steamer in weeks arrived in Chattanooga on the 30th, hailed by the beleaguered army as the opening of the "cracker line." Grant made Smith his own chief engineer.

The siege of Chattanooga was by no means lifted, but it could no longer suffice to guarantee Bragg's success there, especially since Burnside's Army of the Ohio threatened to reinforce Grant at Chattanooga, and Sherman was hastening across northern Alabama from Memphis toward Chattanooga. A new Confederate strategy was devised by Jefferson Davis, namely, that Bragg should detach Longstreet's corps to retake Knoxville and restore rail communications to Virginia, while Bragg held fast in his entrenchments overlooking Chattanooga. This was a risky division of his forces, but Bragg had no choice but to comply. Longstreet took 10,000 troops by rail to a position south of Knoxville during early November and was joined by 5,000 cavalry under Wheeler. They failed to cut off the withdrawal of Burnside's 12,000 men into the hastily-constructed defenses of Knoxville on the 17th. Longstreet now laid siege to the city, but without heavy siege guns he would have to assault the place, so he waited until reinforcements joined him from Bragg.

Grant would not be diverted to strengthen Burnside; if Bragg could be dislodged, Grant could then go to Burnside's assistance. Although Grant planned to attack Bragg when Sherman's army arrived on November 20, autumn rains forced a postponement. Grant, however, discovering that several rebel units had been pulled off Missionary Ridge – Bragg's right – had Thomas on the 23rd investigate while Granger's 4th Corps rushed

Previous pages: from the heights of Lookout Mountain, Bragg's cannon shell Grant's camps at Chattanooga during November 1863.

Budding artist Thomas Nast portrays Hooker's attack on Lookout Mountain, November 24, 1863. The heavy river mist and smoke from the guns inspired the attack's romantic title "Battle Above the Clouds."

Scaling the heights of Missionary Ridge, November 25, 1863, Brigadier General Absalom Baird's division of Midwestern troops captures the guns of Brigadier General J. Patton Anderson's division. These cannon could not be depressed low enough to fire on the Yankees.

CHATTANOOGA UNDER SIEGE

by **B. S. Batchelor**, Private, 2nd Minnesota Infantry

October 1863

The 2nd Minn. was camped on a small rise of ground near the four large hospitals that were built by the Confederacy and afterward occupied by our army. The rebels had a piece of artillery planted on Lookout Mountain which they named the Lady Davis, and it made it lively for us a good many times. … As a number of [my] comrades … were playing marbles, quite a number of the boys gathered around and became interested in the game, when a souvenir in the shape of a solid shot came from the mountain without any warning. It passed just above our heads and made a flying visit to a small campfire just back of us, where a German of our company was making a cup of coffee of two days' rations, which consisted of about two tablespoonfuls – and all that he could get until the next issue.

The ball struck in the fire under the coffee kettle. That coffee kettle shot up in the air like a skyrocket, and the little campfire was no more. But there stood the German covered with dirt and ashes, and so mad that he did not know what his name was. He soon recovered and swore in three different languages at the same time. He was angry enough to go up on old Lookout Mountain and throw that gun into the Tennessee River. But, as time is a great soother, he got over his passion and laughed with the rest of us and was thankful that no greater damage was done. The kettle came down with the smell of coffee yet lingering about its precious sides.

A Confederate view of Chattanooga from Lookout Mountain, as drawn during the siege by an engineer of General Braxton Bragg's staff.

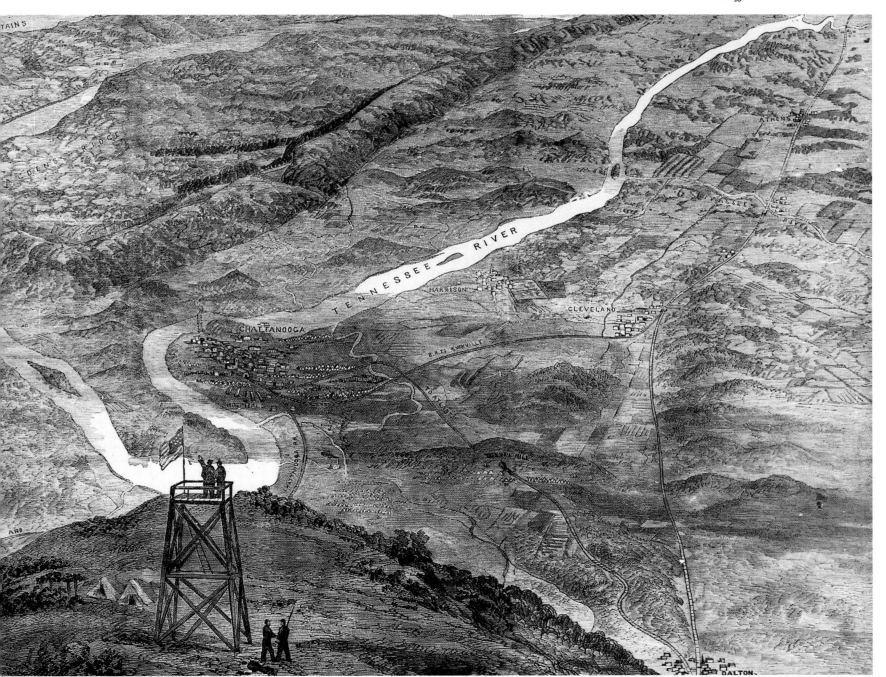

THE TENNESSEE VALLEY

Two Yankee buglers on the march.

This fallen "Johnny Reb" (right), his rolled blanket across his chest, bespeaks the cost of the Civil War in human terms.

Facing page: "Ingenious Devices of Soldiers in the Camp and on Campaign" was the contemporary caption to this interesting piece illustrating Civil War army life.

forward and seized Orchard Knob, a rise of ground midway between the centers of the opposing armies. This sudden attack prompted Bragg to rush three full divisions from his far left at Lookout Mountain to reinforce the right end of Missionary Ridge. This was prudent, for it protected the rail line to Knoxville and was obviously the target of Grant's planned attack. Grant sent Sherman's Army of the Tennessee to that quarter, reinforced by Howard's 11th Corps from Hooker.

On November 24, the Battle of Chattanooga unfolded, but more from Grant and his men seizing opportunities than following his plan of battle. By dawn, Sherman

was preparing for an afternoon assault on the Confederate right under Hardee at Missionary Ridge. During the morning, on the Union right, Hooker's three divisions moved against the 1,100-foot-high Lookout Mountain, held by two Southern brigades, with two more near the base. The fighting developed amidst a thick river haze which obscured most of the mountain, but the Union forces steadily ascended the heights and wrested control of them by midafternoon – an action romantically retold as the "Battle above the Clouds." Meanwhile, just past the noon hour, Sherman advanced with four divisions against the rebel right and easily gained the northern extremity of Missionary Ridge.

Marche du Trompette

During the night, he made ready for the main assault next day, to be followed by Thomas attacking the ridge and Hooker approaching from the valley which separated Lookout Mountain from the ridge.

On the 25th Sherman launched his attack, only to be repelled by a stiff Confederate defense throughout the morning and well into the afternoon. Grant kept the Army of the Cumberland in close support on Sherman's flank but did not commit Thomas in the center until progress was reported from either flank. This came from Hooker in midafternoon when his troops drove

WATERSKIN, AND MODE OF CARRYING IT.

SIGNALING WITH A PIECE OF LOOKING-GLASS.

CUTTING COARSE FORAGE INTO CHAFF.

HOW TO SECURE A PRISONER.

SLED MADE OUT OF A BOUGH.

BRIDGING ACROSS A GAP.

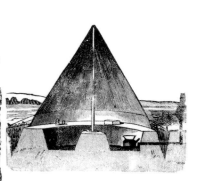

SECTION OF TENT WITH FIREPLACE.

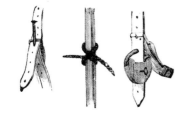

1. A BROKEN TONGUE MENDED. 2. FASTENING ROPES. 3. A STRAP PADLOCKED.

DESCENDING A STEEP HILL.

FRAMEWORK FOR SMALL TENT.

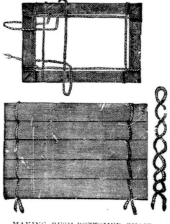

MAKING RUSH-BOTTOMED CHAIR.

UNDERGROUND TENT WITH TWO STORIES.

SHELTER AGAINST A DRIVING WIND.

MODE OF DISTILLING SEA-WATER.

SAFE MODE OF SLEEPING WITH A LOADED GUN.

BATTLE OF MISSIONARY RIDGE

by **W. M. Boroughs**, Lieutenant, Company E, 24th Alabama Infantry   November 25, 1863

... On they came, the grandest army of blue ever witnessed by the veterans on the ridge. When they arrived within two or three hundred yards of the base of the ridge, they moved at the double quick, and soon broke into a run. As line after line came, they lay down at the foot of the ridge.... [Then I noticed] one regiment was slowly and steadily advancing up the ridge, directly in front of Anderson's brigade. Major Pocher, of the 10th S.C., came up to our part of the line and remarked, "The enemy do not appear to be advancing on this part of the line." I called his attention to the regiment on our left, now halfway up the ridge, and he directed us to fire on them. Just then, Captain Hazard came up and asked Major Pocher where he could send a detail for ammunition. The Major turned

to answer when a dull, heavy thud and an exclamation of "oh!" attracted our attention, and the gallant South Carolinian fell full length on his face.

All this time the Federal regiment continued to advance in front of Anderson's brigade. The battery in our rear could now bring upon them an enfilading fire, and with every discharge someone would fall, but still the others would cluster around their colors.... Knowing the material of which [Anderson's] brigade was composed, I remarked to someone near me, "Whenever that Yankee regiment reaches the crest of the ridge, they will be swept out of existence in the flash of a gun."

However, one of those incomprehensible things happened which frequently turned the tide of success in our civil war. When this regiment reached the crest. . .,

A Union gunboat flotilla attacked and captured Galveston, Texas, in October 1862, only to be attacked itself the following January 1. Rebel gunboats (left center) are seen destroying the grounded sidewheeler Westfield; *they also capture the* Harriet Lane *(far left) and drive off the rest, freeing Galveston of Yankee rule.*

Previous pages: on September 8, 1863, two Union gunboats, the sidewheeler Clifton *(left) and screw steamer* Sachem *(right), spearhead a drive by the 19th Corps toward Beaumont, Texas, but are hit and disabled by Confederate batteries defending Sabine Pass. Both vessels had to strike their colors, and the expedition withdrew. The inlet remained a haven for blockade runners.*

in the defenders of Breckinridge's left on the ridge. Grant now ordered Thomas to commit four divisions against the rebel rifle pits at the base of Missionary Ridge in the center. They rushed forward and easily overwhelmed the defenders. Instead of reforming as ordered, however, the bluecoats found themselves exposed to rebel fire from the heights directly down onto them. Spontaneously, partly inspired by Phil Sheridan, they charged up the slopes and were gratified to find that the Confederate cannon could not be depressed at a sufficiently low angle to bear upon them. The spirited attack fascinated and somewhat unnerved Bragg's men, who disputed their steady advance.

The rebel center broke and fled, crumbling also before Hooker's attack on their left. Oddly, the main assault force under Sherman remained stymied by Hardee and the Confederate right, enabling these troops to cover Bragg's general retirement into Georgia during the night. Of Bragg's 64,000 men engaged, 6,600 were casualties, against nearly 5,900 of Grant's 56,000

there did not appear to be more than fifty or sixty huddled around their flag. The gallant band hurled themselves with a yell upon the lines of Anderson's old brigade of Mississippi veterans. Not a shot was fired, but with one impulse they swept them out of their works, and the little band of Federals took possession of the battery, waved their flag over it, and trained the guns so as to rake our lines. Their comrades swarmed up the ridge to their support, and the Confederate line gave way to the right and left, and the battle was won for the Union through the gallantry of that single regiment [which would be impossible to identify from the many scaling the heights more or less simultaneously].

Congressman and Massachusetts governor Nathaniel P. Banks received a major general's commission early in the war but twice fell victim to Stonewall Jackson's superior generalship in Virginia during 1862. An acceptable administrative commander, he took too long to capture Port Hudson in 1863 and also fumbled badly in the Red River campaign of 1864.

A Federal regiment erects log huts for its winter quarters. Elevated tents such as those in the foreground assured dry beds.

ATTACK UPON FORT SANDERS

November 29, 1863

by **Charles W. Walton**, Captain, U.S. Volunteers

[Samuel N.] Benjamin's [2nd U.S. Artillery] and [William W.] Buckley's [1st R. I. Artillery] favorite batteries of six guns each were mounted in the opening [of the fort] on solid floorings, the trees were cut down in the immediate front, and, by an ingenious plan of Lieutenant Benjamin's, thick [telegraph] wires were stretched from stump to stump about knee-high to trip the enemy as they approached, while a deep ditch, almost impossible to leap over, encircled the fort. ...

Across the railroad, up the gentle slope, and through the stumps they came, while our guns were making havoc among their ranks. On they came, never faltering, with that well-known yell; the stumps that the wires were attached to are reached, and down they fall amid charges of grape and canister [and]. . .the steady fire of the infantry. ... They filled the ditch. ... Lighted shells with short fuses and hand grenades were thrown over in the ditch, and in another moment through the smoke we discovered another brigade closed en masse rushing on to meet the same fate. ... Yells mingled with groans filled the air as they fell, and ... they broke and fled to the rear. ...

Such a spectacle I never want to witness again! Men literally torn to pieces lay all around. ... Arms and legs torn from their bodies lay scattered around, while at every footstep we trod in pools of blood. ... Over a hundred dead bodies were taken from the ditch alone. ...

The Union sternwheel gunboat Signal *tows barges filled with wood, brick, stone, and scrap metal, destined for use in the construction of the dam at the falls of the Red River, at the beginning of May 1864. While carrying dispatches downriver, she and the gunboat* Covington *were destroyed by rebel artillery and infantry fire.*

troops. Just after the battle, two Southern cavalry brigades from southwestern Virginia joined Longstreet for the assault on Knoxville's fortifications on the 29th. Longstreet, however, was thoroughly repulsed by Burnside's defenders. Grant immediately dispatched Sherman with two corps to assist Burnside, whereupon Longstreet lifted his siege and retired to spend the winter in the Tennessee foothills of the Smoky Mountains.

Absolute Union control of Chattanooga and Knoxville severed direct Confederate rail connections between the Eastern and Western theaters and gave the Union an advance base for a major offensive into the very heart of the Confederacy. Jefferson Davis had shown faulty strategic acumen, while Bragg and Longstreet had been inferior leaders, quarreling between themselves and with many of their subordinates. Late in December Davis finally replaced Bragg with Johnston as head of the Army of Tennessee and, of all things, recalled Bragg to Richmond to be his own military adviser. For the Union, however, the victory at Chattanooga had been the final proof of Grant's mettle. In March 1864 Lincoln appointed him General-in-Chief of all the Union armies with the rank of lieutenant general. Grant made his headquarters with the Army of the Potomac, although Meade remained tactical head in the field, and Halleck became Grant's chief of staff at the War Department. Sherman replaced Grant in the West.

Whatever Grant envisioned for the ultimate strategy by which to win the war, world affairs began to intrude. During 1863 France blockaded and invaded Mexico, placing an Austrian puppet – the Archduke Maximilian – on the throne of the feeble Mexican state, although resisted thereafter by the guerrilla operations of Mexican patriots. France preferred a Confederate victory in the American war, encouraged by possible Southern recognition of its puppet Mexican government. Illicit trade across the Rio Grande River between Mexican Matamoras and Brownsville, Texas on the Gulf was

305

Porter's gunboats pass the dam near Alexandria, Louisiana, on May 13, 1864, to escape from the low waters of the Red River.

somewhat helping the Confederacy, leading to a Union amphibious expedition in November which occupied Brazos Santiago Island and Brownsville and moved up the Texas coast to Corpus Christi. Although this operation added pressure against the shipment of goods across the Rio Grande, it had no impact on the French presence in Mexico. President Lincoln, alarmed at the flagrant French violation of the 40-year-old Monroe Doctrine forbidding European intervention in Latin America, insisted on an offensive into Texas to impress the French of Union displeasure with its invasion. Beyond that, however, the United States could not spare major forces to deal with the Mexican question until the end of the war.

In January 1864 General Banks, commander of the Department of the Gulf, laid plans to move from the Mississippi River up the Red River to Shreveport, thence into eastern Texas. In March the campaign began with Banks proceeding upriver with 17,000 troops to Alexandria, Louisiana, preceded by 10,000 troops under Major General Andrew J. Smith in transports from Vicksburg and Admiral Porter's squadron of 13 ironclads and seven gunboats. Banks was also supposed to be joined by another Federal force from Arkansas, but it moved too slowly and was forced back to Little Rock by aggressive Confederate actions during April.

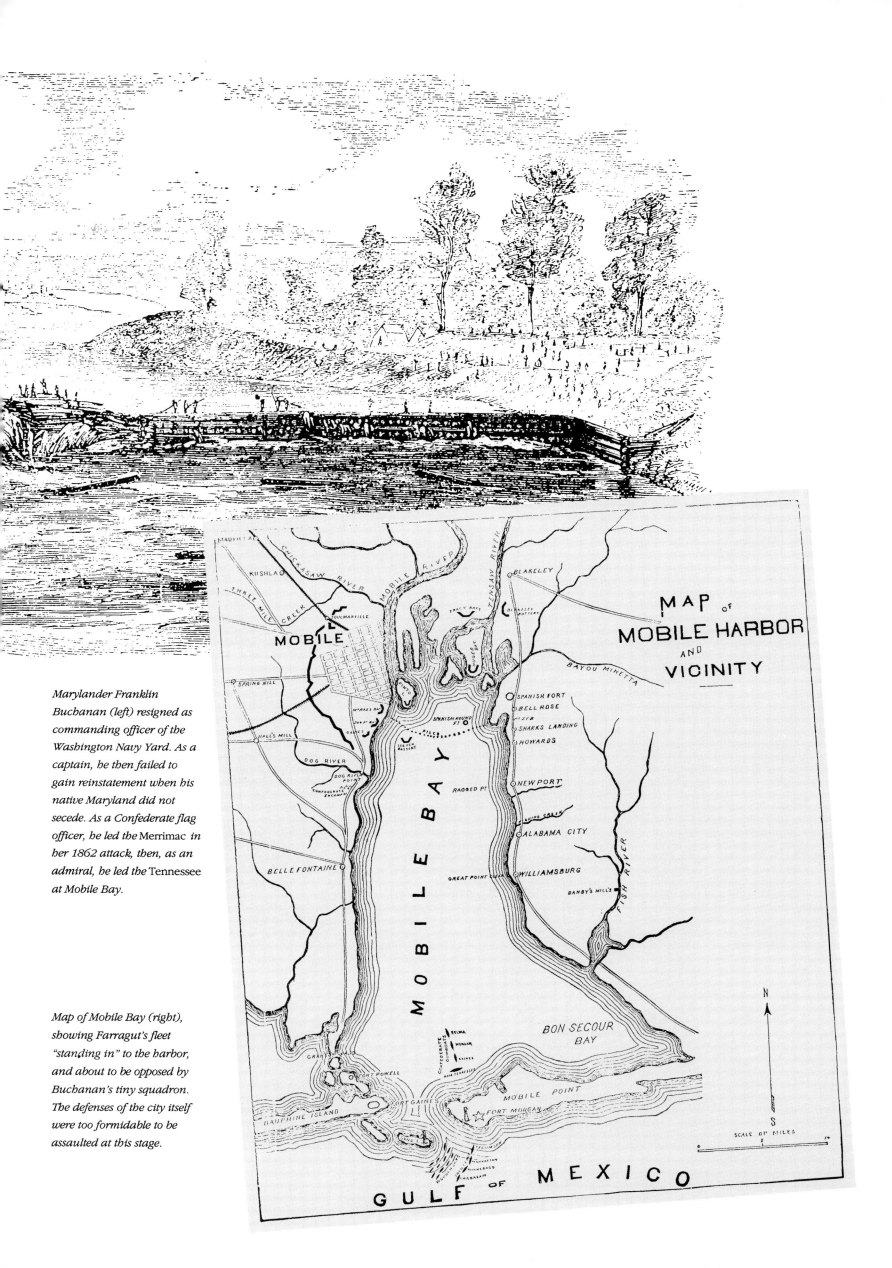

Marylander Franklin Buchanan (left) resigned as commanding officer of the Washington Navy Yard. As a captain, he then failed to gain reinstatement when his native Maryland did not secede. As a Confederate flag officer, he led the Merrimac in her 1862 attack, then, as an admiral, he led the Tennessee at Mobile Bay.

Map of Mobile Bay (right), showing Farragut's fleet "standing in" to the harbor, and about to be opposed by Buchanan's tiny squadron. The defenses of the city itself were too formidable to be assaulted at this stage.

MAP OF MOBILE HARBOR AND VICINITY

MOBILE

MOBILE BAY

BON SECOUR BAY

GULF OF MEXICO

THE
TENNESSEE
VALLEY

Farragut's fleet passes the forts and underwater mines ("torpedoes") to enter Mobile Bay, August 5, 1864. Preceded by the monitors are the sail-screw steamers (left to right) Hartford, Brooklyn, Richmond, Lackawanna, Monongahela, *and* Ossipee, *each screening a more vulnerable sidewheeler from the guns of Fort Morgan.*

The C.S.S. Tennessee *surrenders to the U.S.S.* Hartford, *which flies Farragut's two-star rear admiral's flag. The other Union warships are the gunboat* Itasca *next to the flagship, the brand new twin-turreted monitor* Chickasaw *(right), and (from left) the screw sloops* Ossipee, Brooklyn, *and* Richmond.

Banks pressed on, in spite of low water, and forced the Louisiana troops of Major General Richard Taylor to retreat to Mansfield, some 50 miles below Shreveport. The Confederate Trans-Mississippi commander, Kirby Smith, concentrated reinforcements from Arkansas and Texas, enabling Taylor to defeat Banks at Sabine Cross Roads near Mansfield on April 8. Taylor pursued but was driven back by A. J. Smith's troops at Pleasant Hill next day. Banks now elected to abandon the drive on Shreveport but was harassed by rebel attempts to cut him off and by perilously low water which threatened to entrap Porter's ships. Confederate underwater torpedoes and batteries along the shore sank the largest ironclad and several lesser vessels. The Red had become so low at Alexandria that the squadron did not escape until army engineers fabricated dams, raising the water level enabling Porter to proceed on May 13.

At point blank range, the guns of Farragut's flagship Hartford *exchange blows with the rebel ironclad* Tennessee *during the Battle of Mobile Bay, August 5, 1864. Farragut himself can be seen on the main shroud lines, secured to them, against his wishes, by a line. He damned the guns as well as the torpedoes.*

The Confederate sidewheel gunboat Selma, *her open gun deck exposed, surrenders to the Union sidewheeler* Metacomet *after a running flight which lasted an hour following the main battle. Masked by the* Hartford *while entering Mobile Bay,* Metacomet *had been released by Farragut to overtake the* Selma.

309

THE TENNESSEE VALLEY

The Union army and navy had to fight all the way to the Mississippi – a disastrous campaign in every respect. Banks resigned from the army and returned to his normal career in politics.

The Confederate Trans-Mississippi – "Kirby Smithdom" – still found itself in dire strategic and economic straits. Even though the Union garrison evacuated Brownsville in the spring of 1864 in favor of Brazos Santiago Island, warring French and Mexican factions interfered with the Confederate importation of military goods from Matamoros, whose long overland logistics were further plagued by Indian and outlaw attacks. This being the case, Smith had to rely on blockade runners between Havana and Galveston, a run continually plagued by the West Gulf Blockading Squadron. The district was simply cut off from the rest of the Confederacy and most of the world. All that Smith could hope to do was whittle away at Union forces across his borders. When several units around New Orleans were sealifted to Sherman and Grant in the summer of 1864, Smith sent Taylor across the Mississippi

to operate in eastern Louisiana but without success. And in September Smith sent Sterling Price with 12,000 men to conquer Missouri, where Price fought more than forty engagements before being defeated at Westport by S. R. Curtis and Alfred Pleasonton on October 23. Retreating into Kansas, Price was defeated again at Marais des Cygnes two days later before escaping back to Arkansas via the Indian Territory. Kirby Smith could do no more west of the great river.

East of the Mississippi along the Gulf coast, the Union navy bent every effort to choke off blockade running to and from St. Marks at the crook in the Florida coast beyond Pensacola and at Mobile. Early in 1864 the East Gulf Blockading Squadron finally sealed off St. Marks, even as a Union expeditionary force took Jacksonville on the Atlantic coast, although its progress inland was checked at the battle of Olustee in February. All seaborne efforts then focused on Mobile, where successful runners progressively increased their activities, despite Rear Admiral Farragut's great desire to close the port. With Gulf operations focused on

Fort Morgan, whose inner citadel and outer walls are seen below, commanded the approaches to Mobile Bay and survived Farragut's initial attack but was then besieged and battered into surrender by Union naval guns and army siege guns on August 23, 1864.

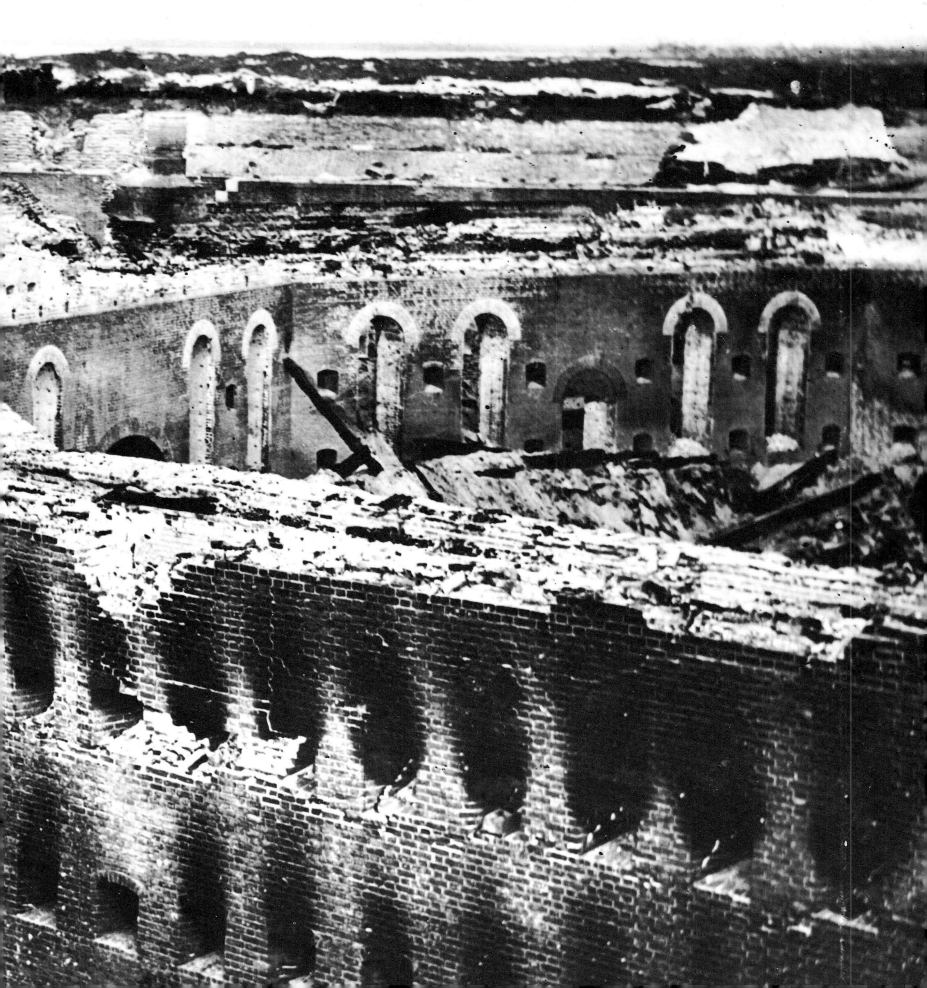

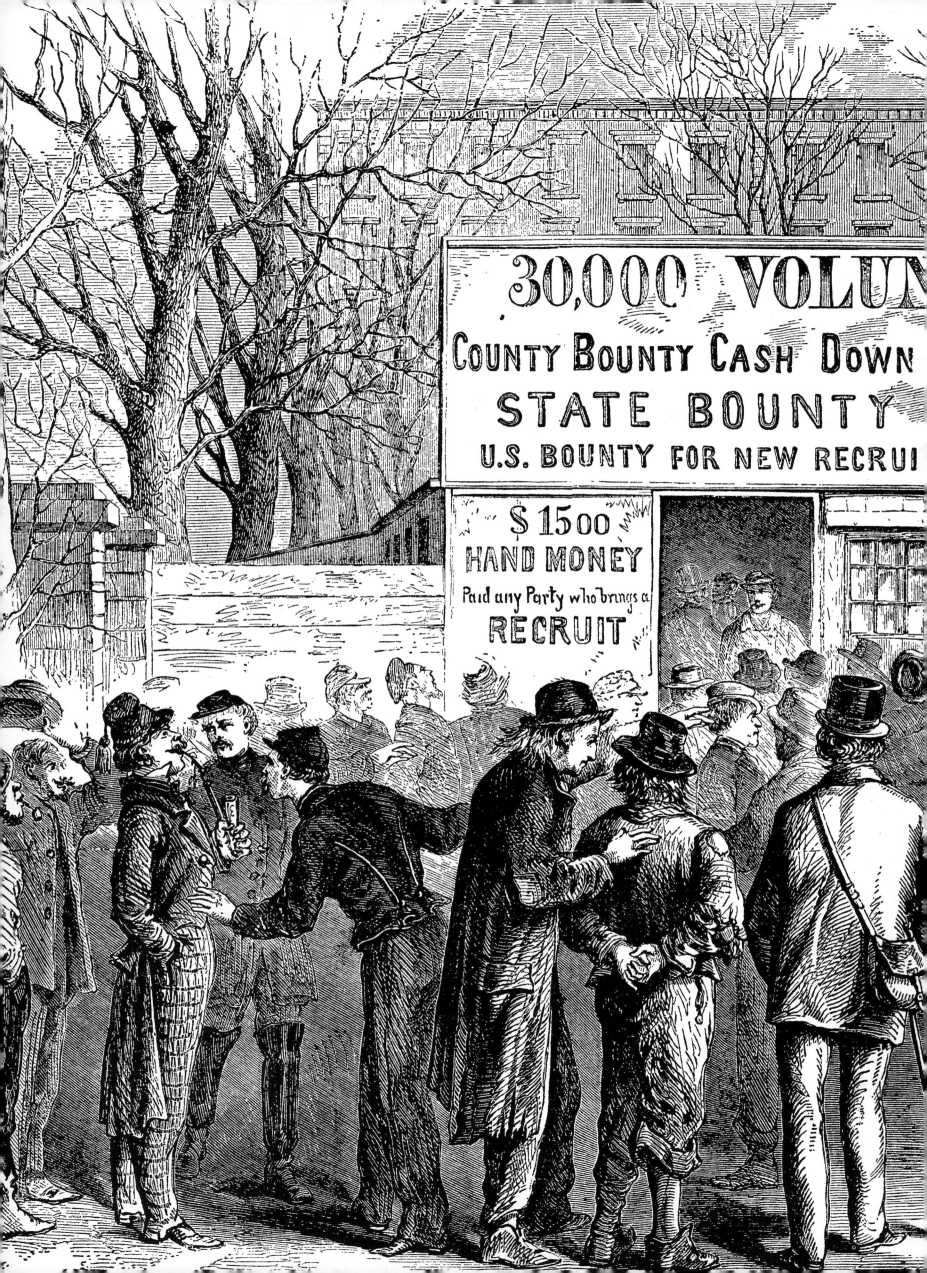

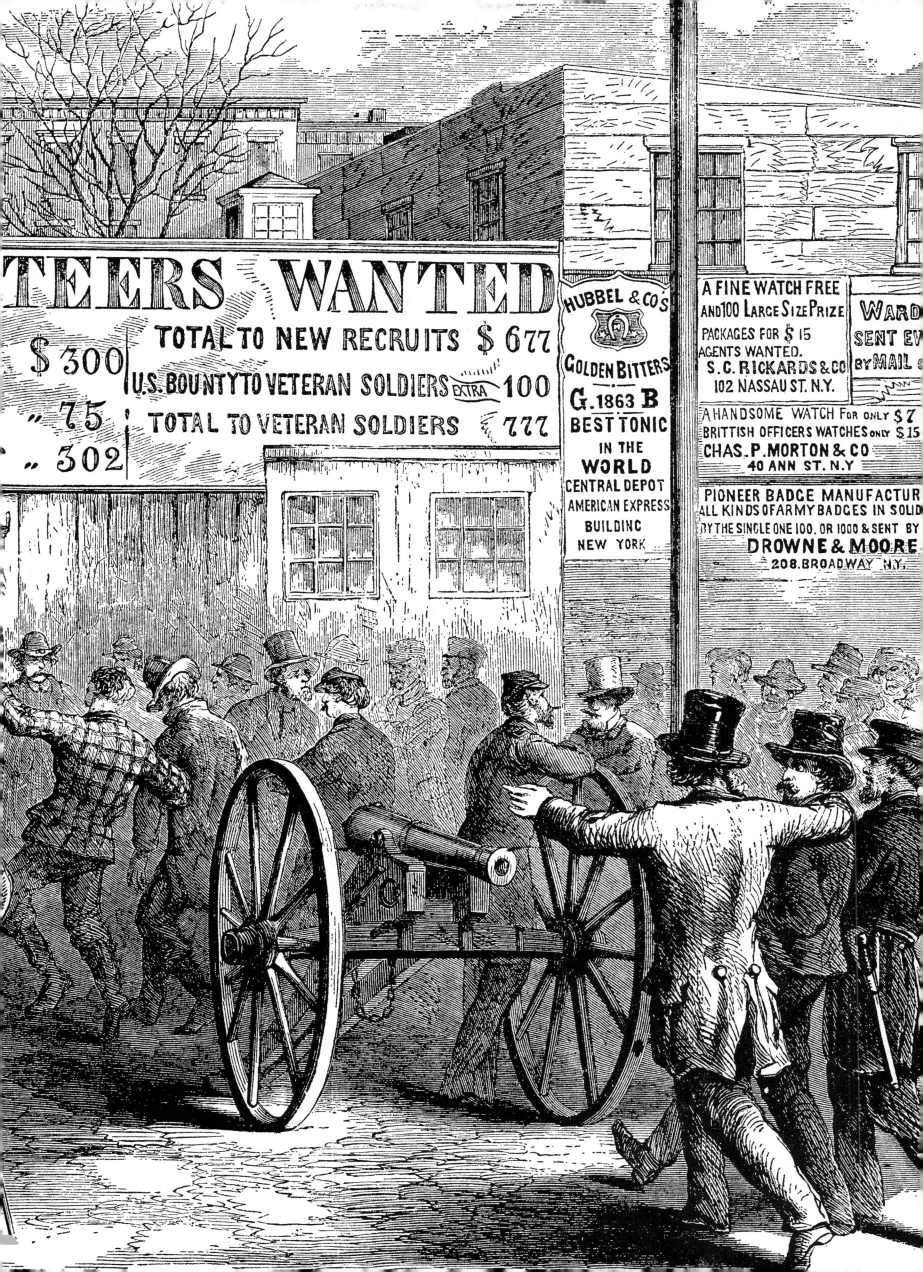

THE TENNESSEE VALLEY

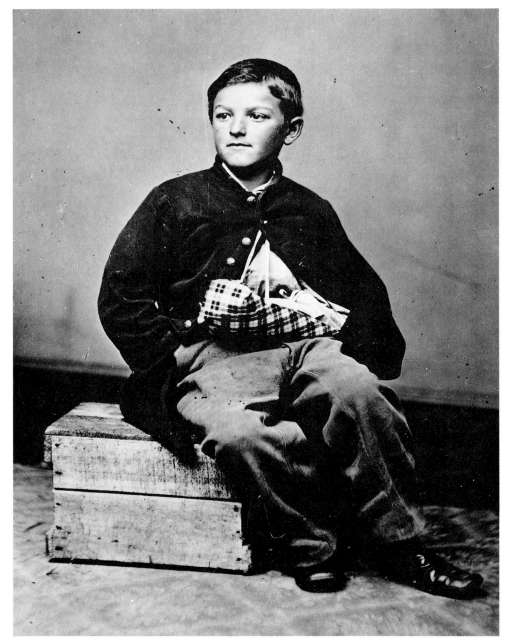

William Black (left) was one of more than a thousand Union boy soldiers who were fifteen years of age and under. He confidently displays his wounded arm.

Northern envelopes display patriotic covers and three-cent George Washington stamps. The second envelope from the top suggests a Christmas tree of Old Glory flags, each representing a loyal state.

"Old Abe" (right) and his young son Tad. The President's oldest boy, Robert Todd Lincoln, graduated from Harvard in 1864 at the age of twenty-one and joined General Grant's staff.

Texas and the Red River campaign, however, he could do nothing until the summer of 1864. Then he moved with alacrity, hoping to destroy rebel ironclads at Mobile – the ram *Tennessee* and several more under construction, all commanded by Admiral Franklin Buchanan, the Confederacy's ranking naval officer.

The Battle of Mobile Bay began on August 3, 1864 when Farragut landed Granger's 13th Corps on the outer islet containing Fort Gaines to besiege it. Two days later, Farragut in the steam frigate *Hartford* ran the batteries of Gaines and Fort Morgan opposite it with his four monitors and thirteen other wooden ships. The monitor *Tecumseh* struck an underwater torpedo and sank quickly, but Farragut pressed on with the ringing pronouncement, "Damn the Torpedoes! Full speed ahead!" Buchanan then sallied forth in the *Tennessee* with three wooden gunboats but proved no match for Farragut's armada. Rammed and pounded, the *Tennessee* went out of control and had to strike her colors. Fort Gaines surrendered on the 8th, enabling General Granger to lay siege to Fort Morgan, utilizing siege guns brought in from New Orleans. Under a combined army-navy bombardment, Granger's infantry moved forward on August 22, whereupon the fort capitulated next day. Although the city of Mobile remained in Confederate hands, it ceased to exist as a seaport. It had never been as prominent as Wilmington or Charleston, but its closure nevertheless hurt the South, especially when news of the naval battle reached the Confederacy's creditors in Europe. Farragut, for his achievement, received promotion to vice admiral – first in the Navy's history.

With the noose tightening around the Confederacy, the task facing U.S. Grant during the spring of 1864 was to devise and execute a grand strategy by which to destroy the Confederacy. For this, he was eminently suited.

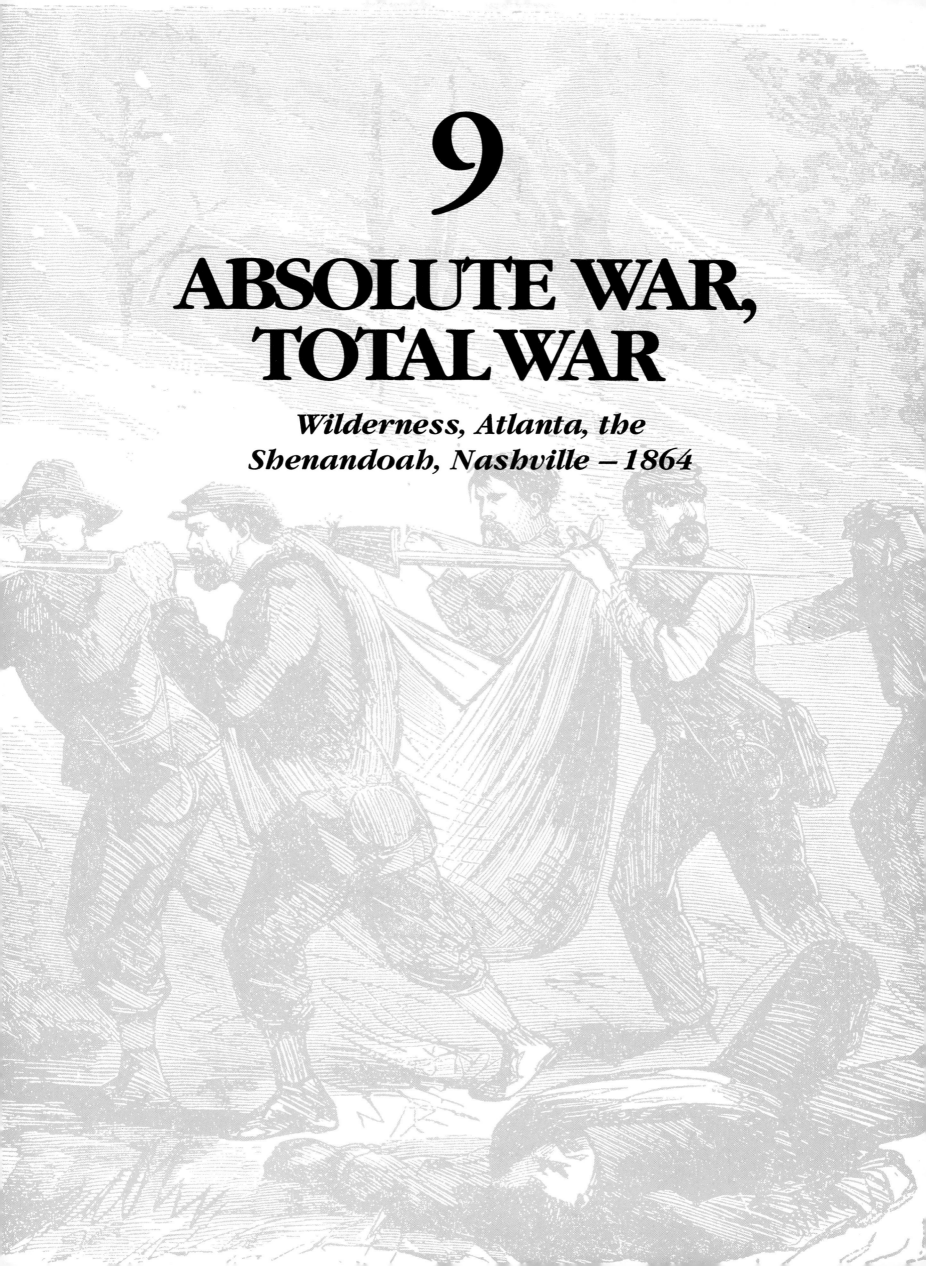

9
ABSOLUTE WAR, TOTAL WAR

Wilderness, Atlanta, the Shenandoah, Nashville – 1864

ABSOLUTE WAR, TOTAL WAR

After assuming command of the Union armies, Lieutenant General Grant journeyed to Nashville where, in mid-March 1864, he and his Western commander, Sherman, decided upon the grand strategy for winning the war. They agreed that the principal objectives were the destruction of Lee's army in northern Virginia and Johnston's in northern Georgia. Attacking simultaneously on as many fronts as possible, the armies of the North were not only to destroy their opponents in battle but to inflict all possible damage to the Confederacy's "war resources." This meant the food-producing areas as well as the sources of munitions. Three principal Southern "breadbaskets" remained: Virginia's Shenandoah Valley, central Georgia and Alabama, and the ports of Wilmington and Charleston. Such total war had to be waged absolutely, not only to break the Southern peoples' will to resist but to sustain that of the North by constant victories. Politically, success would guarantee Lincoln's re-election in November against an antiwar

One of Meade's troopers gets a shave from a comrade in arms attended by a black helper, while others clean their rifles, at the Army of the Potomac's winter quarters near Culpeper, Virginia, on the Rapidan River. Sketch by Edwin Forbes.

Unable to feed themselves over the winter, Southern families living behind Union lines had to be fed by the Federal army commissary. Forbes sketched these ladies coming into a camp in northern Virginia. Such dependence upon the enemy subtly ate away at the people's confidence in the Confederate government.

318

party seeking to make peace. Neither Grant nor Sherman had any illusions about the difficulties of this grand campaign. Their respect for their opponents was too great to warrant overconfidence.

Grant's overall plan was the long-awaited strategy of concentration. At the head of Meade's Army of the Potomac, Grant would hammer away at Lee in Virginia, continuing the stalemate to hold Lee down if he could not actually defeat him. Sherman's Western armies would then provide the hitting element, driving Johnston back on Atlanta and eventually reaching the seacoast somewhere, splitting the Confederacy into thirds as Vicksburg had cut it in half and hopefully destroying Johnston's Army of Tennessee in the process. In the execution of the grand campaign, Grant would deny the Shenandoah breadbasket to Lee, and Sherman would lay waste to Georgia or Alabama. Ever crucial to the plan was the maritime dimension. Grant would keep the Army of the Potomac with its back to the Chesapeake Bay and naval support as McClellan

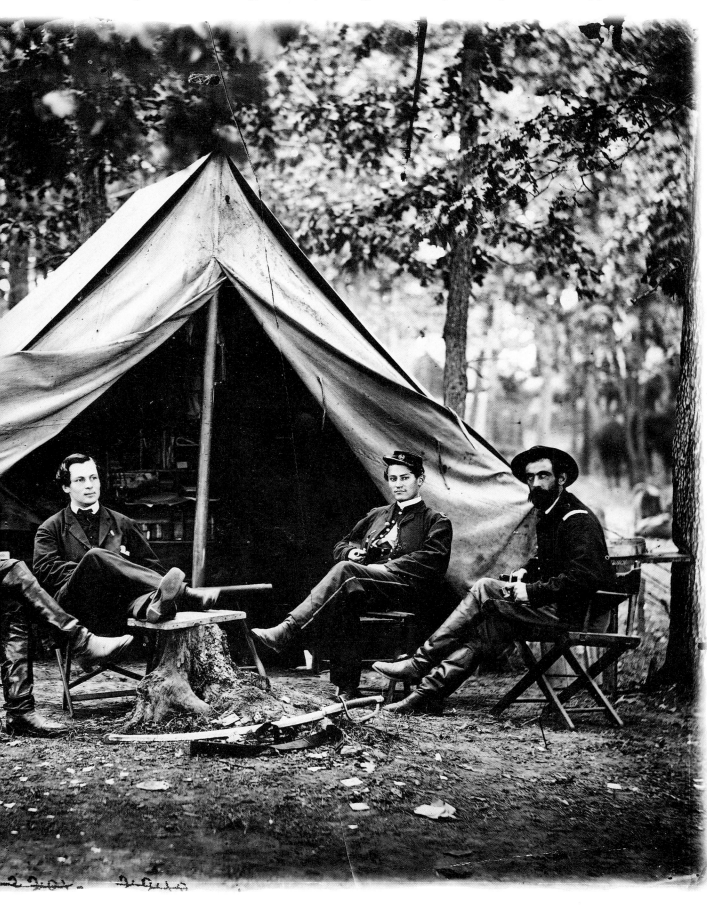

From early 1863 till the war's end, Colonel George H. Sharpe (left) headed the Army of the Potomac's Bureau of Military Information: the scouting and spy service whose agents penetrated rebel lines despite the threat of execution if captured. Three agents are the other subjects of this April 1864 photo, taken on the eve of the Wilderness campaign.

ABSOLUTE WAR, TOTAL WAR

THE SOUTHERN ENEMY IN 1864

By **William T. Sherman**, Major General Commanding, Military Division of the Mississippi

[In May 1864, Grant and I] had at our front [enemy] generals to whom in early life we had been taught to look – educated and experienced soldiers like ourselves, not likely to make any mistakes, and each of whom had as strong an army as could be collected from the mass of the Southern people – of the same blood as ourselves, brave, confident, and well equipped; in addition to which they had the most decided advantage of operating in their own difficult country of mountain, forest, ravine, and river, affording admirable opportunities for defense, besides the other equally important advantage that we had to invade the country of our unqualified enemy and expose our long lines of supply to the guerrillas of an "exasperated people." Again, as we advanced we had to leave guards to bridges, stations, and intermediate depots, diminishing the fighting force, while our enemy gained strength by picking up his detachments as he fell back, and had railroads to bring supplies and reinforcements from his rear.

I instance these facts to offset the common assertion that we of the North won the war by brute force, and not by courage and skill.

Officers pose at the neatly appointed headquarters of the Army of the Potomac at Brandy Station, scene of the 1863 cavalry battle and the army's winter quarters between Culpeper and the Rappahannock River. Uniforms are spotless, the plank boardwalk protects against mud, and the folding chairs look comfortable in the February 1864 sun.

had done in the Peninsular campaign. Sherman, no longer near navigable rivers, must reach the Atlantic or Gulf coast to obtain supplies from the Navy. The rivers and coastal waters would be exploited along with the railroads to shift troops between theaters.

The strategy of the Confederacy remained limited and defensive, directed as usual by Jefferson Davis who had no intention of yielding supreme military authority to any general as Lincoln had to Grant – not even to Lee, although he frequently drew on Lee's advice. Lee remained in charge only of the Virginia theater but could be counted on to take advantage of opportunities to strike against Grant's rear. Johnston in the West was even planning on mounting another counterattack into Tennessee. Such bold action, if successful, held out the only hope for a negotiated peace and possible foreign recognition, because manpower and military material lost in new campaigns could not be replaced easily.

Grant and Sherman began the offensive simultaneously, the first week in May 1864, and intended

Brigadier General James S. Wadsworth's division engages Ewell's Corps in the Battle of the Wilderness, May 6, 1864. Wadsworth, who had gone on leave to run, unsuccessfully, for governor of New York in the autumn of 1862, was mortally wounded in this battle and died two days later.

Overleaf: cannonades and musketry at the Battle of the Wilderness set fire to the dry underbrush, creating a veritable hell for the wounded of both armies. This etching by Forbes shows a Federal battery and infantry column moving forward at night, the burning tree having been deliberately torched to provide light.

Union troops evacuate their less fortunate wounded comrades on a makeshift stretcher: rifles bound together with a blanket slung between them.

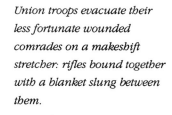

321

ABSOLUTE WAR, TOTAL WAR

to keep up the pressure relentlessly, no longer affording the South a breathing space between campaigns as in the past. Furthermore, Grant took a page out of the brief McClellan-Pope scheme of attacking Lee from two directions at the same time. Reinforcing forces still on the Peninsula into the Army of the James under Ben Butler, he had Butler move against Petersburg, south of Richmond, with the 15,000 men of the 10th and 13th Corps. Unfortunately, Butler, although able to cut some rail lines, was outmaneuvered by Beauregard who with 18,000 men in two weeks during May managed to "bottle up" Butler's army in the curl of the James River known as Bermuda Hundred near Drewry's Bluff. Also, to secure the Shenandoah Valley, Grant had the German emigré Major General Franz Sigel march into the Valley with 6,500 men, only to be driven back by Breckinridge at New Market on May 15. Without success in either quarter, Grant had to depend on the Army of the Potomac to accomplish his task.

Reinforced by Burnside's 9th Corps transferred from Tennessee, Grant began the Wilderness campaign with seasoned corps commanders: Hancock, 2nd; Warren, 5th; Sedgwick, 6th; and Sheridan, brought in from the West to lead the Cavalry Corps. Crossing the Rappahannock on May 4 into the Wilderness around the Chancellorsville battlefield of exactly one year before, the more than 100,000 Federal troops were immediately attacked by Lee's 60,000 under the same corps commanders Lee had had at Gettysburg: Longstreet, 1st; Ewell, 2nd; Hill, 3rd; and Stuart, Cavalry. Lee, hoping to disrupt Grant's forces in the thick woods as he had Hooker a year before, attacked furiously in the two-day Battle of the Wilderness, May 5-7. Grant counterattacked, and the fight seesawed with heavy casualties, particularly when the woods caught fire from the cannonade and many of the wounded were burned to death. Grant lost the battle and suffered nearly 18,000 casualties, Lee less than half that, including Longstreet, badly wounded by his own men near the spot where Stonewall Jackson had fallen under similar circumstances the year before. He was replaced by Richard H. Anderson, and Jubal Early filled in for Hill who became sick.

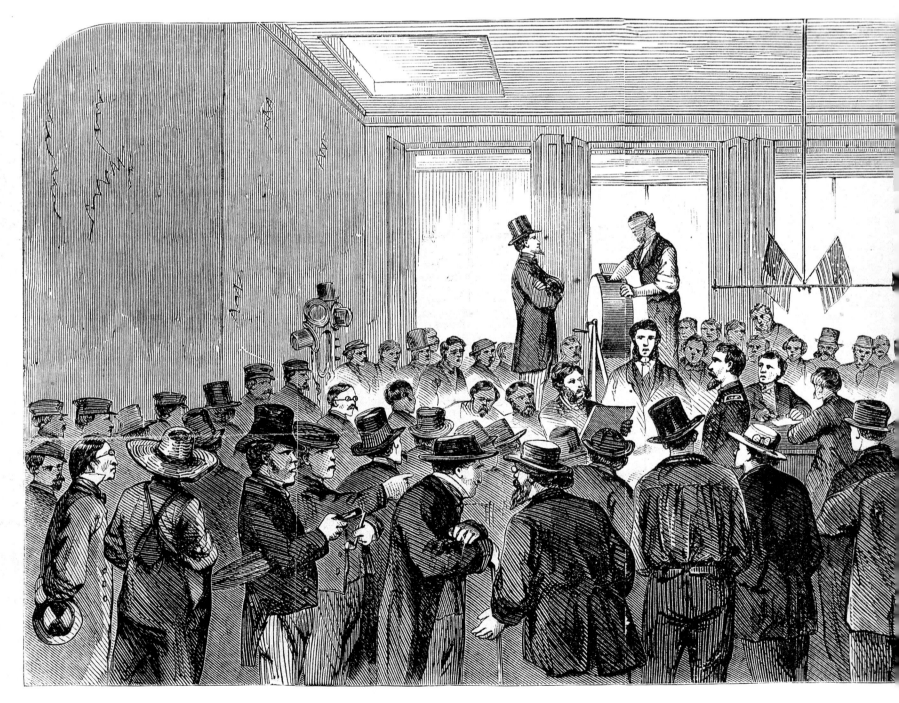

Hancock's 2nd Corps hammers away at the "Bloody Angle" – Ewell's exposed salient at Spotsylvania, May 12, 1864.

"Uncle John" was the affectionate nickname given to Major General John Sedgwick by his men. Sedgwick commanded the 6th Corps at Chancellorsville, Gettysburg, and the Wilderness, until brought down by a rebel sharpshooter at Spotsylvania Court House, May 9, 1864.

Grant, however, still with overwhelming strength, maneuvered around Lee's right flank toward Spotsylvania Court House, keeping his communications secure back to Fredericksburg on the Rappahannock. Lee won the race to the village on May 8, due partly to the aggressive activity of his trusted cavalryman, Jeb Stuart. Grant detached Sheridan with the Cavalry Corps to seek out and punish Stuart's command, while Grant pounded against Lee's right flank. As the main battle raged on the 9th, 6th Corps commander Sedgwick was

Cold Harbor — rifle pits —

Pioneer asleep. Worn Out!
In Chickahomine Swamp June 1864.

Musician Alexander Meinung, of the 26th North Carolina Infantry, sketched this Confederate bridge and road builder during Lee's futile attempt to stop Grant crossing the James River to the east and south of Petersburg and Richmond.

killed, and many others with him, but Grant did not let up. In the midst of it, on the 11th, he telegraphed Halleck in Washington that he intended "to fight it out on this line if it takes all summer." The thrusts and counterthrusts created an exposed salient in the rebel center, held by Ewell's corps, against which Grant hurled the 20,000 men of Hancock's 2nd Corps on the 12th. The furious assault succeeded but with so many casualties that the scene of the disputed salient was dubbed the "Bloody Angle." Then Grant shifted southeastward against Lee's right that resulted in another solid week of fighting before the long Battle of Spotsylvania Court House came to an end. Northern losses were 11,000, but a nearly equal number of Yankee reinforcements arrived late in the battle.

With an almost unlimited reservoir of recruits and draftees to draw upon, in contrast to Lee, Grant continued moving southward, shifting his base on the Rappahannock from Fredericksburg further downriver to Port Royal. Lee had no choice but to parallel his movements, blocking him at the North Anna River to protect Richmond, probing and skirmishing all the while. Sheridan, meanwhile, had headed toward Richmond with 10,000 horses on a raid designed to flush out Jeb Stuart. As Sheridan's men destroyed railroads, rolling stock, and foodstuffs intended for Lee's army, Stuart followed in pursuit, confronting Sheridan's approach to Yellow Tavern on May 11. In the battle that ensued, Custer's Michigan cavalry brigade carried the day; one of its men, a 48-year-old marksman, felled Stuart with a pistol shot. The famous horseman died next day. Sheridan abandoned his mission against Richmond as impracticable but pressed on to the Peninsula where he briefly joined Butler. On the 17th he headed north to rejoin Grant and finally linked up a week later, having circled Lee's army. Grant then had Sheridan lead the rest of the army across the Pamunkey River, clashing frequently with rebel cavalry during May 26-31 as Grant took up a new position facing Lee at Totopotomoy Creek.

Both armies then turned further south toward Cold Harbor and a battle which would surpass Shiloh, Antietam, and Chickamauga in its bloodletting. Lee's army of 59,000 veterans was now led by Dick Anderson,

A Federal battery duels with distant Southern guns at Cold Harbor, June 2, 1864. Artist A. R. Waud has also sketched the intervening infantry pits stretching across the open fields and a rebel shell exploding in the left foreground.

In this fanciful Currier & Ives lithograph, the attack of Grant's troops on Lee's position at Cold Harbor, June 1, 1864, appears almost antiseptic. The opposite was actually true, Cold Harbor being perhaps the bloodiest battle of the war.

ABSOLUTE WAR, TOTAL WAR

WITH CUSTER AT YELLOW TAVERN

by **L. E. Tripp**, First Sergeant, 5th Michigan Cavalry   May 11, 1864

Finally our brigade was ordered to the front, where we found a large field with a rail fence running … through the middle, with woods mostly on three sides. … Our regiment and the 6th Mich. were moved down on the north side of the field in the woods, where we formed and dismounted for a charge across the field. … When we were about to leap the fence into the field (for we were under fire at the time) the colonel [Russell A. Alger] said: "Now, boys, keep a good line, for General Sheridan is watching us." (General Sheridan and quite a body of troops were on an elevation to our right overlooking the field.). … My tent-mate and friend Daniel F. Miller remarked, "Now, Tripp, let's keep together."

We had not advanced over twenty yards, I think, before a murderous crossfire was opened upon us out of the woods on our left and rear. Words cannot picture the scene that followed out there in that level field, without any chance of cover. We were trying to return the fire, shooting in three different directions. Poor Miller received his death wound while on one knee shooting in the direction that the left of our line

had come from. Our brave and noble Custer rode up on his horse in that field among us – always cool – with the words: "Lie down, men – lie down. We'll fix them! I have sent two regiments around on the flank." His words of cheer and sympathy to the wounded were deeply appreciated. …

Right there in that field I think General Custer decided on taking that battery [firing on us]. Custer's brigade (the 1st, 5th, 6th, and 7th Mich. Cavalry) were now all engaged, but the 1st Vt. had formerly belonged to our brigade, and to it Custer went for help. … The 1st Vt. went, and there was an advance all along the line. The battery was taken. (One of Private Tripp's fellow troopers in the 5th, John A. Huff, had been the best shot in Berdan's Sharpshooters the first two years of the war and mortally wounded Jeb Stuart in this battle, only to be killed himself two weeks later. Custer fell in his famous stand against the Indians at the Little Big Horn in 1876. Colonel Alger served as Secretary of War during the Spanish–American War in 1898.)

329

ABSOLUTE WAR, TOTAL WAR

1st Corps; Jubal Early, who replaced Ewell, injured at the Bloody Angle, 2nd; A. P. Hill, returned from sick leave, 3rd; and Wade Hampton, successor to Jeb Stuart with the Cavalry. Grant not only swelled his ranks with constant replacements but now absorbed Baldy Smith's 18th Corps of Butler's Army of the James near Cold Harbor. With no fewer than 108,000 effective troops at his disposal, Grant battled Lee for position on June 1, then launched a frontal attack all along the line at Cold Harbor on the 3rd. The several Union corps moved erratically, however, exposing their flanks to enfilading Southern artillery and rifle fire that cut down perhaps 7,000 Federal troops in a manner of minutes. By nightfall, the exhausted armies stood only a hundred yards apart, and there they stayed until midmonth.

The Wilderness campaign was over. Lee had beaten Grant in most of the pitched battles, but Grant now faced Richmond from the east and decided to cross the James to attack Petersburg and Richmond from the east and south. With the Navy to support him, his crossing could not be prevented. So Lee lost the campaign in the strategic sense; he had failed to stop Grant's advance. Both armies had suffered tremendous casualties – Lee 32,000, Grant 50,000 – but only Grant could replace them.

With victory in sight, Grant ordered Sheridan to make a diversionary raid north of Richmond and Butler to attack Petersburg while the Army of the Potomac crossed the James. Sheridan, however, was defeated at Trevillian Station by Hampton on June 11-12 and Butler before Petersburg by Beauregard on the 9th and again on June 15-18, even as part of Grant's army crossed the James and assisted him. Lee's main forces began arriving inside Petersburg and Richmond on the 18th – to frustrate Grant's plan. Grant had no choice but to lay siege to the two cities, a stratagem that would require many months. He also linked up with the Navy, controlling the James River, and established a permanent base at City Point on that river. Unlike his siege of Vicksburg, however, Grant could not isolate Lee from his supply lines. With the fertile Shenandoah Valley at his back, and the railroad to Wilmington intact west of the city, Lee could continue to supply his army indefinitely. He also had the James River Squadron of three formidable ironclads and several gunboats at his disposal and the Tredegar iron works to forge weapons.

As the siege lines formed around Petersburg by both armies, promising continuous fighting and probes, Lee came up with one last stratagem by which to break the

As if these 24-pound howitzers of Company L, 2nd New York Heavy Artillery at Fort C. F. Smith were not enough to defend Washington, the gunners have been equipped with rifles and 18-inch steel bayonets. Washington was ringed by fifty-seven such forts.

"Sheridan's Ride" rallied the Army of the Shenandoah to repulse Early's attack at Cedar Creek, Virginia, October 19, 1864. Sheridan, a feisty Irishman and son of

an immigrant couple, proved such an aggressive leader that he emerged from the war as number three in the triad of

top Union leaders, alongside Grant and Sherman.

REPULSE OF THE STAR BRIGADE AT COLD HARBOR

June 3, 1864

by **Pinckney D. Bowles**, Colonel, 4th Alabama Infantry, who led Law's Brigade after Brigadier General E.M. Law was wounded.

I found on bringing my [five Alabama] regiments into the [breast]works that the men were four deep. I ordered three of every four of the men to set themselves under cover of the fortifications and load for the fourth one, who was to stand at the works and fire his gun and then hand it back to those in the rear to reload while he was to have a freshly-loaded piece as rapidly as he could fire. [A fast reload of a muzzle-loaded rifle musket was about ten seconds.]

We were not long waiting. Soon the woods in our front resounded with cold, mechanical huzzas, as if

from myriad voices, and a general advance was made along the whole line. I ordered my men to hold their fire until the Federals came within 70 yards of our works, when I gave the command to fire. ... Our artillery was not idle, but firing double-shotted canister, and at the distance of 100 yards was cutting wide swaths through their lines at every fire, literally mowing them down by the dozen, while heads, arms, legs, and muskets were seen flying high in [the] air at every discharge.

We were not long in discovering that there was no child's play awaiting us. We were opposed to a brave, determined, and gallant foe [Brigadier General George T. Stannard's Star Brigade of the 18th Corps—the 23rd, 25th, 27th Mass., 9th N. J., and 55th Pa. infantry regiments]. The wide lanes made in their column were quickly closed, while on, on they came, swaying first to the right and then to the left, like great waves of the sea ..., hurrying ... nearer and nearer to our works. There was a ravine with a marsh in [Brigadier] General [G.T.]

Early's raiders upset local trade by breaking the dikes of the Chesapeake and Ohio Canal, which ran northwest from Washington, parallel to the Potomac River.

Union cavalry drives back Early's infantry at the battle of Winchester, Virginia, September 19, 1864.

Anderson's front. Here the enemy surged to the right to obtain shelter from the musketry of my men, only to be raked by the artillery and leaden hail from Anderson's [Georgia] brigade.

At this point the dead were piled upon each other five and six deep, and the blood ran down the gully past our lines. Such invincible resolution I never saw before or since. They advanced again and again, only to be shot down until the ground was blue with the dead and wounded. ... (Of the 900 or so men who participated in the charge of the Star Brigade, 98 were killed; 356 wounded, including General Stannard; and 38 captured. Of the charge, Private W.P. Derby of the 27th Massachusetts quoted the French general who had observed the charge of the British Light Brigade at Balaklava in the Crimean War a decade before: "It was doubtless magnificent, but such a waste of men is not war!")

siege. He ordered Jubal Early to lead his 2nd Corps of 14,000 men up the Shenandoah to attack Washington, D. C. itself. Since similar maneuvers by Stonewall Jackson had caused Lincoln to withdraw troops from McClellan before Richmond in 1862, it might work again. Departing late in June 1864, Early attacked several Union garrisons in the Valley before crossing the Potomac on July 5, alerting Grant to the danger. The Navy sealifted one division to Washington, while Early occupied Frederick, Maryland. This division joined General Lew Wallace's two defensive brigades at Monocacy Creek, southeast of Frederick. On the 9th Early attacked and drove back Wallace's 6,000 men to Baltimore. The Battle of Monocacy, however, bought Grant added time to transport Major General Horatio G. Wright's 6th Corps by water from City Point to Washington. It arrived at noon of the 11th, just as

Currier & Ives lithographs did much to sustain the Northern people's support of the war effort throughout the war. This particular lithograph glamorizes Sheridan's victory at Cedar Creek.

Early's skirmishers entered the Washington suburb of Silver Spring, Maryland. This timely reinforcement convinced Early to abandon any attack on the city and recross the Potomac. With Grant believing Early would rejoin Lee, Early defeated several Federal units in the upper Shenandoah Valley then moved north again to capture several towns in western Maryland and burn Chambersburg, Pennsylvania on July 30 – an uncharacteristic application of total war by the Confederacy.

Grant now determined to rid himself of the Early menace and in the process lay waste to the Shenandoah Valley, thus crippling Lee in two ways. At the beginning of August he appointed Sheridan to command of a new Army of the Shenandoah, 48,000 troops comprised of the 6th Corps and cavalry from Meade's army, the 19th Corps brought by sea from New Orleans, and Brigadier

General George Crook's two divisions from West Virginia. Early received some reinforcements as the two opposing forces felt each other out in the environs of Harpers Ferry during August and September. Then, when Early split his force to move north again, Sheridan's full army struck and defeated 11,000 men of Early's force at Winchester in the Valley on September 19 and again at Fisher's Hill three days later. With Early on the run, Sheridan began to withdraw in early October, only to have Early launch a surprise attack on his army at Cedar Creek on the 19th, driving it back. Sheridan, 14 miles away at Winchester, came dashing back ("Sheridan's Ride" became a popular poem), rallied his troops and crushed Early's 18,000-man army. With Early finally neutralized, Sheridan's army proceeded to plunder Lee's granary of the Shenandoah so completely, according to Grant's orders, "that a crow

Seen astride Sam, a half-thoroughbred bay and one of several horses that he owned, William Tecumseh Sherman displays his own erect bearing. Having been closely associated with Grant since early 1862, Sherman was the logical choice to succeed him in the West. There Sherman waged total war against the South of his prewar affections.

ABSOLUTE WAR, TOTAL WAR

Popular "Black Jack" Logan (right), affectionately nicknamed for his ample black hair and mustache, receives his men's cheers on the drive toward Atlanta. From Fort Donelson to the end of the war, the former Congressman ably led first a brigade, then a division, and finally the 15th Corps in the Army of the Tennessee.

After his successes at First Bull Run and on the Peninsula, General Joseph E. Johnston (above) became the only logical candidate to direct Confederate fortunes in the Western theater. The impatient Jefferson Davis preferred the younger Braxton Bragg and John Bell Hood, but always went back to Johnston, unfortunately too late for it to matter.

flying across the Valley would have to carry its rations with it." Both generals kept token forces in the area, but the 6th Corps rejoined Grant, and Lee had to rely mostly on the rail connection to Wilmington in order to withstand the siege of Petersburg.

Whereas Grant had both the masterful Lee and often blundering subordinate generals to inhibit his inexorable advance on Richmond, Sherman in the West had neither for the Atlanta campaign. His three armies of 100,000 men were commanded not only by veteran professionals from both theaters but by aggressive volunteer generals who had learned their skills under the inspired leadership of Grant, Sherman, and Thomas. Their opponent, Joe Johnston, though not a Lee, was the second most talented general in the Confederate Army and his corps commanders were solid fighters. With an army of some 53,000 men, Johnston would be gradually reinforced by Western units rallying to the defense of Atlanta. Founded as a railroad center sixty miles northwest of Milledgeville, the state capital,

Atlanta also boasted munitions factories and leaped to prominence after the fall of Chattanooga. Linked by rail to supply centers in Alabama and the Carolinas, Atlanta held the key to the survival of Johnston's army.

Sherman, like Grant, began his movement south in early May 1864 and used the same tactic of extending his longer lines around Johnston's flank after every pitched battle, forcing the smaller Army of Tennessee to fall back on Atlanta. He initially skirted Johnston's entrenchments westward around Dalton with McPherson's army as Thomas' moved directly down the Chattanooga–Atlanta rail line. Johnston withdrew on the 12th to Resaca, where he contested Sherman's forces over the following three days before Sherman again turned his left flank and captured the manufacturing town of Rome. The Confederates fell back to solid defensive positions first at Cassville then Allatoona Pass, but Sherman struck again at the battle of New Hope Church (or Dallas), May 25-27, took Allatoona Pass, and extended his lines on Johnston's

McPherson's Army of the Tennessee drives back part of the rebel Army of Tennessee at the battle of Resaca, May 14, 1864, at the start of the Atlanta campaign.

COMMANDS IN THE ATLANTA CAMPAIGN

MILITARY DIVISION OF THE MISSISSIPPI
Major General William T. Sherman (USMA 1840)

Army of the Cumberland
Major General George H. Thomas (USMA 1840)

4th Corps
Major General Oliver O. Howard (USMA 1854)

14th Corps
Major General John M. Palmer (lawyer, politician)

20th Corps
Major General Joseph Hooker (USMA 1837)

Cavalry Corps
Brigadier General Washington L. Elliott (USMA nongraduate; regular army)

Army of the Tennessee
Major General James B. McPherson (USMA 1853)

15th Corps
Major General John A. Logan (lawyer, politician)

16th Corps
Major General Grenville M. Dodge (railroad constructor)

17th Corps
Major General Frank P. Blair, Jr. (lawyer, politician)

Army of the Ohio (23rd Corps)
Major General John M. Schofield (USMA 1853)

ARMY OF TENNESSEE
General Joseph E. Johnston (USMA 1829)

Hardee's Corps
Lieutenant General William J. Hardee (USMA 1838)

Hood's Corps
Lieutenant General John B. Hood (USMA 1853)

Cavalry Corps
Major General Joseph Wheeler (USMA 1859)

Polk's Corps, Army of Mississippi
Lieutenant General Leonidas Polk (USMA 1827; clergyman)

Sherman's army required thousands of supply wagons during its operations in northern Georgia. Having to move these through the mountains during the summer rains greatly slowed Sherman's advance.

339

ABSOLUTE WAR, TOTAL WAR

Previous pages: Sherman's men halt to rest and refresh themselves at a farm in Georgia. The reason that so many lithographic prints exist of the Union armies and so few of the Confederate is that the South lacked real illustrated newspapers such as Leslie's *and* Harper's.

To isolate Hood's army in Atlanta, Sherman's troops (below) destroy the railroad between Rough and Ready and Jonesboro, south of the city.

right or eastward flank. Sherman received more troops to guard his communications back to Chattanooga, necessary because Forrest's cavalry was now active in northern Mississippi, soundly defeating a Union force at Brice's Cross Roads on June 10. Johnston's army meanwhile swelled to perhaps 67,000 fresh troops, enabling him to slow Sherman's eastward envelopment but during which Polk was killed. Heavy rains inhibited these operations, and Johnston entrenched at Kennesaw Mountain, where Sherman decided on a frontal assault instead of the usual tedious maneuvering. This was crushed on June 27, leading Sherman to turn Johnston's flank again and force him back to the Chattahooche River on the outskirts of Atlanta.

At the same time as Grant and Lee were settling into their siege lines at Petersburg and Early was moving on Washington, Johnston's 60,000-man army stood ready to hold Atlanta and Forrest threatened Grant's base at Memphis. But Sherman turned Johnston's flank yet again on July 9, forcing him back on Atlanta's Peach Tree Creek, and five days later Forrest's cavalry was beaten near Tupelo, Mississippi by an expedition under A.J. Smith. Johnston may not have been a Lee, but Jefferson Davis was no Grant as a strategist, for on July 17, tired over Johnston's steady but quite inevitable retreat, Davis relieved Johnston of command. His replacement was corps commander John B. Hood, known for his aggressiveness under Lee in Virginia, at Antietam and Gettysburg, and at Chickamauga, where he had suffered the loss of a leg. Davis wanted Hood to fight for Atlanta, and Hood gladly complied – with disastrous results.

As Thomas' and Schofield's armies moved directly on Atlanta and McPherson swung through Decatur from the east, Hood attacked Thomas in the battle of Peach Tree Creek on July 20 but was driven back inside the fortifications of Atlanta. Hood then sent Hardee and Wheeler's cavalry against McPherson's flank east of the city in the Battle of Atlanta two days later, only to be repulsed. Hood suffered some 8,000 casualties against

343

LEIUT. GEN. E. KIRBY SMITH.

LEIUT. GEN. W. J. HARDEE.

MAJ. GEN. J. B. HOOD.

GEN. BRAXTON BRAGG.

GEN. JOHN H. MORGAN.

MAJ. GEN. FORREST.

LEIUT. GEN. L. POLK.

half that for the Union, but McPherson was killed and replaced at the head of the Army of the Tennessee by Howard. (Hooker felt he deserved the post and quit in a huff, succeeded by Slocum.) Now besieged inside Atlanta from the north and east, Hood released Wheeler on a cavalry raid to cut Sherman's railroads, which Wheeler did between Atlanta, Chattanooga, Knoxville, and Nashville from August 10 to September 10. Forrest meanwhile raided Memphis. Sherman responded to these forays by trying to cut Hood's railroad at Jonesboro south of Atlanta. After three attempts by smaller forces failed, Sherman wheeled his three armies to the west and south of Atlanta. Hood attacked them on August 31 at Jonesboro and continued to engage next day while he evacuated Atlanta, no longer defensible. Sherman pursued Hood to Lovejoy but found him too well positioned to attack.

Sherman and Hood correctly reasoned that communications held the key to success – namely, that Sherman could not hold his long rail lines back to Chattanooga and Nashville if Hood and Forrest moved against them, which Sherman fully and quite rightly expected them to do. He therefore sent Thomas back to Nashville, with Schofield's Army of the Ohio to be Thomas' major fighting force, reinforced by other units concentrated there via river steamer and railroad. Sherman in the meantime decided to abandon Atlanta, cut his communications, and live off the fertile countryside in a drive into central Alabama, southern Georgia, or toward the coast around Savannah. While Sherman considered these options and prepared for

Facing page: Confederate generals of the Western theater in a montage commissioned at the end of the war by Edward A. Pollard, wartime editor of the Richmond Examiner, for a history of the war entitled The Lost Cause. *The engraver made their blouses much too dark for rebel gray, and misspelled "lieutenant" general, a rank also held by Nathan Bedford Forrest. Hood became a full general; Morgan, a major general.*

Visualized as picture-book soldiers by a Currier & Ives artist, Sherman's troops occupy the abandoned city of Atlanta on September 2, 1864.

his march, Hood swung west of Atlanta toward Tennessee, hoping to force Sherman to abandon the city. When one of Hood's divisions surrounded the supply base at Allatoona on October 5, Brigadier General John M. Corse successfully held the place until Sherman arrived. Sherman positioned his main force west of Rome, but still holding Atlanta, while Hood moved into northern Alabama to await the completion of Forrest's latest raid. Forrest's cavalry had penetrated into Tennessee as far as Fort Henry on the Kentucky line, capturing and destroying Union supply depots and river transports before joining Hood in mid-November. The Army of Tennessee, almost 40,000 strong, then crossed into that state en route to Nashville.

Sherman did not follow him. Returning to Atlanta, he evacuated the civilians, burned the city on November 15 to prevent its utilization by the enemy, and set out across Georgia toward the seacoast (portrayed in the book and 1939 film *Gone With the Wind*). His 62,000 men were arranged into Howard's Army of the Tennessee, the 15th and 17th Corps of the right wing, and Slocum's new Army of Georgia, the 14th and 20th Corps of the left, plus Kilpatrick's cavalry division. The only opposition was Wheeler's cavalry and some militia, no more than 13,000 in all, which could only skirmish along the way. By living off the land without a fixed supply line, Sherman's troops shattered military convention, the only recent precedent being during Grant's operations against Vicksburg. What they and their horses did not consume, they destroyed, both to eliminate the Georgia breadbasket and to shatter the will of the people in this most dramatic demonstration of total war. Sherman's March to the Sea also cut the east-west railroads, thus isolating the southeastern Confederacy. Georgia "howled," which Sherman had

Atlanta burns as Sherman renders it useless to the enemy and his armies strike out for the sea, November 15, 1864.

Sherman's men destroy the railroad tracks at Atlanta during their occupation of the city in September and October 1864, thereby ending its role as a Confederate railhead.

ABSOLUTE WAR, TOTAL WAR

Sherman insured that central Georgia could no longer sustain the Confederacy by destroying its railroad tracks (right) as he went. Cross-ties were piled into bonfires, then sections of track were laid over them, softened, and finally twisted around tree trunks.

BATTLE OF ALLATOONA

by **J. J. Whitney**, M.D., Assistant Surgeon, 18th Wisconsin Infantry   October 5, 1864

Soon the cannonading ceased, and an officer from [Major] General [S. G.] French came under a flag of truce. ... After saluting [General Corse, the officer] handed him a letter ...,which read about as follows: "General: I now have you surrounded. My force [7,000 men] is far superior to yours [1,900 men]. To prevent the unnecessary effusion of blood I summon you to surrender immediately." General Corse coolly and firmly said: "Say to General French that I will not surrender, and that he can begin the unnecessary effusion of blood whenever he pleases." The aide returned, and within ten minutes the gray columns were seen marching up and over the hills by the left flank. ...

The enemy...charged on thin lines and carried our outposts by the weight and momentum of numbers.... Corse was everywhere – walking around outside and on top of the parapets – going through the embrasures – everywhere speaking words of assurance and plucky defiance. "It is hot, boys, but remember Vicksburg! We shall not surrender!" The writer was near the general when ... a ball struck him and he fell backward bleeding.... A surgeon gave him a little stimulant and a handkerchief was placed around his torn temple and ear, and he rallied from the swoon and arose to his feet. ...

Not many minutes elapsed before the enemy were seen rallying for a grand charge on our interior defenses and the fort itself. General Sherman was on Lookout Mountain, away northward 15 miles. Signal flags were continually waving, up and down, to the right and left, carrying the burning words of Sherman, "Hold on! Hold the fort! Never give up!" The other returning: "We never will– we cannot surrender. I am short an ear and part of a cheek bone, but all b—l can't whip us."

... The general placed [magazine loaded, 15-shot] Henry [repeating] rifles in the trenches and under the parapets. ... In a bayonet charge, ... hand-to-hand they fought, and the enemy encountered the Henry rifles. Down the embankment they fell. ... [Soon] the battle was won. And now came the sad work of the surgeons. We were but few in number, but our labor was fearfully great. Two humane Confederate surgeons were left with us, and together side by side for six days and nights we labored. ...

Sherman's "Left Wing," comprising the 14th and 20th Corps, leaves the burning city on November 15, 1864, passing two of "Sherman's sentinels," the chimneys of once-grand mansions. The men of the Left called themselves the Army of Georgia, a name that was later officially adopted. Its commander, Major General Henry W. Slocum, had been Sherman's roommate at West Point.

SHERMAN'S BUMMERS

by **F. Y. Hedley**, Lieutenant and Adjutant, 32nd   Illinois   Infantry   November-December 1864

[Central Georgia] was a section of country which the war had not disturbed until this moment. It was literally a land overflowing with milk and honey, and well was it for the army that such was the case. ... The emergency produced the forager, commonly known as "the Bummer." He was not a development, he was a creation. ... [In addition to] regular foraging parties ..., every regiment in the army sent out an independent foraging party, whose duty it was to see that its particular command was furnished with all the delicacies the country afforded. These men were the most adventuresome in the army, and in their keen competition to outdo each other, ... they took great risks. ...

When the Bummer left the column on his first day's excursion, he either went on foot, having just quitted the ranks, or bareback on some broken-down horse or mule which had been turned out from the wagon [ammunition] train utterly exhausted. At the first farm house he came to, he looked about for a fresh mount. If it was to be had, he helped himself; if not, ...

nine times out of ten some darkey belonging to the place would pilot him to where the stock was hidden in the woods or swamp. Then he would search the place for provisions and soon have his animal, and perhaps two or three others, loaded down with poultry, meats, meal, sweet potatoes, honey, sorghum, and frequently a jug of apple-jack; or he would find a wagon and load it, with the aid of a few negroes, and hitch together mules and horses indiscriminantly. ...

If the negroes on the place told stories of great cruelty they had suffered, or of bitter hostility to the Union, or if there were bloodhounds about which had been used to run down slaves, the injury was generally avenged by the torch. Where the Bummer found women and children, he was usually as courteous as circumstances admitted. ...,a wily diplomat [who]. . .learned all that was to be known of the neighbors farther down the road, whom he expected to "raid" the next day. ... Information under this head was usually yielded more willingly than upon any other subject; for it is a curious trait of human nature that a man (or woman) who has been robbed, or swindled in a trade, takes a keen enjoyment, perhaps disguised, in seeing his fellows made fully as miserable as himself.

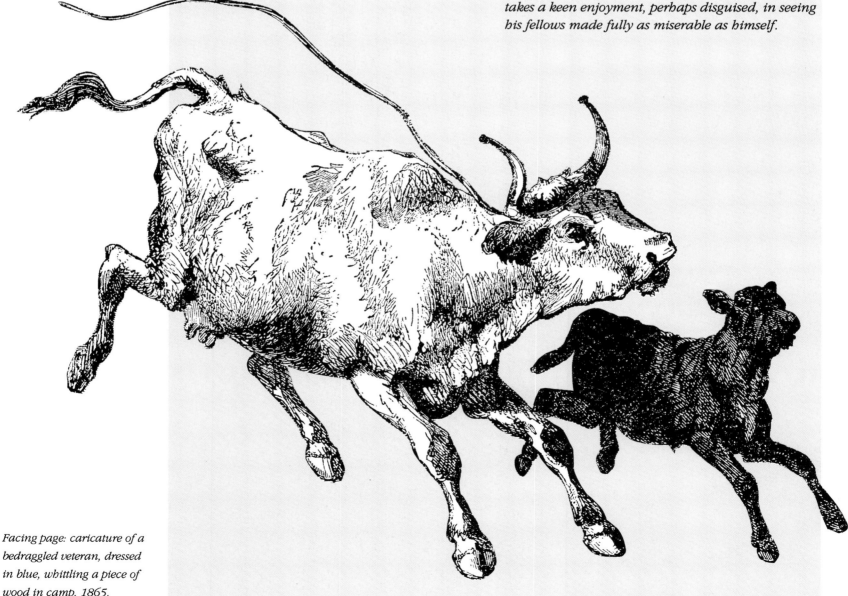

Facing page: caricature of a bedraggled veteran, dressed in blue, whittling a piece of wood in camp, 1865.

ABSOLUTE WAR, TOTAL WAR

The sheet music for "Marching Through Georgia" was illustrated by this scene of charging Union cavalry. The only real fighting during the March to the Sea took place when rebel cavalry, under Major General "Fighting Joe" Wheeler, skirmished along Sherman's flanks; the Southerners were always outnumbered and outfought.

Previous pages: two brigades of Negro troops assault Overton Hill, the final Confederate defensive right flank position, on December 16, 1864, only to be driven back with heavy losses. The 13th U.S. Colored Infantry suffered 221 casualties, the highest for any regiment at Nashville. Thomas' simultaneous attack on the left, however, crushed Hood's army.

predicted, as he cut his swath 60 miles wide and 300 miles across the state. Needless to say, freebooting foragers often exceeded their instructions to punish the people and the land, not uncommon in any war, although very few of the victims were physically abused. Reaching Savannah on December 10, Sherman used one division to attack and capture Fort McAllister on the 13th, whereupon the rebels evacuated the city a week later. Sherman reestablished his supply line with Admiral Dahlgren's fleet.

Hood, meanwhile, pressed deep into Tennessee, forcing Schofield's 32,000-man army back into the town of Franklin, where Hood launched a frontal attack on November 30. Though outnumbering Schofield, Hood's charge cost him over 6,000 casualties, thrice those of Schofield, who then pulled back toward Nashville. Hood took up position south of that city, his 25,000 troops too few in number for making an assault on Thomas' fortifications and army twice the size of his own. But neither did Thomas attack. The "Rock of Chickamauga" waited until Wilson's cavalry obtained sufficient mounts, time during which Forrest successfully

raided Yankee outposts around Murfreesboro. Grant grew so impatient that he was about to relieve Thomas, when the latter executed his attack on December 15. Utilizing tactics of concentration, he feinted with one division on the rebel right to distract Hood while wheeling around Hood's left with his main force. Hood fell back to higher ground, but next day Thomas' army enveloped the left flank and fell on Hood's line of retreat – the most perfect example of Napoleonic tactics during the entire war. The number of killed and wounded on both sides was slight, but Thomas captured 4,500 men and left the rest of Hood's obliterated army to straggle back to Mississippi, no longer an effective fighting force and cut off from the eastern Confederacy.

By Christmas of 1864, all that remained under major Confederate control east of the Mississippi was Lee's army, besieged at Petersburg, and the Carolinas, with their closely-blockaded ports of Wilmington and Charleston. What was more, the people of the North had handily re-elected "Honest Abe" in November against the peace party nominee, General McClellan. The Confederacy was on its knees – down, but still not out.

354

Iowa, Minnesota, and Minnesota, and Missouri troops of Scottish immigrant Brigadier General John McArthur's division attack and envelop Hood's left flank at Nashville, December 15, 1864.

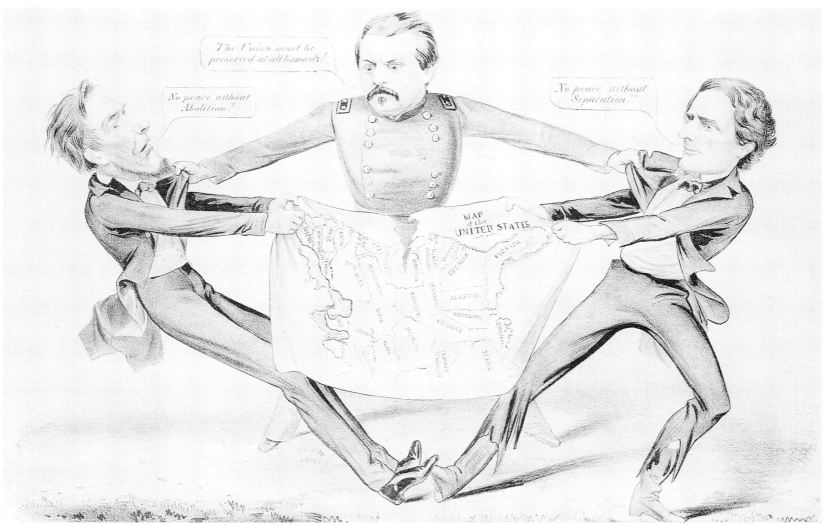

Democratic Presidential candidate McClellan is caricatured by Currier & Ives trying to make peace between Lincoln and Davis. "The True Issue, or that's what the matter," ran the caption. Lincoln's Republicans, calling themselves the National Union Party, soundly defeated the still-popular general.

10

ABSOLUTE TRIUMPH

Petersburg, the Carolinas,
Appomattox – 1864-65

ABSOLUTE TRIUMPH

The willpower of the Southern people to resist the Union invasion held the key to the survival of the Confederacy. To shatter the credibility of that government in the eyes of its populace, Sherman's armies had ravaged Georgia with impunity, as had Sheridan's in the Shenandoah, along with Grant's murderous attacks in the Wilderness of Virginia. Internally, however, the political hold of the Jefferson Davis regime contributed to the psychological demise of Southern resolve. Consistently undermined by but often accommodating fire-eater critics like Senator Louis T. Wigfall, who demanded absolute and arbitrary rule by the planter aristocracy, Davis virtually ignored the Confederate Congress and ran the war effort under one-man rule. He imposed harsh edicts and sponsored tough laws, particularly over conscription, and seemed to be oblivious to the suffering of his people. Mounting quarrels among politicians discredited Davis' government so much that one of Lee's division commanders in the last days of the war remarked to Lee that, ever since Gettysburg, the men in the army had been fighting mostly out of loyalty to Lee. And as the women left behind were increasingly victimized by government agents and remained threatened by

starvation, they convinced their menfolk to leave the army and come home. Without the manpower, the armies could not fight. As the morale of the armies and the people collapsed, the Confederacy was doomed.

Neither could the C.S.A. combat the moral superiority of the Union's crusading ideals of democratic government and universal freedom. States' rights and slavery had no future in a world shifting toward both liberal principles and centralized, industrial nations. Thus an attempted peace settlement at Hampton Roads between President Lincoln and Secretary of State Seward for the Union and Vice President Alexander H.

Stephens and two other Confederate political leaders on February 3, 1865 failed when the latter insisted on independence and the perpetuation of slavery. Needing manpower, however, the South finally accepted the idea of mobilizing its blacks; that same month its Congress passed a labor troop bill to arm 40,000 slaves for support duties. No concession was provided for giving such draftees their freedom, although General Lee advocated eventual emancipation for all the slaves. By abandoning one major premise for its very existence, however, the Confederacy's war aims became completely hollow – and the sacrifices of its people

The Northern arms industry continued to develop ever more powerful weapons; the largest gun was this 20-inch smoothbore designed by T.J. Rodman and built at Fort Pitt, Pittsburgh, in 1864. The 117,000-pound cannon, mounted at Fort Hamilton, was never fired in anger.

meaningless. The ruling aristocracy desperately flailed about, trying to survive intact, while the disillusioned and hard-pressed yeoman farmers who manned the armies deserted in increasing numbers. By the beginning of 1865 absolute Union victory was only a matter of time.

Inasmuch as the army had become the raison d'être of the dying nation, and because Jefferson Davis had failed as a military strategist and manager, he yielded to the obvious necessity of appointing General Robert E. Lee to be General-in-Chief of all the Confederate armies on February 9, 1865 – much too late to affect the outcome of the war. Lee remained in

the field with the Army of Northern Virginia. One of Lee's first acts, two weeks later, was to reappoint Joe Johnston to command of the shattered Army of Tennessee. Although neither Confederate army had sufficient manpower, they did not lack for equipment, arms, or foodstuffs. Beef, bacon, guns, ammunition, shoes, and uniform cloth had been run through the blockade with such regularity that both armies were easily reequipped at the beginning of the year, while Lee's army had a large enough stockpile of supplies in Virginia and North Carolina to last at least through April. As long as Wilmington and Charleston held out,

In 1865, the central signal station atop the Winder Building in Washington enabled the high command to transmit messages both to local defensive forces and to army and navy forces beyond the capital.

and the rail connections between them and Petersburg remained intact, Lee's and Johnston's men could continue the fight.

For the Union, and supreme commander Grant, the strategy for 1865 was clear. The Navy's economic blockade had been a failure. Whatever its indirect effect by keeping up pressure on Southern resources, it had not stopped the blockade runners from supplying the Southern armies with most of the necessary military goods. Neither had it eliminated rebel high seas naval operations; as late as the autumn of 1864 two Confederate raiders ran out of Wilmington and sank

Yankee merchant shipping off Long Island Sound and the Delaware Capes. And in January 1865 the cruiser *Shenandoah* reached Melbourne, Australia to begin operations against Union whaling ships in the Pacific, while the new ironclad ram *Stonewall* left Europe to attack the blockading fleet. Over 1,000 of the 1,300 attempts by merchant sail-steamers to run the blockade in both directions succeeded during the course of the war. To be sure, 221 of the vessels were captured or destroyed, but some four-fifths of the supplies coming in made it, and 400,000 bales of cotton were run out. The U.S. Navy had captured New Orleans in 1862 and

A 100-pound Parrott rifled gun protects the northern outskirts of Washington at Fort Totten in 1865, by which time such defenses had become unnecessary.

Union army transports, embarking the 24th and 25th Corps, sail out from the Chesapeake Bay into wintry Atlantic seas early in January 1865 en route to assault Fort Fisher, which guarded the approaches to Wilmington, N.C. Drawing by Waud.

361

ABSOLUTE TRIUMPH

The 26th U.S. Colored Infantry, complete with white gloves, musters on parade at Camp William Penn in Philadelphia in 1865. This regiment had suffered heavy losses at Honey Hill, South Carolina, the previous November, while trying to assist Sherman's approach to Savannah.

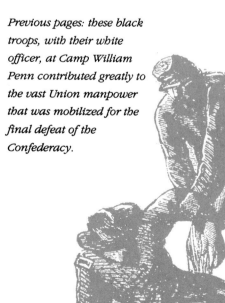

Previous pages: these black troops, with their white officer, at Camp William Penn contributed greatly to the vast Union manpower that was mobilized for the final defeat of the Confederacy.

Above: under cover of a naval barrage, Major General Alfred H. Terry's amphibious troops assault Fort Fisher, January 15, 1865. Spearheading the attack is a brigade comprising four New York regiments under Colonel N. Martin Curtis, who received four wounds and lost an eye in the hand-to-hand combat.

in combined operations with the army had seized the forts guarding the approaches to Savannah in 1862 and Mobile in 1864, thereby neutralizing both ports. Direct military-naval action therefore appeared to be the only recourse to closing Wilmington and Charleston as well, thus starving Lee's and Johnston's armies into submission.

The Union strategy for 1865 was consequently threefold. First, the strategy of concentration would continue, Grant holding down Lee's army before Petersburg and Richmond while Sherman relentlessly pushed back Johnston's army in the Western theater. Second, Sherman would drive north from Savannah into South and North Carolina, plundering the countryside of supplies as he had in Georgia, cutting the rail lines to Lee, and capturing Charleston. Sherman might even continue on to link up with Grant and between them destroy Lee's army. Third, an army-navy amphibious assault would seize the approaches to Wilmington, capture that port, and link up with Sherman. Concurrently, cavalry raids would mop up the bypassed foodproducing regions, especially in Alabama, where coastal forces would take the city of Mobile, afterwhich

the Trans-Mississippi region could be overrun.

The Union held the upper hand in all respects. Its moral crusade had excited the peoples of the North and the world, and no fewer than 300,000 blacks had enlisted in 166 "colored" regiments to add to the virtually unlimited supplies of Yankee manpower. Many black troops had already seen heavy action – and butchery at the hands of Southern troops who hated all that they represented. In December 1864 the white and black troops of the 10th and 18th Corps were separated into a new all-white 24th Corps and all-black (with white officers) 25th Corps. To move the many troops between theaters, absolute control of the continent's rivers and coastal waters augmented the ubiquitous railroads. General Thomas' victorious army at Nashville was released to apply pressure on the other theaters. The 4th Corps moved to eastern Tennessee to head off any attempt by Lee or Johnston to escape thence, while Stoneman in December led a cavalry raid which cleared that region of rebel forces and destroyed supplies in southwestern Virginia. The next month Schofield's 23rd Corps left Nashville by river steamer

The assault on Fort Fisher included U.S. Navy bluejackets and U.S. Marines, who all suffered heavy casualties.

365

SOLDIER SONGS ON THE MARCH

By adopting their own lyrics to a traditional tune or accepting some of the professionally composed songs as their own, the men of the blue and the gray buoyed their spirits with music on the march. A no more sad lot existed than Hood's broken Army of Tennessee retreating from Nashville during December 1864 and January 1865 in search of "Uncle Joe" Johnston to lead them again. To the popular melody "Yellow Rose of Texas," they fashioned these words:

And now I'm going Southward,
For my heart is full of woe,
I'm going back to Georgia
To find my "Uncle Joe."
You may sing about your dearest maid,
And sing of Rosalie,
But the gallant Hood of Texas
Played hell in Tennessee

The prolific Yankee songwriter Henry Clay Work captured the mood of triumph from Sherman's March to the Sea in his 1865 tune, adopted by the Bummers and the Northern public alike, "Marching Through Georgia." The fifth and final verse, plus chorus, were:

So we made a thoroughfare for Freedom and her train,
Sixty miles in latitude – three hundred to the main;
Treason fled before us, for resistance was in vain,
While we were marching through Georgia.
"Hurrah! Hurrah! we bring the Jubilee!
Hurrah! Hurrah! the flag that makes you free!"
So we sang the chorus from Atlanta to the sea,
While we were marching through Georgia.

The best thought of all was the final march home, vividly portrayed in 1863 by the bandmaster of the 24th Massachusetts Infantry, Patrick Sarsfield Gilmore, and probably adapted from an old folk tune of his native Ireland, as "When Johnny Comes Marching Home":

When Johnny comes marching home again,
Hurrah, hurrah!
We'll give him a hearty welcome then,
Hurrah, hurrah!
The men will cheer, the boys will shout.
The ladies, they will all turn out,
And we'll all feel gay,
When Johnny comes marching home.

The interior of the large Battery Buchanan at Fort Fisher. Defended solely by North Carolina artillery and a naval detachment, Fort Fisher withstood Butler's inept attack in December but was no match for the combined Terry-Porter arms in the January battle.

Yankee merchant schooners lie at anchor on the James River during the nine-month-long siege of Petersburg and Richmond, awaiting their turn to unload supplies at City Point, Grant's base of operations. Smaller craft have been converted into hulks, in which cargo could be stored until transferred onto these Army supply wagons.

A contemporary painting portrays the ruined Fort Fisher after its capture, which cut off the last overseas supply source for Lee's army. Union casualties numbered nearly 1,000, half those of the rebel defenders.

ABSOLUTE
TRIUMPH

Union bombproof bunkers provided protection both for the troops and for the well from which they drew fresh water.

In the Yankee siege lines, a company kitchen made of logs and mud. By the autumn of 1864, black soldiers were becoming a common fixture of the armies of the Potomac and the James.

18th Corps sharpshooters aim through tiny tunnels, which allows them to pick off the defenders of Petersburg without exposing themselves to enemy fire. 1864 sketch by Waud.

up the Ohio to Cincinnati, then went by rail to Washington to reinforce Grant. From there, however, it was diverted by steamer to the North Carolina coast to set up a base of operations for Sherman's approaching army.

To seal off Wilmington, Grant assigned General Ben Butler's Army of the James – the new 24th and 25th Corps – to move by sea and with Admiral Porter's fleet to assault and capture Fort Fisher at the entrance of the Cape Fear River below Wilmington. When Lee learned of the move, he rushed a division of 6,000 men by rail to Wilmington to reinforce the big fort. Butler's assault by his force of nearly equal size on Christmas Eve and Day 1864 bore little fruit, however, and the expeditionary

force withdrew. This gave Grant cause to sack the incompetent Butler and replace him with Major General Alfred H. Terry of the 24th Corps for another attempt. Porter began his bombardment of Fort Fisher at midnight of January 12, 1865 with the largest Union fleet of the war – five ironclads and 48 other ships mounting 627 naval guns. Under cover of the devastating barrage, during which two shells hit per second, Terry's 8,000 troops came ashore, joined by a makeshift naval brigade of 2,300 sailors and U.S. Marines. Although this unit suffered heavy losses during the main assault on the 15th, the 1,500-man garrison surrendered after hand-to-hand fighting. The division from Lee's army never came up to support the defenders, the final miscue by General Braxton Bragg in his new job as a departmental commander. Schofield now arrived by sea with the 23rd Corps and began the advance up the Cape Fear River against Wilmington. The port was sealed off, leaving only Charleston to supply goods from overseas.

Sherman now undertook the Carolinas campaign. After a division of the 19th Corps arrived by sea from the Army of the Shenandoah to hold Savannah, he divided his forces of 60,000 men to confuse the enemy about his intentions. In late January, the Navy sealifted Howard's Army of the Tennessee – the 15th and 17th Corps – to the Port Royal blockading base to give the impression that Sherman would advance on Charleston. On February 1 Slocum's Army of Georgia – the 14th and 20th Corps – crossed the Savannah River into South Carolina, suggesting an upriver advance on Augusta, Georgia. Meanwhile, the remnant of the Army of Tennessee under Beauregard was rushed overland mostly by rail from Tupelo, Mississippi, via Mobile, Macon, and the devastated Georgia countryside to

Augusta, where its two-week odyssey ended on January 31. Beauregard, with only 22,500 troops, contemplated defending either Augusta or Charleston, whereupon Sherman fooled him by driving straight up the middle toward Columbia, South Carolina, cutting the Augusta and Charleston railroad on February 7. Outflanked, Beauregard evacuated Charleston and Augusta and fell back toward North Carolina. On the 17th Sherman's two armies occupied Columbia, which however was devastated by a fire, and the next day Charleston was occupied by Union naval and landing forces. Lee's supply lines were now cut.

The inexorable advance of Sherman's forces through muddy, rain-soaked South Carolina forced the tiny reconstituted Army of Tennessee to abandon Cheraw, South Carolina, in favor of Fayetteville, North Carolina. Commanded by Johnston, with Beauregard second-in-command, this army found a third Union force threatening its eastward flank. Schofield's 30,000 men, the reorganized Army of the Ohio of the 10th and 23rd Corps, occupied Wilmington on February 22 and

SHERMAN AND THE NAVY

To coordinate his Carolina campaign, General Sherman held discussions with Rear Admiral John A.B. Dahlgren, whose South Atlantic Blockading Squadron would support his armies. Attending the meeting was the captain of the gunboat *Pontiac*, Lieutenant Commander Stephen B. Luce. What Luce heard changed his life and the Navy forever:

General Sherman indicated in a few short pithy sentences and by the aid of a map his plan of campaign. … "When I get on solid ground," he said (for much of that part of the country was inundated), "somebody will have to get out of the way. … You navy fellows have been hammering away at Charleston for the past three years. But just wait until I get into South Carolina; I will cut her communications and Charleston will fall into your hands like a ripe pear."…

After hearing General Sherman's clear exposition

… the scales seem to have fallen from my eyes. … It dawned upon me that there were certain fundamental principles underlying military operations which it were well to look into.… There was then I learned such a thing as a military problem, and there was a way of solving it; or what was equally important, a way of determining whether or not it was susceptible of solution.… In other words, the Civil War demonstrates conclusively the necessity of a War College and general staff.

(That it did. As rear admiral, Luce founded the U.S. Naval War College in 1884 and brought in Captain Alfred Thayer Mahan to initiate systematic strategic thinking and planning in the Navy. Though the Army's Sherman had provided the spark, the Navy continued to dominate American strategic thought until World War II.)

Shovels (left) replace rifles to dig the siege lines before Petersburg. The coal miners of Lieutenant Colonel Henry Pleasant's 48th Pennsylvania Infantry dug a mine under a rebel battery. They detonated 8,000 pounds of black powder in the mine before dawn, July 30, 1864, but Burnside's follow-up assault was repulsed with heavy losses.

The Union signal tower (above) at Point of Rocks, Virginia, watches over an area from the Appomattox River as far as Grant's base at City Point, five miles to the east on the James River, during the siege of Petersburg.

ABSOLUTE TRIUMPH

Two hand-pulled portable steam engines adorn this well-constructed wharf at City Point, early in 1865. The wheel atop the front could be fitted to a winch for unloading cargo from the barges in the water. Such machine power was just one example of the Civil War as the first modern industrialized, technological war.

THE BURNING OF COLUMBIA

February 17, 1865

by **Ira B. Sampson**, Captain, 2nd Massachusetts Heavy Artillery. (A prisoner of war, Sampson was moved with 1,500 other Union officers from Savannah to Charleston and finally Columbia, as rebel forces withdrew before Sherman's advance. He escaped on February 14, 1865, was given succor by an old Negro couple, and awaited the approach of Sherman's army.)

The morning of the 17th of February opened with the hasty evacuation and attempt to burn the city of Columbia ...; [and] a body of Wheeler's rebel cavalry ... [fired] several buildings, including the railroad depot and warehouses, filled with grain and other stores, and then passed across the fields on the outskirts of the city and disappeared. There was no chance of a mistake as to who they were or what their intention was in firing the buildings. ... A little before noon ... I jumped from [my hiding place] and was presented to an officer of one of Iowa's brave regiments. With one bound I was in his arms, [overjoyed]. ...

The streets were lined with broken bales of cotton, and from the amount consumed there was no escape

from the conclusion that it must have been fired some time previous to the coming of the Union forces by the rebels before their retreat. It was so stated to me by a number of citizens. The fire from the first had been urged on by a high wind, but during the excitement attending the evacuation of the enemy and occupation by the Union army, little attention had been paid to the progress of the flames.

It soon became evident that it would require energetic work to stop the conflagration. The Iowa brigade aided by others battled bravely against its advance, but the strong wind carried the burning brands far and wide with destructive effect. It was plain that the fire was beyond control, and but for the presence of an army of disciplined men there could hardly have been a building left to mark its former site. I never worked harder than that night in saving life and property, and it was in sight of the hated stockade where but a few hours previous I had been confined as an outlaw. When the morning of the 18th dawned the fire was stayed. ...

This somewhat whimsical rendering of Grant's troops besieging Petersburg and Richmond shows some Yankees enjoying their pipes and playing cards while drawing rebel fire. Both sides developed an unwritten rule to cease firing whenever a man announced he had to relieve himself in an exposed area!

Confederate sabotage apparently caused this detonation of the Union ammunition depot (left) at City Point, August 11, 1864, inflicting considerable damage.

pushed up the coast to turn the blockading station of New Bern into the new operating base for Sherman. Bragg's one available division failed to arrest this movement in a series of skirmishes in early March and withdrew to join Johnston, now headquartered at Raleigh. Sherman passed through Fayetteville, his army moving in three separate columns.

After Hardee's Corps was repulsed by Slocum's Army of Georgia at Averasboro on March 16, Johnston threw most of his 21,000-man army against Slocum at Bentonville three days later. Slocum's troops held their ground, however, and on the 21st Sherman used Howard's Army of the Tennessee to join Slocum in driving Johnston back. Schofield's Army of the Ohio joined Sherman next day, and they occupied Goldsboro on the 23rd – 80,000 strong and well-supplied from the sea. At the same time, Stoneman mounted a raid with 4,000 cavalry from East Tennessee into southwestern Virginia and western North Carolina, tearing up railroads before reaching Hendersonville in mid-April. Sherman paused to consult with Grant.

Grant's siege of Petersburg and Richmond had deprived Lee of making any significant counterthrusts after the destruction of Early's corps in the Shenandoah during the autumn of 1864. By the beginning of the year Lee's army numbered slightly over 50,000 men, organized into the four infantry corps of Longstreet, John B. Gordon, Hill, and Anderson, as well as Fitzhugh Lee's cavalry (Wade Hampton had been transferred to command of Johnston's cavalry). Lee also had the twelve-vessel James River Squadron of Flag Officer John K. Mitchell, which tried to break through the Union gunboats on the James with three ironclads late in January only to have two run aground in the low water, spoiling the attempt. Mitchell was replaced by Rear Admiral Raphael Semmes, recent skipper of the celebrated cruiser *Alabama*. Grant besieged Lee with over 100,000 men in Meade's Army of the Potomac (2nd, 5th, 6th, and 9th Corps) and Major General Edward O.C. Ord's Army of the James (24th and 25th Corps). Sheridan's 10,000-man Army of the Shenandoah (three divisions of cavalry) initiated a raid throughout Virginia at the end of February, destroying the remnant of Early's command at Waynesboro in the Shenandoah on March 2 and railroad track to the southeast, rejoining Grant before Petersburg on the 28th.

In a final effort to reach City Point and relieve the pressure on Petersburg, Major General John B. Gordon leads an assault against Fort Stedman near the eastern end of Grant's lines, March 25, 1865. The Southerners succeeded in taking the fort but were driven out by Meade's counterattack. Axes are used to clear paths.

Rebel infantry positioned behind felled trees take pot shots at Sherman's forces as they cross a swamp on the march into South Carolina in early February 1865.

Southern troops marveled at the speedy efficiency of Yankee engineers in overcoming such watery obstacles.

Previous pages: Union forces enter Richmond on April 3, 1865, cheered by a few Union sympathizers and slaves, and watched ruefully by others. It had taken nearly four years of fighting to capture the seat of the rebel government.

Richmond burns (above) as government officials, citizens, and troops flee south across the James River on the night of April 2, 1865. Ironclads of Admiral Semmes' James River Squadron were also put to the torch.

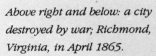

Above right and below: a city destroyed by war; Richmond, Virginia, in April 1865.

ABSOLUTE TRIUMPH

After the capture of Richmond, a disabled locomotive serves as a photographic prop for Federal soldiers.

Both Grant and Lee could see only one possible strategy for the South: Lee uniting with Johnston in North Carolina for joint operations against the Union armies. Desertions daily depleted Lee's lines, seriously weakening his strength, while his supplies dwindled. A futile frontal assault on Fort Stedman on March 25 only resulted in more losses. If Lee could swing west around Grant's left flank, the life of the Army of Northern Virginia might be prolonged. While Lee prepared for the maneuver, Grant struck first, anticipating it. On March 29, the day after Sheridan returned from his raid, Grant sent Sheridan's cavalry and the 2nd and 5th Corps against Lee's right flank to the west, hoping to force Lee to abandon Petersburg. Lee rushed Pickett's division to Five Forks to protect the Southside railroad, essential for his rejoining Johnston

in North Carolina. After clashing on the 31st, the two forces met in the pitched Battle of Five Forks on April 1. Sheridan managed to exploit Pickett's separation from the rest of Lee's army to crush Pickett and capture over 5,000 men, half of Pickett's division.

Grant, realizing that Lee could no longer hold Petersburg, launched a full-scale attack all along Lee's defenses early on April 2 – more than 60,000 troops which broke through at several points, driving back some 19,000 rebels. A.P. Hill was killed trying to hold his sector, and fellow corps commanders Longstreet and Gordon covered the evacuation of Petersburg during the night. As Davis and the government fled Richmond, the torch was put to ammunition magazines, bridges, and warships of the James River Squadron; the explosions started fires around the two already battered

The ruins of Richmond, resembling an old movie set, in April 1865.

Overleaf: the remains of a Confederate supply train intercepted at Appomattox Station during the final retreat.

DESERTIONS FROM LEE'S ARMY

by **Joel Zener**, Private, 20th Indiana Infantry (Letter to brother)

Hd Qrs 3rd Div. 2nd A.C.
February 24th/65
Gen Sherman seems very successful. Charleston and Columbia follow Savannah, and to day Grant sends an official report that Wilmington is also ours. bully for Sherman.

Reports are quite current to day that Petersburg is being evacuated but whether there is any truth in the rumor I cannot say. deserters from the rebel army come in every night. the number to our div[ision] alone of late will average some 5 are a night, 5 came last night[,] 12 night before, &c. The soldiers bring their guns and equipment, generly and the cavalry men their horses. Government pays them for such as is serviceable. At City Point Somewhere between 50 and 100 arrive daily. Our prospects certainly look better now than ever before.

We have been expecting to be attackted by old Lee here upon the extreme left for the last few days. deserters have reported such to be his intention. The troops have been & are now under orders to be ready to move at a moments notice. ... (By the time this letter was written, at least 100,000 deserters had recently left the Confederate armies, just as a similar number had after Gettysburg and Vicksburg. The overall rate of desertion in the Confederate army throughout the war was one in eight, for the Union one in ten.)

ABSOLUTE TRIUMPH

General Lee, attended by his aide Colonel Charles Marshall (standing), surrenders to Grant at Appomattox Court House, April 9, 1865. Seated behind Grant are clean-shaven Major General Wesley Merritt, the Cavalry Corps commander, and Grant's military secretary, Lieutenant Colonel Ely S. Parker, a Seneca Indian. Brigadier General George A. Custer stands at far right with staff officers.

The earthenware inkwell and pen used by Lee to sign the instrument of surrender. Although general in chief of all the Confederate armies since February 1865, Lee chose to surrender only the Army of Northern Virginia.

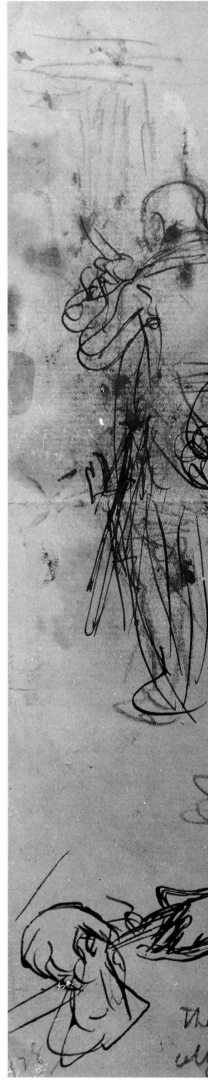

cities. A squad of 40 Union cavalrymen of Major General Godfrey Weitzel's 25th Corps headquarters escort occupied the abandoned rebel capital before dawn of the 3rd, the government having fled westward endeavoring to reach North Carolina, as was Lee's army. With Richmond and Petersburg gone, Virginia was lost. Lee no longer had a base of operations and thus no lines of communication over which supplies and ammunition could pass. The end was in sight; escaping to join Johnston would only postpone the inevitable.

The two armies marched and rode on parallel courses westward, with minor clashes of cavalry along the way. Sheridan's horse raced in the van of Grant's huge 113,000-man army, endeavoring to block Lee's 40,000 or so veterans from reaching the Danville and Richmond railroad, along which it might escape southward. But Sheridan got there first, moving along the Appomattox River to Jetersville on April 5, leaving one last possible escape route to the southwest. Before Lee could do anything, however, Grant attacked the marching army near Saylor's Creek next day and succeeded in isolating and swallowing up a major chunk of Lee's army, taking over 7,000 prisoners.

A rough sketch by Thomas Nast of a dejected Lee, who had just uttered his memorable explanation for capitulating: "Peace – the sole object of all."

385

ABSOLUTE TRIUMPH

The parole signed by General Lee and his staff officers.

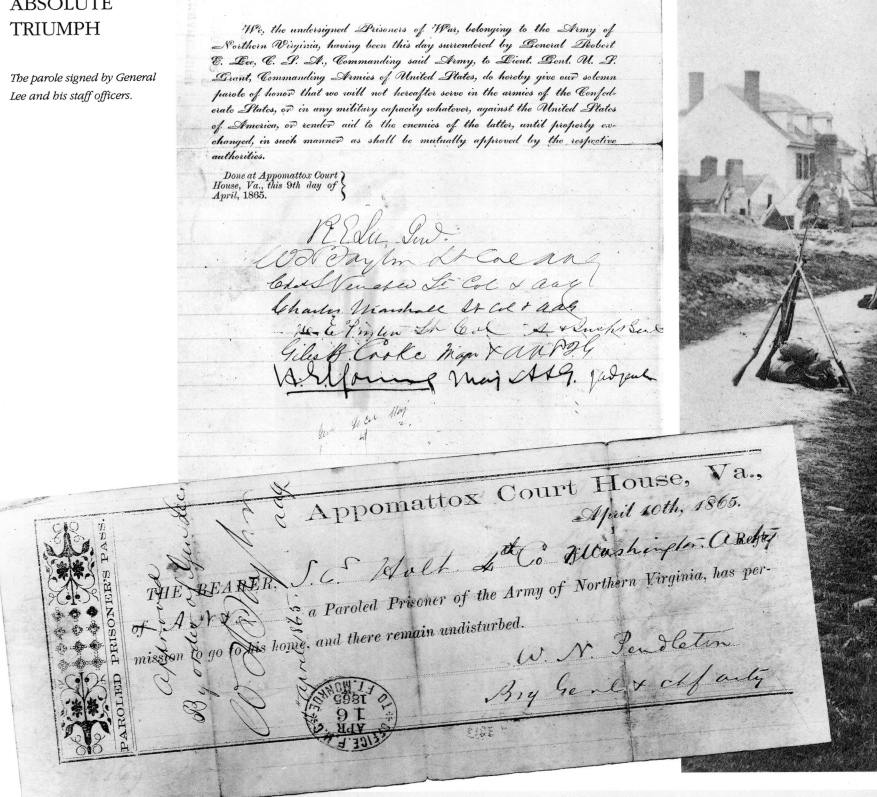

We, the undersigned Prisoners of War, belonging to the Army of Northern Virginia, having been this day surrendered by General Robert E. Lee, C. S. A., Commanding said Army, to Lieut. Genl. U. S. Grant, Commanding Armies of United States, do hereby give our solemn parole of honor that we will not hereafter serve in the armies of the Confederate States, or in any military capacity whatever, against the United States of America, or render aid to the enemies of the latter, until properly exchanged, in such manner as shall be mutually approved by the respective authorities.

Done at Appomattox Court House, Va., this 9th day of April, 1865.

Hastily printed passes enabled the surrendered troops of the Army of Northern Virginia, such as this veteran of New Orleans' elite Washington Artillery, to return home unmolested by other Confederate forces still in the field. The signatories are two of Lee's staff officers.

THE BATTLE OF SAYLOR'S CREEK

by **Archibald Hopkins**, Colonel, 37th Massachusetts Infantry   April 6, 1865

As we rose the crest, a crashing volley from an invisible enemy tore through the pines over our heads. The misdirected aim was most fortunate for us. Before the enemy could reload we were close upon them. At the word every man poured in seven shots from his Spencer [repeating carbine], at easy speaking distance and with deadly effect. . . [giving] us the advantage, and the enemy, broken into confused groups, were driven back into the ravine in a huddled mass. We gathered at its mouth and gave them such a terrible raking fire that they soon began to show white handkerchiefs in token of surrender, and our firing ceased. . . .

A corporal, who was noted for his quiet promptitude and unvarying good behavior, found himself confronted by a rebel officer whose surrender he demanded. The officer refused, and the corporal fired, shooting him through the body. As he fell the corporal bent over and told him that he was sorry he had to shoot him, and that he was a Christian, and if he wished he would pray with

Union signatories to the parole of General Lee and his staff officers.

him. The officer eagerly assented, and the corporal knelt amidst the drifting smoke and flying missiles and the shouts and groans of the combatants, and offered a fervent prayer for the soul of his dying foeman. When he had finished they shook hands, and the officer gave the corporal his sword as a memento and asked him to write to his wife what had befallen him. ...

As the shadows fell, and the evening breeze rose and sighed a requiem through the swaying pines, all sounds of conflict died away, and we made our bivouac close at hand.

The within named men will not be disturbed by United States authorities, so long as they observe their parole and the laws in force where they may reside.

George W. Hartsie

ABSOLUTE TRIUMPH

Sheridan continued to circle in front of the Army of Northern Virginia, his division under Custer capturing a wagon train of supplies at Appomattox Station on the 8th. Reduced to eating parched corn, and unable to dislodge two Federal army corps closing around them next morning at Appomattox Courthouse, Lee's men were finally licked for good. There was no escape.

The two commanders met at the residence of one Wilbur McLean on the early afternoon of April 9, 1865 – the squat, 5-foot-8 browned-haired 43-year-old Grant in a slightly muddied plain blue uniform, and Lee at 59 years, 6-feet, silver-gray-haired, and majestically attired in a new grey uniform – having selected it as his best one when abandoning the rest of his baggage during the flight. Lee surrendered his last 28,000 men, to the universal joy of the Union forces. Grant allowed the defeated soldiers to retain their privately-owned horses, for he realized these men were small farmers who would need to plow their fields for a spring planting. Now paroled, the surrendered men could return home unmolested, as long as they observed the laws of the land. Lee's final strength – even excluding the 6,200 casualties and nearly 3,800 deserters over the final week of operations – was not very different from the first big battle, at Bull Run (and where, incidentally, the unfortunate Mr. McLean had had an earlier house hit by cannon fire). But Grant's well-equipped and well-fed army of quadruple that size – minus the nearly 11,000

Robert E. Lee photographed by Matthew Brady in Richmond, shortly after the surrender. With quiet dignity, Lee set the example for his defeated comrades to bury their wartime emotions and rebuild the South as part of the American Union.

ABSOLUTE TRIUMPH

casualties of the Appomattox campaign – showed how far modern warfare had developed in four years.

Lee's surrender spelled the demise of the Confederacy, but other aspects of the final strategy, already in motion, completed the final victory. Jefferson Davis escaped to Danville and then to Johnston's army in North Carolina, whereas Abraham Lincoln was assassinated by the fanatical actor John Wilkes Booth on April 14, dying the next day. The Vice President, Andrew Johnson of eastern Tennessee, took up the reigns of reunifying the nation. General Johnston saw no point in continuing the fight against the 200,000 troops which could be arrayed against him, and he asked Sherman for terms of surrender on the 13th. But because Sherman's terms were too generous toward the rebels in the eyes of the government, Grant had to visit Sherman to insure Johnston surrendered on the same terms given Lee. The official capitulation of the 31,000-man Army of Tennessee occurred at Durham Station, North Carolina on April 26. Jeff Davis and his party had fled further south, hoping to reach Texas to continue the fight.

The final mop-up of rebel forces in Alabama occurred in a dual operation – a full-scale coastal assault and a dramatic cavalry raid. On March 17 Major General Edward R.S. Canby mounted a pincers movement

THE FINISH AT APPOMATTOX

April 9, 1865

by **David Craft**, Chaplain, 141st Pennsylvania Infantry. (Several members of this regiment were forebears of the author of this book.)

The Brigade remained in line to advance but were held in position hour after hour. They had planted themselves across the line of the enemy's retreat. A little past noon a flag of truce came into the lines announcing that General Lee was about to surrender his entire army, which was done at four o'clock in the afternoon. Our regiment had reached Clover Hill when the joyful news was received.

Words cannot describe the scene of wild excitement which ensued. Cheer after cheer made the woods ring. Men shouted themselves hoarse. All feeling of animosity was forgotten in the tide of joyous victory which swept through the ranks. Every man knew the end of hard marches and severe fighting was at hand and their homes and loved ones were near. With a soldier's generosity, the victors, though themselves short of rations, shared their stores with the vanquished. . . .

THE NEW YORK HERALD.

WHOLE NO. 10459. NEW YORK, SATURDAY, APRIL 15, 1865. PRICE, FOUR CENTS.

IMPORTANT.

ASSASSINATION
OF
PRESIDENT LINCOLN

The President Shot at the Theatre
Last Evening.

SECRETARY SEWARD

DAGGERED IN HIS BED

BUT

NOT MORTALLY WOUNDED.

Clarence and Frederick
Seward Badly Hurt.

ESCAPE OF THE ASSASSINS.

Intense Excitement In
Washington.

SCENE AT THE DEATHBED OF MR.
LINCOLN.

J. Wilkes Booth, the Actor, the Alleged
Assassin of the President,

&c.,   &c.,   &c.

THE OFFICIAL DISPATCH.

WAR DEPARTMENT,
WASHINGTON, APRIL 15—1:30 A. M.
Major General Dix, New York:

This evening at about 9:30 P. M., at Ford's Theatre, the President, while sitting in his private box with Mrs. Lincoln, Mrs. Harris and Major Rathbun, was shot by an assassin, who suddenly entered the box and approached behind the President.

The assassin then leaped upon the stage, brandishing a large dagger or knife, and made his escape in the rear of the theatre.

The pistol ball entered the back of the President's head and penetrated nearly through the head. The wound is mortal.

The President has been insensible ever since it was inflicted, and is now dying.

About the same hour an assassin, whether the same or not, entered Mr. Seward's apartments, and under pretence of having a prescription was shown to the Secretary's sick chamber. The assassin immediately rushed to the bed and inflicted two or three stabs on the throat and two on the face.

It is hoped the wounds may not be mortal. My apprehension is that they will prove fatal.

The nurse alarmed Mr. Frederick Seward, who was in an adjoining room, and he hastened to the door of his father's room, when he met the assassin, who inflicted upon him one or more dangerous wounds. The recovery of Frederick Seward is doubtful.

It is not probable that the President will live through the night.

General Grant and his wife were advertised to be at the theatre this evening, but he started to Burlington at six o'clock this evening.

At a cabinet meeting, at which General Grant was present, the subject of the state of the country and the prospect of a speedy peace was discussed. The President was very cheerful and hopeful, and spoke very kindly of General Lee and others of the confederacy, and of the establishment of government in Virginia.

All the members of the Cabinet except Mr. Seward are now in attendance upon the President.

I have seen Mr. Seward, but he and Frederick were both unconscious.

EDWIN M. STANTON,
Secretary of War.

THE HERALD DISPATCHES.

WASHINGTON, April 14, 1865.
Assassination has been inaugurated in Washington. The bowie knife and pistol have been applied to President Lincoln and Secretary Seward. The former was shot in the throat while at Ford's Theatre to-night. Mr. Seward was badly cut about the throat, while in bed at his residence.

SECOND DISPATCH.

WASHINGTON, April 14, 1865.
An attempt was made about ten o'clock this evening to assassinate the President and Secretary Seward. The President was shot at Ford's Theatre. Result not yet known. Mr. Seward's throat was cut, and his son badly injured. There is intense excitement here.

Details of the Assassination.
WASHINGTON, April 14, 1865.

Washington was thrown into an intense excitement a few minutes before eleven o'clock this evening, by the announcement that the President and Secretary Seward had been assassinated and were dead.

The wildest excitement prevailed in all parts of the city. Men, women and children, old and young, rushed to and fro, and the rumors were magnified until we had nearly every member of the Cabinet killed. Some time elapsed before authentic data could be ascertained in regard to the affair.

The president and Mrs. Lincoln were at Ford's Theatre, listening to the performance of the American Cousin, occupying a box in the second tier. At the close of the third act a person entered the box occupied by the President and shot Mr. Lincoln in the head. The shot entered the back of his head and came out above the temple.

The assassin then jumped from the box upon the stage and ran across to the other side, exhibiting a dagger in his hand, flourishing it in a tragical manner, shouting the same words repeated by the desperado at Mr. Seward's house, adding to it, "The South is avenged," and then escaped from the back entrance to the stage, but in his passage dropped his pistol and his hat.

Mr. Lincoln fell forward in his seat and Mrs. Lincoln fainted.

The moment the astonished audience could realize what had happened the President was taken and carried to Mr. Peterson's house on Tenth Street, opposite to the theatre. Medical aid was immediately sent for, and the wound was first supposed to be fatal, and it was announced that he could not live; but at half-past twelve it is still alive, though in a precarious condition.

As the assassin ran across the stage Col. J. B. Stewart, of this city, who was occupying one of the front seats in the orchestra, on the same side of the house as the box occupied by Mr. Lincoln, sprang to the stage and followed him; but he was obstructed in his passage across the stage by the fright of the actors and reached the back door about three seconds after the assassin had passed out. Col. Stewart got in the street just in time to see him mount his horse and ride away.

The operation shows that the whole thing was a preconcerted plan. The person who fired the pistol was a man about thirty years of age, about five feet nine, spare built, fair skin, dark hair, apparently bushy, with a large moustache.

Laura Keene and the leader of the orchestra recognized him as J. Wilkes Booth the actor, and a rabid secessionist. Whoever he was, it is plainly evident that he thoroughly understood the theatre, and all the approaches and modes of escape to the stage.

A person not familiar with the theatre could not have possibly made his escape so well and quickly.

The alarm was sounded in every quarter. Mr. Stanton was notified and immediately left his house.

All the other members of the cabinet escaped attack.

Cavalrymen were sent out in all directions, and dispatches were sent to all the fortifications, and it is thought they will be captured.

About half-past ten o'clock this evening, a tall, well-dressed man made his appearance at Secretary Seward's residence, and applied for admission. He was refused admission by the servant when the desperado stated that he had a prescription from the Surgeon General and that he was ordered to deliver it in person. He was still refused, except upon the written order of the physician. This he pretended to show and pushed by the servant and rushed up stairs to Mr. Seward's room. He was met at the door by Mr. Fred Seward, who notified him that he was master of the house, and would take charge of the medicine. After a few words had passed between them he dodged by Fred Seward and rushed to the Secretary's bed and struck him in the neck with a dagger, and also in the breast.

It was supposed at first that Mr. Seward was killed instantly, but it was found afterwards that the wound was not mortal.

Major William H. Seward, Jr., paymaster, was in the room and rushed to the defence of his father and was badly cut in the side by the assassin, but not fatally.

The Surgeon is reported to escape from the house, and was prepared for escape by having a horse at the door. He immediately mounted his horse and sang out the motto of the State of Virginia, "Sic Semper Tyrannus," and rode off.

Surgeon General Barnes was immediately sent for, and he examined Mr. Seward and pronounced him safe. His wounds were not fatal. The jugular vein was not cut, nor the wound in the breast deep enough to be fatal.

WASHINGTON, April 15—1 A. M.

The streets in the vicinity of Ford's Theatre are densely crowded by an anxious and excited crowd. A guard has been placed across Tenth street and F and E streets, and only official persons and particular friends of the President are allowed to pass.

The scene at the house where the President lies is extremis is very affecting. Even Secretary Stanton is affected to tears. When the news spread through the city that the President had been shot, the people, with pale faces and compressed lips, crowded every place where there was the slightest chance of obtaining information in regard to the affair.

After the President was shot, Lieutenant Rathbun caught the assassin by the arm, who immediately cut him with a knife, and jumped from the box, as before stated.

The popular affection for Mr. Lincoln has been shown by this diabolical assassination, which will bring eternal infamy, not only upon its authors and abettors, but upon the hellish cause which they desire to avenge.

Vice-President Johnson arrived at the White House, where the President lies, about one o'clock and will remain with him to the last.

The President's family are in attendance upon him also.

As soon as intelligence could be got to the War Department, the electric telegraph and the magnetic Corps were put in requisition to endeavor to prevent the escape of the assassins, and all the troops around Washington are under arms.

Popular report points to a somewhat celebrated actor of known secession proclivities as the assassin, but it would be unjust to name him until some further evidence of his guilt is obtained. It is rumored that the person should be in his custody.

ONE O'CLOCK A. M.

The President is perfectly senseless, and there is not the slightest hope that he will live until morning. Physicians believe he will die before morning. All of his Cabinet except Secretary Seward are with him. Speaker Colfax, Senator Farwell, of Maine, and many other gentlemen are also at the house awaiting the final result.

The scene at the President's bedside is described by one who witnessed it is most affecting. It was surrounded by the Cabinet minister, all of whom were bathed in tears, not even excepting Mr. Stanton, who, when informed by Surgeon General Barnes, that the President could not recover until morning, exclaimed, "Oh, no, General; no, no," and with an impulse natural as it was unaffected, immediately sat down on a chair near his bedside and wept like a child.

Senator Sumner was seated on the right of the President's couch, near the head, holding the right hand of the President in his own. He was sobbing like a woman, with his head bowed down almost on the pillow of the bed on which the President was lying.

TWO O'CLOCK A. M.

The President is still alive, but there is no improvement in his condition.

THE PRESS DISPATCHES.

WASHINGTON, April 15—12:30 A. M.
The President was shot in a theatre to-night, and perhaps mortally wounded.

SECOND DISPATCH.

WASHINGTON, April 15—1 A. M.
The President is not expected to live through the night.
He was shot at a theatre.
Secretary Seward was also assassinated. No arteries...

Additional Details of the Assassination.

WASHINGTON, April 15—1:20 A. M.
President Lincoln and wife, with other friends, this evening visited Ford's Theatre, for the purpose of witnessing the performance of the American Cousin.

It was announced in the papers that General Grant would also be present, but that gentleman took the late train of cars for New Jersey.

The theatre was densely crowded, and all seemed delighted with the scene before them.

During the third act, and while there was a temporary pause for one of the actors to enter, a sharp report of a pistol was heard, which merely attracted attention, but suggested nothing serious, until a man rushed to the front of the President's box, waving a long dagger in his right hand, and exclaiming, "Sic semper Tyrannis," and immediately leaped from the box, which was in the second tier, to the stage beneath, and ran across to the opposite side, making his escape, amid the bewilderment of the audience, from the rear of the theatre, and disappearing in the back.

The screams of Mrs. Lincoln first disclosed the fact to the audience that the President had been shot, when all present rose to their feet rushing towards the stage, many exclaiming, "Hang him! hang him!"

The excitement was of the wildest possible description, and of course there was an immediate rush towards the President's box.

There was a rush towards the President's box, when cries were heard : "Stand back and give him air." "Has any one stimulants?"

On a hasty examination it was found that the President had been shot through the head, above the back of the temporal bone, and that some of the brain was oozing out.

He was removed to a private house opposite the theatre, and the Surgeon General of the Army was sent for to attend to his condition.

On an examination of the private box it was discovered on the back of the cushioned rocking chair on which the President had been sitting, also on the partition and on the floor, a quantity of clotted blood.

A military guard was stationed at the private residence to which the President had been conveyed. An immense crowd was in front of it, and deeply anxious to learn the condition of the President. It had been previously announced that the wound was mortal, but all hoped otherwise. The shock to the community was terrible.

The President was in a state of syncope, totally insensible, and breathing slowly. The blood oozed from the wound in the back of his head.

The surgeons exhausted every possible effort of medical skill, but all hope was gone.

The parting of his family from the dying President is too sad for description.

The President and Mrs. Lincoln did not start for the theatre until fifteen minutes after eight o'clock. Speaker Colfax was at the White House at the time and the President stated to him that he was going. Mrs. Lincoln had not been well, but because the papers had announced that General Grant and they were to be present, and General Grant had gone North, he did not wish the audience to be disappointed. He went with apparent reluctance, and urged Mr. Colfax to go with him, but that gentleman had made other engagements, and with Mr. Ashmun, of Massachusetts, bid him good by.

When the excitement at the theatre was at its wildest height reports were circulated that Secretary Seward had also been assassinated.

On reaching the gentleman's residence a crowd and a military guard were found at the door, and on entering it was ascertained that the reports were based on fact.

Everybody there was so excited that scarcely an intelligible account could be gathered. But the facts are substantially as follows:—

About ten o'clock a man rang the bell, and the call having been answered by a colored servant, he said he had come from Dr. Verdi, Secretary Seward's family physician, with a prescription, at the same time holding in his hand a small piece of paper folded, and saying, in answer to a refusal, that he must see the Secretary, as he was entrusted with particular directions concerning the medicine.

He still insisted on going up, although repeatedly informed that no one could enter the chamber. The man pushed the servant aside, and walked hastily towards the Secretary's room, and was then met by Mr. Frederick Seward, of whom he demanded to see the Secretary, making the same representation which he did to the servant.

What further passed in the way of colloquy is not known; but the man struck him on the head with a billy, severely injuring the skull and felling him almost senseless.

The assassin then rushed into the chamber and attacked Major Seward, Paymaster United States Army, and Mr. Hansell, a messenger of the State Department, and two male nurses, disabling them all.

He then rushed upon the Secretary, who was lying in bed in the same room, and inflicted three stabs in the neck, but severing, it is thought, no arteries, though he bled profusely.

The assassin then rushed down stairs, mounted his horse at the door and rode off before an alarm could be sounded, and in the same manner as the assassin of the President.

It is believed that the injuries of the Secretary are not fatal nor those of either of the others, although both the Secretary and the Assistant Secretary are very seriously injured.

Secretaries Stanton and Welles, and other prominent officers of the Government, called at Secretary Seward's to inquire into his condition, and there learned of the assassination of the President.

They then proceeded to the house where the President was lying, exhibiting of course intense anxiety and solicitude.

An immense crowd was gathered in front of the President's house, all anxious to obtain the latest information of the condition of their loved ones.

It was a touching scene.

The entire city to-night presents a scene of wild excitement, accompanied by violent expressions of indignation, and the profoundest sorrow; many shed tears.

The military authorities have despatched mounted patrols in every direction, in order, if possible, to arrest the assassins. The whole metropolitan police are like wise vigilant for the same purpose.

The attacks, both at the theatre and at Secretary Seward's, took place at about the same hour — ten o'clock — thus showing a preconcerted plan to assassinate these two gentlemen. Some evidence of the guilt of the party is in the possession of the police, showing that the President was to have been the victim of the assassination.

Vice President Johnson is in the city, and his hotel quarters are guarded by troops.

EXTRA.
8:10 A. M.

New York, Saturday, April 15, 1865.

DEATH
OF
THE PRESIDENT.

Further Details of the
Great Crime.

ADDITIONAL DISPATCHES FROM THE
SECRETARY OF WAR.

What is Known of the Assassins.

THE OFFICIAL DISPATCHES.

WAR DEPARTMENT,
WASHINGTON, April 15—9:10 A. M.
Major General Dix, New York:

The President continues insensible and sinking.

Secretary Seward remains without change. Frederick Seward's skull is fractured in two places, besides a severe cut upon the head. The attendant is still alive but hopeless. Major Seward's wounds are not dangerous.

It is now ascertained with reasonable certainty that two assassins were engaged in the horrible crime, Wilkes Booth being the one that shot the President, and the other, an accomplice, whose name is not known, but whose description is so clear that he can hardly escape.

It appears from a letter found in Booth's trunk that the murder was planned before the 4th of March, but fell through then, because the accomplice backed out until Richmond could be heard from.

Booth and his accomplice were at the livery stable at six o'clock this evening, and left there with their horses at ten o'clock, or shortly before that hour.

It would appear that they had for several days been seeking their chance, but for some unknown reason it was not carried into effect until last night.

One of the assassins has evidently made his way to Baltimore and the other has not yet been traced.

EDWIN M. STANTON,
Secretary of War.

THE PRESIDENT DEAD.

WAR DEPARTMENT,
WASHINGTON, April 15—7:30 A. M.
Major General Dix, New York:—

Abraham Lincoln died this morning at twenty-two minutes past 7 o'clock.

EDWIN M. STANTON,
Secretary of War.

IMPORTANT FROM SOUTH AMERICA.

Surrender of Montevideo to Gen. Flores.

Brazil in Possession of the City, &c.

The Brazilian mail arrived at Lisbon April 2, bringing the following advices:—

Montevideo has surrendered to General Flores. The Brazilians now (March 11) occupy the city.

RIO DE JANEIRO, March 11, 1865.
Coffee—Sales of good first at 6,700. Shipments, 100,000 bags. Freight, 85/32 to 85/8.

BAHIA, March 11, 1865.
Exchange 25 5/8 a 25 3/4.

PERNAMBUCO, March 11, 1865.
Exchange 25 1/4. Cotton nominal.
Exchange 26 1-2 a 27.

News From San Francisco.

SAN FRANCISCO, April 12, 1865.
The exports of treasure for the quarter just ended, show a falling off of about six and a half million as compared with the same period last year.

SAN FRANCISCO, April 14, 1865.
The Pacific mail steamship Sacramento sailed to-day, with a large number of passengers for New York, and $1,353,000 in treasure, of which nearly $700,000 go to New York.

The steamship Moses Taylor sailed for San Juan Del Sur, with numerous passengers.

The market continues variable and unsettled, and traders pursue a continuous policy. Prices of Eastern goods are slowly falling.

Sailed, ship Flying Eagle, for Boston.

New Orleans Markets.

NEW ORLEANS, April 8.
VIA CAIRO, April 14, 1865.

The New Orleans markets are at a stand still. Low middling cotton is quoted at 49c per pound, and good superfine flour at $9 per bbl.

THE REBELS.

JEFF. DAVIS AT DANVILLE.

His Latest Appeal to his
Deluded Followers.

He Thinks the Fall of Richmond a Blessing in
Disguise as it Leaves the Rebel Armies
Free to Move From Point to Point.

HE VAINLY PROMISES TO HOLD VIR-
GINIA AT ALL HAZARDS.

Lee and His Army Supposed to
Be Safe.

BRECKINRIDGE AND THE REST OF DAVIS'
CABINET REACH DANVILLE SAFELY.

The Organ of Gov. Vance of North Carolina,
Advises the Submission of the Rebels
to President Lincoln's Terms.
&c.,   &c.,   &c.

JEFF. DAVIS' LAST PROCLAMATION.

VIRGINIA TO BE HELD BY THE REBELS AT ALL HAZARDS.

DANVILLE, VA., April 5, 1865.

The General-in-Chief found it necessary to make such movements of his troops as to uncover the Capital. It would be unwise to conceal the mental and material injury to our cause resulting from the occupation of our capital by the enemy. It is equally unwise and unworthy of us to allow our own energies to falter and our efforts to become relaxed under reverses, however calamitous they may be. For many months the largest and fairest army of the confederacy, under conditions of a leader whose presence inspired equal confidence in his troops and the people, has been greatly trammelled by the necessity of keeping constant watch over the approaches to the capital, and has thus been forced to forego more than one opportunity for promising enterprise. It is for us, my countrymen, to show by our bearing under reverses, how wretched has been the self-deception of those who have believed us conquered, to endure misfortune that will ever encounter dangers with courage.

We have now entered upon a new phase of the struggle. Relieved from the necessity of guarding particular points, our army will be free to move from point to point to strike the enemy in detail far from his base. Let us but will it and we are free.

Animated by that confidence in spirit and fortitude which never yet failed me, I announce to you, fellow countrymen, that it is my purpose to maintain your cause with my whole heart and soul; that I will never consent to abandon to the enemy one foot of the soil of any one of the States of the Confederacy...

JEFFERSON DAVIS.

The Evacuation of the Rebel Capital.

THE FIRST REBEL ACCOUNT OF HOW THE CITY WAS ABANDONED.

[From the Danville (Va.) Register, April 5.]

Persons who left the capital Sunday night and Monday morning represent that the scene which followed the evacuation of the city by our troops beggars description...

High Prices in an Overstocked Market.

[From the Raleigh Confederate, April 7.]

Our market on the arrival of the Weldon train to-day was literally crammed with shad...

Exchange of Rebel General Vance.

[From the Asheville (N. C.) News.]

The exchange of prisoners seems to go steadily on...

City Intelligence.

against the city of Mobile, 45,000 men of the 13th and 16th Corps converging from Forts Morgan and Gaines at the harbor entrance and from Pensacola, supported by the Navy. The operation against the 10,000 defending troops and five gunboats lasted two weeks and culminated with a final assault on fortifications at Blakely, taking its 3,400 defenders on April 9. Canby occupied Mobile three days later, while the surviving Confederate troops retired toward Montgomery. But they could not find refuge there, for Major General James H. Wilson had mounted a raiding expedition across central Alabama.

Leaving the northwest corner of that state on March 22, Wilson and his cavalry crossed the Tennessee 9,000 strong and moved against Selma, to which place and to Macon Confederate weapons factories had been relocated from Atlanta before its fall. Routing Forrest's and other rebel forces concentrating against him, Wilson assaulted and took Selma on April 2. One of his

brigades captured Tuscaloosa three days later, and on the 12th the city of Montgomery surrendered to Wilson. Crossing into Georgia, the cavalrymen took Columbus on the 16th and Macon on the 20th. Next day, Wilson received orders from Sherman to cease hostilities. His command had taken nearly 7,000 prisoners, 15 locomotives plus 250 cars, munitions factories, and the Selma navy yard.

Wilson's and Canby's operations finished off Confederate opposition east of the Mississippi, and on May 4 Lieutenant General Dick Taylor formally surrendered the more than 42,000 troops still under arms throughout the region to Canby. Rebel naval units on Alabama's rivers capitulated on May 10, the same day that part of Wilson's force received the surrender of Tallahassee, Florida and 8,000 troops there. Also on the 10th, two regiments of Wilson's cavalry captured Jefferson Davis at Irwinsville, Georgia. With his seizure died any hope of relocating the Confederate government

General Joe Johnston surrenders the Army of Tennessee to General William T. Sherman at Durham Station, North Carolina, April 26, 1865.

This Northern political cartoon depicts "Moving Day in Richmond": the Confederate government going to the dogs, and losing all of its constituent states in the process. Crown, scepter, and rifle are worthless, with the freedman thumbing his nose and a mutt lifting his leg on "wastepaper" rebel currency.

west of the Mississippi River.

Conditions in the Trans-Mississippi District had deteriorated into a nearly chaotic state by the beginning of the year. Despite the fact that blockade runners managed to run between Galveston and Havana as late as May 24, 1865, Kirby Smith's harsh draft policies and commandeering of goods for the army had led to widespread dissatisfaction and almost mutinous troops. Smith had no recourse but to surrender, which he did to Canby on the 26th – officially some 17,500 men plus another 8,000 in Arkansas. When Galveston hauled down the rebel flag on June 2, the Confederacy ceased to exist. Any resistance would have been futile, particularly since Sheridan was hurrying to Texas with part of his Cavalry Corps and Weitzel's 25th Army Corps to make a show of force along the Rio Grande against Maximilian's French puppet government in Mexico. Indeed, the last battle of the Civil War occurred on a ranch near Brownsville on May 11-12, and part of

Sheridan's force kept watch over various rebel units escaping across Texas to Mexico, rather than surrender. The largest unit was Brigadier General J.O. "Jo" Shelby's remnant brigade which marched all the way from Arkansas to the Rio Grande, crossing over on July 4 to join Maximilian's army. The French intervention in Mexico would collapse two years later.

The last Confederate forces to receive the word of the final defeat were naval. The powerful ocean-going ironclad ram *Stonewall* reached Havana

ABSOLUTE DEFEAT

by **Reuben S. Norton**, merchant of Rome, Georgia, January 1, 1863. (Too old to fight – in his mid fifties – Norton was one of the few men to remain in his war-torn town throughout the conflict. He kept a running diary, from which the following excerpts are drawn. His daughter eventually married Billy Towers.)

January 1, 1863
This is the day President Lincoln says the Negroes shall be free. Everything is quiet, the hiring of servants going on, and at an advance of full 25% over last year, and sales are fully 1/3 higher than 12 months ago.

January 6, 1863
... Boys from 9 to 14 years sold for from $800 to $1,400; women as high as $1,500, men up to $1,600. (Cash.)

August 4, 1863
President Lincoln has issued his Proclamation saying

he will protect his negro soldiers, and put them on an Equality with our White men. Things must be drawing to a Focus: steal our Slaves, arm them against us, turn them against their masters, and then, claim for them treatment as 'Prisoners of war'!

November 25, 1863
To day, a White man cannot pass up and down Broad Street without a Permit. A Negro can. Times are changing.

June 8, 1864 [Under Union army occupation]
... Most of the servants, both in town and in the Country, are leaving their Masters and coming in to better their condition. ...

June 18, 1864
This evening, the first shipment of negroes took place, 300 women and children, more than half of those, I should think, under 12. Said to be destined to

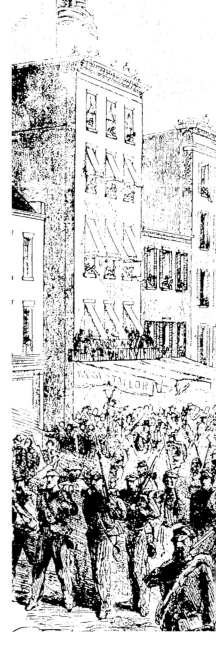

The Civil War provided the political foundation for a generation of American presidents, the last being William McKinley (above), portrayed enlisting in the 23rd Ohio Infantry in 1861; he attained the rank of brevet major. Union generals who became president were Andrew Johnson, U.S. Grant,

Rutherford B. Hayes, James A. Garfield, and Benjamin Harrison.

The grand review of Grant's and Sherman's victorious armies (right) down Pennsylvania Avenue in Washington took two days, May 23 and 24, 1865, after which the men were mustered out of volunteer service to return home.

from Europe in May but had to be immediately turned over to Spanish authorities. The commerce raider *Shenandoah*, operating in the distant Bering Sea against Yankee whalers, refused to believe news of Lee's surrender from one of his captures on June 23 and took 21 more whaling ships before learning the truth from a British vessel on August 2. Captain James I. Waddell then secured his guns and made a 17,000-mile voyage around the Horn, avoiding contact with any vessel, until he reached Liverpool and surrendered to the British navy on November 6, 1865. By that time, some 800,000 troops had been discharged from the Union volunteer army, and the rest were posted throughout the South on occupation duty.

By waging total and absolute war, the Federal government had finally crushed the rebellion of the Southern states. The political vision and direction for the ultimate victory had been due to Abraham Lincoln, final credit for the successful strategy and military operations to Grant and Sherman. Only by such extreme measures as emancipation and the utter destruction of the socio-economic system of the South did the Union force the Southern whites to accept the future.

AFTERWORD

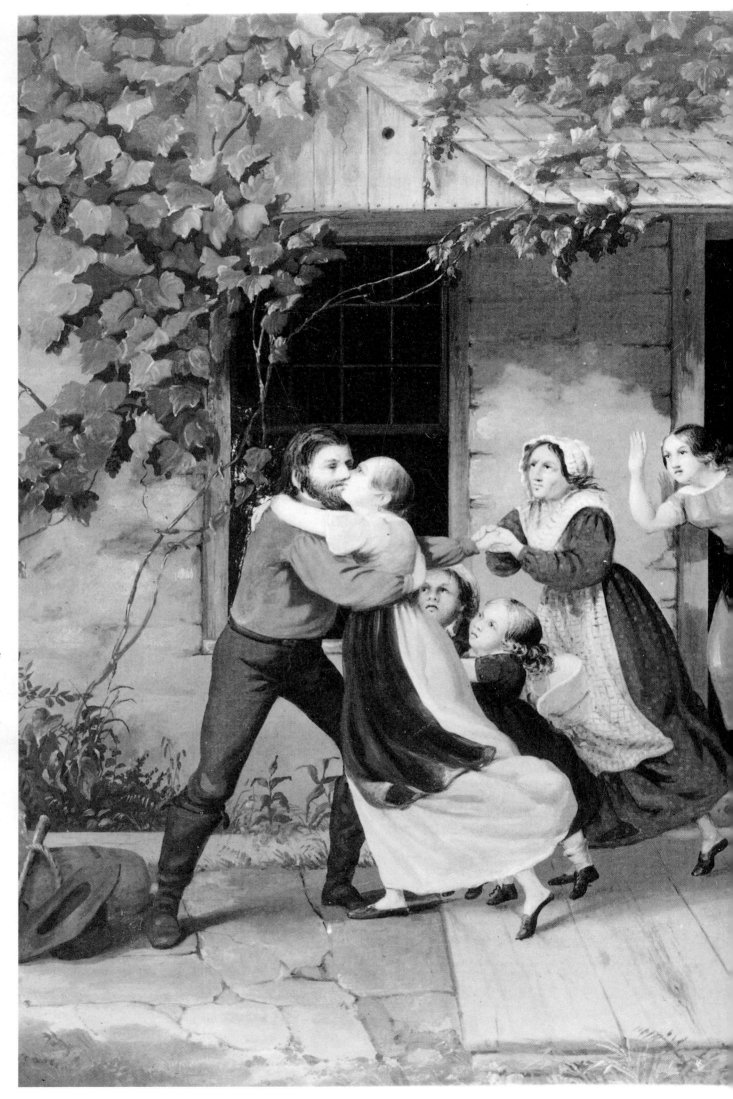

The Soldier's Return *by A.D.O. Braviere seems melodramatic to modern eyes but it captures the feelings of universal relief at the end of America's bloodiest war. Ninety years after the birth of the republic, it was finally unified for all time.*

The Civil War once and for all time unified the United States into the powerful political and economic colossus that it has been ever since. At the cost of perhaps 625,000 deaths – not to mention the countless maimed – a new era was forged through the sacrifice and suffering of both sides. From the struggle emerged myths and folklore that were purely American, neither shared nor appreciated by other nations. It was, in effect, "our war" and national epic.

But the trials of the defeated white South and newly liberated blacks did not end at Appomattox. The wretched era of Reconstruction rocked national and regional politics for another generation, while a string of mediocre politicians achieved high office at every level, North and South, including the Presidency, right up to the end of the century largely on the strength of their military service during the war. The civil rights of black Americans did not even begin to achieve fruition until the middle of the 20th century, an issue still not completely resolved in American society to this day.

The greatest legacy of the war, however, was not only the unification of the country on the national level but the inspiration that the outcome of the war gave for democratic principles on a global scale – through two world wars, a cold war, modern communications, and the active American example to this nation's former enemies and emerging peoples throughout the world.

Still in all, like any war, it was a tragedy in human suffering that no amount of romanticizing or flag-waving can minimize. The men who fought and died were brothers of different beliefs who by their actions made this great nation even greater. That achievement is their own ultimate legacy.

DON'T JUDGE HASTILY

by **Joshua L. Chamberlain**, Brevet Major General, U.S. Volunteers, Governor of Maine, President of Bowdoin College

One of the saddest things I know of is that epitaph which the Virginia father, gathering up the remnant left him after the ravages of war, and setting himself as best he could into the new situation, placed upon a stone he raised as a memorial of his old home. On one face of it he inscribed these words: "To the sacred memory of my eldest boy, who fell fighting for the stars and stripes." On the opposite side he wrote, "To the sacred memory of my youngest boy, who fell fighting for the lost cause." And between them on the third face: "God only knows which was right!"

I pity that man's sorrow and perplexity. But there is a double question there as to the "right," of which he dared not judge. The motive in the young men's minds was one thing, and the justice of the cause was another. God alone knows the heart, and He alone can judge men's motives.

Selected Sources

Black, Robert C. *The Railroads of the Confederacy*. Chapel Hill: University of North Carolina Press, 1952.

Boatner, Mark Mayo, III. *The Civil War Dictionary*. New York: David McKay, 1959.

Brewer, James H. *The Confederate Negro: Virginia's Craftsmen and Military Laborers, 1861-1865*. Durham, N.C.: Duke University Press, 1969.

Cohen, Stan. *Hands Across the Wall: The 50th and 75th Reunions of the Gettysburg Battle*. Missoula, Mt.: Pictorial Histories, 1982.

Craft, David. *History of the One Hundred Forty-First Regiment, Pennsylvania Volunteers, 1862-1865*. Towanda, Pa.: Reporter-Journal Printing Co., 1885.

Crawford, Richard, compiler. *The Civil War Songbook*. New York: Dover, 1977.

Dictionary of American Naval Fighting Ships, 8 volumes. Washington: Naval Historical Center, 1959-1981, especially Vol. II, Appendix II, "Confederate Forces Afloat."

Durkin, Joseph T. *Confederate Navy Chief: Stephen R. Mallory*. 1954. Columbia: University of South Carolina Press reprint, 1987.

Faust, Drew Gilpin. "Altars of Sacrifice: Confederate Women and the Narratives of War," *Journal of American History* (March 1990).

Hamm, Charles. "Songs of the Civil War." New World Records (LP NW 202 Stereo) Anthology of American Music, 1976.

Hayes, John D., "Captain Fox - *He* Is the Navy Department," *U.S. Naval Institute Proceedings* (September 1965). "Sea Power in the Civil War," *U.S. Naval Institute Proceedings* (November 1961).

Hedley, F. Y. *Marching Through Georgia*. Chicago: R. R. Donnelley & Sons, 1887.

Hogg, Ian V. *Weapons of the Civil War*. New York: Military Press, 1987.

Johnson, Robert Underwood, and Clarence Clough Buel. *Battles and Leaders of the Civil War*, 4 volumes, 1887. New York: Thomas Yoseloff reprint, 1956.

King, Alvy L. *Louis T. Wigfall: Southern Fire-eater*. Baton Rouge: Louisiana State University Press, 1970.

King, Will. C., ed. *Camp-Fire Sketches and Battle-Field Echoes*, 1887.

Marszalek, John F. "Where Did Winfield Scott Find His Anaconda?" *Lincoln Herald* (Summer 1987).

McPherson, James M. *Battle Cry of Freedom: The Civil War Era*. New York: Oxford University Press, 1988.

Mearns, David C. *The Lincoln Papers* (to July 4, 1861). Garden City, N.Y.: Doubleday, 1948.

Miller, Francis Trevelyan. *The Photographic History of the Civil War*, 10 volumes, 1911. New York: Thomas Yoseloff reprint, 1957.

Minnigh, L. W. *Gettysburg: What They Did Here*. Gettysburg, Pa.: Bookmart, 1954.

Mitchel, F. A. *Ormsby MacKnight Mitchel: Astronomer and General*. Boston: Houghton, Mifflin, 1887.

Moore, Frank, ed. *The Portrait Gallery of the War*. New York: D. Van Nostrand, 1865.

Murray, Williamson. "What Took the North So Long?" *Military History Quarterly* (Summer 1989).

Reynolds, Clark G. *Command of the Sea: The History and Strategy of Maritime Empires*, Vol. 2, rev. ed. Malabar, Fla.: Robert Krieger, 1983.

Reynolds, Clark G. *Famous American Admirals*. New York: Van Nostrand Reinhold, 1978.

Ropp, Theodore. *War in the Modern World*. Durham, N. C.: Duke University Press, 1959.

Russell, William Howard. *My Diary North and South*. London: Burnham, 1863.

Shattuck, Gardiner H., Jr. *A Shield and a Hiding Place: The Religious Life of the Civil War Armies*. Macon, Ga.: Mercer University Press, 1987.

Street, James. *The Civil War: An Unvarnished Account*. New York: Dial, 1953.

Stuart, Reginald C. "Cavalry Raids in the West: Case Studies of Civil War Cavalry Raids," *Tennessee Historical Quarterly* (1971).

Whitman, Walt. *Leaves of Grass*. New York: Doubleday, Doran, 1940.

Wiley, Bell Irvin. *The Life of Johnny Reb*. Indianapolis: Bobbs –Merrill, 1943.

Wise, Stephen R. *Lifeline of the Confederacy: Blockade Running During the Civil War*. Columbia: University of South Carolina Press, 1988.